M000305051

$0 ORIGINAL $20
RECEIPT

SPRINGER SERIES ON SOCIAL WORK

Albert R. Roberts, DSW, PhD, Series Editor
Professor of Social Work and Criminal Justice, School of Arts and Sciences, Rutgers The State University of New Jersey

Advisory Board: Jose Ashford, PhD, Barbara Berkman, PhD, Elaine P. Congress, DSW, Sophia F. Dziegielewski, PhD, C. Aaron McNeece, PhD, Kenneth R. Yeager, PhD

Helping Victims of Violent Crime

Assessment, Treatment, and Evidence-Based Practice

DIANE L. GREEN, PhD

ALBERT R. ROBERTS, DSW, PhD

SPRINGER PUBLISHING COMPANY

New York

Springer Publishing Company, LLC
11 West 42nd Street
New York, NY 10036
www.springerpub.com

Acquisitions Editor: Jennifer Perillo
Project Manager: Kelly J. Applegate
Cover design: Joanne E. Honigman
Composition: Publication Services

08 09 10 11 12 / 5 4 3 2 1

Library of Congress Cataloging-in-Publication Data

Green, Diane L.
  Helping victims of violent crime : assessment, treatment, and evidence-based practice / Diane L. Green, Albert R. Roberts.
    p. ; cm. – (Springer series on social work)

  ISBN 978-0-8261-2508-8 (hardcover)
  1. Victims of violent crimes—Mental health.   2. Crisis intervention (Mental health services)   3. Evidence-based psychiatry.   I. Roberts, Albert R.   II. Title.   III. Series: Springer series on social work (Unnumbered)

  [DNLM: 1. Crime Victims—psychology.   2. Crisis Intervention—methods. 3. Violence—psychology. WM 401 G795h 2008]
  RC569.5.V55G74 2008
  362.88–dc22

                                                                                    2008013398

Printed in the United States of America by Bang Printing.

Dedication

This book is dedicated to the many thousands of victim advocates and counselors who have devoted their careers to victims and families, and who work tirelessly to improve the lives of all survivors.

Diane Green dedicates this book to her mother, Lois Green, and in loving memory of her father James Russell Green, Jr., for their love, support, and understanding throughout the years. Al Roberts dedicates this book in loving memory of his mother and father Evelyn and Harry Roberts who instilled love, compassion, educational pursuits, and perserverance in his first 21 years of life before his parents death from cancer.

Contents

About the Authors

Diane L. Green, PhD, is associate professor of social work, School of Social Work, Florida Atlantic University in Boca Raton, Florida. Dr. Green received her master's degree in social work from the University of Central Florida. She received her PhD from the University of Texas–Austin. For the past 7 years, she has taught psychopathology, victimology, grief and loss, and research at the undergraduate and graduate level in social work at the School of Social Work at Florida Atlantic University. Additionally, she developed an online transition course designed to help undergraduates prepare for the rigors of graduate school. Dr. Green is currently developing a certificate program for undergraduates and graduates in victim advocacy/forensic social work. Her clinical experience has been as clinical director of a behavioral health care system, program administrator in foster care, director of outpatient and intensive outpatient services in a psychiatric hospital, and hospice clinical social worker. Dr. Green has conducted many focus groups with victim assistance providers and leaders in the victim field to develop a manual for and provide training to clinical social workers in assessment and treatment for victims of crime. She was an integral part of Victims Services 2000 in Texas, a program to develop a comprehensive service delivery plan for victims of crime, integrating knowledge gained in interviews with law enforcement leaders (sheriff, chief of police, probation officers, parole officers), victim service providers, and others. The overarching goal was to streamline delivery in order to avoid overlapping services.

Dr. Green has published over 26 national and international articles and 10 chapters in books relating to victims of crime; she has presented her research at over 20 conferences in the United States and abroad. Dr. Green's research has focused on the stress and coping processes for victims of violent and nonviolent crime, the effectiveness of mental health interventions, and grief and loss issues. Dr. Green currently serves on the editorial boards of four different scholarly journals and is a reviewer on over eight peer-reviewed journals. She is on the professional advisory board of Gift from Within, an international nonprofit organization for survivors of trauma and victimization. She is a member of the International Critical Incident Stress Foundation, the National Association of Social Workers, the Society for Social Work and Research, and the National Organization for Victim Assistance.

Albert R. Roberts, DSW, PhD, is professor of criminal justice and social work, School of Arts and Sciences, Livingston College Campus at Rutgers, the State University of New Jersey in Piscataway, NJ (he has been a tenured professor at Rutgers since 1989). Dr. Roberts served as director of faculty and curriculum development for the Interdisciplinary Program in Criminal Justice from 2001 to 2004, and chair of the Administration of Justice Department from 1990 to 1993. Dr. Roberts has over 21 years of administrative experience as department chairperson, program director, project director, and director of social work field placements. During the 1970s and 1980s, he taught at Indiana University, the University of New Haven, Seton Hall University, and Brooklyn College of C.U.N.Y. Dr. Roberts has 36 years of full-time university teaching experience at the undergraduate and graduate level in both criminal justice and social work. His DSW is from the University of Maryland School of Social Work and Community Planning (1978); in 1981, he received a PhD degree from the University of Maryland in social work, with a double specialization in advanced criminology and social research methods. In 1984, Dr. Roberts was the Project Director of the National Institute of Justice's federally funded project on the effectiveness of crisis intervention with violent crime victims at neighborhood offices of the Victim Services Agency (VSA) in New York City. In 1990, Dr. Roberts developed the Seven-Stage Crisis Intervention Model (R-SSCIM), which is used by a growing number of crisis counselors and workers throughout the world. In 2002, he was the recipient of the Richard W. Laity Academic Leadership Award of the Rutgers Council of the American Association of University Professors (AAUP). In addition, Dr. Roberts was the recipient of the Teaching Excellence Award from the Sigma Alpha Kappa chapter of the National Criminal Justice Honor Society in both 1997 and 1998. He is a charter member of the Gamma Epsilon chapter of Alpha Delta Mu National Social Work Honor Society at Indiana University (1985 to the present). He has over 250 publications to his credit, including numerous peer-reviewed journal articles and 38 books. His most recent books are

> *Correctional Counseling and Treatment* (2008)
> *Battered Women and Their Families*, 3rd edition (2007)
> *Handbook of Forensic Mental Health with Victims and Offenders* (2007, David W. Springer, coeditor)
> *Crisis Intervention Handbook: Assessment, Treatment and Research*, 3rd edition (2005)
> *Evidence-Based Practice Manual: Research and Outcome Measures in Health and Human Services* (2004, Kenneth R. Yeager, coeditor)

Professor Roberts is the founding editor-in-chief of the peer-reviewed journal *Brief Treatment and Crisis Intervention* and of the peer-reviewed international journal *Victims & Offenders: Journal of Evidence-Based Policies and Practices*. Dr. Roberts currently serves on the editorial boards of 10 different scholarly journals. He is a member of the Board of Scientific and Professional Advisors, a diplomate in forensic traumatology as well as domestic violence, and a board certified expert in traumatic stress for the American Academy of Experts in Traumatic Stress (AAETS). Professor Roberts serves as a member of the editorial advisory board for *Encyclopedia Americana* (2002 to the present). Dr. Roberts has been the project director or principal investigator on eight different national studies of crisis intervention, suicide prevention, victim/witness assistance, forensic social work, correctional education, juvenile offender treatment, and domestic violence emergency services in the past 25 years.

In March 2008, Dr. Roberts completed the manuscript for the expanded second edition of the *Social Workers' Desk Reference* (SWDR) (the first edition was published in 2002 by Oxford University Press and includes 146 original chapters; the second edition includes approximately 170 original chapters). In addition to being the editor-in-chief of the second edition of the SWDR, he chairs the SWDR editorial board, consisting of 12 associate/section editors. The current edition of the SWDR has received three prestigious library reference awards.

Foreword

At the time that this important text is being published, we find ourselves at a crossroads in both our understanding of, and our capacity to, serve crime victims and survivors. Crime victims and those who serve them can both revel at the great progress that has been made in legislative initiatives and funding to support victims' rights and services, while at the same time be rightly concerned about looming threats to the gains earned for victims during these last few decades. The reality of economic downturns and the resulting budget cutbacks creates an environment that challenges this relatively new field of study and service provision. Fortunately, Drs. Green and Roberts provide us with an extremely useful tool-kit that is well grounded in theory and empirical research, and tempered with substantial practical experience.

Of particular note is the authors' use of an evidence-based approach to presenting state-of-the-art knowledge across a broad range of critical topics. Whether budgetary times are good or not so good, it is imperative that practitioners employ the best information available to provide victims and covictims with the highest quality services. In times of shrinking resources, such efficiencies and effective service provision are even more imperative. This scholarly, yet practice-oriented, book does just that. It provides those in the field with cutting-edge information that will increase their knowledge and allow them to hone their skills and, therefore, enhance their capacity to serve victims.

As noted above, this is an excellent time for a book such as this to be produced. Those in our field are well aware that a stalwart of basic funding for all crime victim services across the nation is under attack, again. The Crime Victims Fund, created by the landmark Victims of Crime Act (VOCA) in 1984, has recently been the target of immediate budget-reduction attempts that would also zero-out any reserves in the fund, which could possibly result in no federal funding for victim services in the near future.

From its modest beginnings in 1984–1985, when it collected $68.3 million for crime victims, the fund has truly represented a sea-changing innovation in program support, in that it is not the taxpayer dollars that is being appropriated, but rather it is the offenders' fines, forfeitures, and special assessments that are collected and distributed to and for victims of crime. The simple elegance of this approach allowed this funding mechanism to be created during a time when virtually no new federal programs were established, and, indeed, many were abolished. Those old enough will remember the mid-1980s as the "Graham-Rudman-Hollings" Balanced Budget Act period. The fact that criminal perpetrators, and not taxpayers, were funding service for victims of crime helped catapult the Crime Victims Fund and make hundreds of millions of dollars available for crime victim compensation and services programs across the country.

Although the accomplishments of the VOCA Crime Victims Fund are impressive—with monies in excess of $500 million currently being distributed each year and total deposits into the fund of approximately $9 billion from 1984 through 2007—they actually represent only a small fraction of the cost of crime to victims. Early Justice Department estimates of these costs for violent crimes alone were approximately $450 billion annually, and it was also estimated that perhaps as many as 10%–20% of all mental health expenditures were attributable to criminal victimization.[1]

Green and Roberts's wonderful book is right on the mark in several other important ways. Their approach is cross-disciplinary, which is essential as we come to understand the complexities of victimization and the myriad needs of crime victims. Interdisciplinary cooperation is essential to provide the necessary assistance to the victims. This book provides a road map for victim advocates, victim service providers, health and mental health workers, criminal justice practitioners and other allied professionals on how to understand their roles in assisting victims as well as how to forge interagency collaboratives that will benefit their clients.

For those focused on program efficacy, the text is replete with examples of interventions with proven effectiveness. For the clinician, this text provides a wealth of information and will serve as a perfect desktop reference. The authors also clearly recognize that the vast array of

---

1. Miller, Ted, Cohen, Mark A., & Wiersema, Brian. (1996, February). *Victim costs and consequences: A new look*. Washington, D.C. National Institute of Justices. U.S. Department of Justice. Washington, D.C.

human experiences involved in victimization and its aftermath cannot be easily summarized in any one compilation, regardless of its length. Their solution is an obvious focus on the development of critical and strategic thinking skills, so that reader will not only be equipped with these skills, but he or she will also benefit from the thought-provoking exercises that will further help them, novice and experienced alike, to be better prepared to confront the real-life issues and challenges that those who wish to help victims face each day.

Finally, the breadth of coverage in this text is truly impressive. Sound theory, research, and practice is reviewed in several traditional areas of victimization such as child abuse, intimate-partner violence, sexual assault, and homicide, all presented against the context of newer areas such as elder abuse, school-based violence, terrorism, and mass victimization. Fundamentals of assessment and intervention are applied adeptly across all these types of victimization, providing the reader with a solid grounding in the most essential areas of criminal victimization that will most likely affect their clients.

Green and Roberts have provided us with a must-read for those who assist victims. This is a major contribution to a field that is coming of age in the context of much uncertainty about programs and resources. This book provides substantial solutions and evidence-based, effective interventions that will truly help crime victims.

Mario Thomas Gaboury, JD, PhD
Professor and Chair of Criminal Justice
Oskar Schindler Humanities Foundation Endowed Professor
University of New Haven, West Haven, Connecticut
President, American Society of Victimology

Preface

Our book represents a distinct departure from other books on crime victims, victimology, and violence prevention. Our book emphasizes practical assessment and intervention strategies with victims of violence, rather than limiting the focus to academic literature reviews. No other book provides step-by-step assessment and treatment methods for crime victims integrated into each chapter. Victim advocates, victim counselors, domestic violence advocates, forensic social workers, forensic psychologists, psychiatric–mental health nurses, and graduate students have been searching for a readable book that includes the latest clinical issues and treatment protocols for helping crime victims. We wrote this book to meet that critical need.

In order to understand what it means to work successfully with victims of crime, practitioners must develop both a foundation of knowledge and skills, and an understanding of the key elements critical to helping victims of violent crime. We wrote this book to provide a framework for learning these necessary skills in a way that emphasizes the uniqueness of each type of crime victim.

This text emphasizes the necessary skills in assessing and intervening with crime victims in order to make decisions, and complete tasks and activities—that is the essence of treatment.

When we look at the dynamics of assessing and supporting a crime victim, it is easy to see why this can be a challenging topic to address. Experience is what is needed, yet this takes time. Until one can obtain this experience, it is up to the textbooks to provide the conceptual foundation and introduction to the skills necessary for understanding and implementing successful treatment of violent crime victims. This text will help with these challenges.

We had three main goals in writing this text:

- **Accuracy.** This book is the result of many years of facilitating, researching, and working with crime victims. It is important to teach skills that are based in research from the fields of social work, criminal justice, public health, and other related disciplines. This book places a clear emphasis on skills but also ensures that those skills are based on rigorous and current research.

- **Understanding of the victim experience.** To describe and explain victimization concepts, this book uses realistic examples to help clarify skill applications. These examples will help distinguish between effective and ineffective assessment and treatment practices, as well as help identify the practices that practitioners may wish to adopt to improve their interactions with violent crime victims.

- **A structured approach.** We have defined violent crime victimization and treatment in terms of key crime types.

Taken as a whole, this framework allows readers to place new information and skills development into a larger context. The title of this book, *Helping Victims of Violent Crime: Assessment, Treatment, and Evidence-Based Practice,* speaks to fundamental components in helping individuals who have been victimized. In this text, readers will discover the unique dynamics of crime victimization; the essential skills that lead to success in helping victims of violent crime; and the roles, tasks, and processes that pave the way for effective work with this population. By examining crime victims from each of these viewpoints, readers will come to understand the dynamic capacity of each interaction. To be competent in helping violent crime victims, as this text emphasizes, practitioners must learn to identify each situation as unique, assess what skills are needed, and effectively apply the appropriate skills. In essence, the goal of this text is to provide a toolbox from which practitioners can draw for any victim situation. The emphasis here is on critical thinking, skills assessment, and practice. In this book, we have documented the latest trends, intervention strategies, and treatment programs for violent crime victims. Unlike most books on violence, this volume provides guidelines and practical applications of crisis intervention and other time-limited treatment approaches for use with victims of violent crime. Because we are in the twenty-first century, with managed care cost-cutting and major health insurance restrictions looming over our clients and patients, the time-limited clinical strategies and programs examined in this book are of paramount importance.

Acknowledgments

Like any production, a book cannot be accomplished without the support of many people who have contributed their time, energy, commitment, and emotional support to make the completion of this venture possible.

We would like to thank Suzanne Deffendall, who worked tirelessly with commitment to the formatting and editing. We would also like to thank Brandy Macaluso for her assistance with the literature search.

We extend our grateful appreciation to the following professionals and organizations for their contributions and for providing critical expertise and cogent information throughout the development of this book: Robert Neimeyer, PhD; Mental Help Net (www.mentalhelp.net); and HospiceNet for their contributions to Chapter 2 on grief and loss. Child Welfare Information Gateway; Judith Cohen, MD (medical director at the Center for Traumatic Stress in Children and Adolescents); Julie Lipovsky, PhD; the Children's Law Center; and Aaron T. Beck, MD, for their contributions to Chapter 5 on child abuse. Sherry Falsetti, PhD, University of Illinois College of Medicine; and the Rape, Abuse and Incest National Network (RAINN) for their contributions to Chapter 7 on sexual assault. Debi Fry, research director, New York City Alliance Against Sexual Assault; Alyssa Rheingold, PhD, Medical University of South Carolina; and the National Organization of Parents of Murdered Children for their contributions to Chapter 8 on homicide. Prevent Elder Abuse for its contribution to Chapter 9 on elder abuse. George Everly, Jr., PhD, for his expertise and contributions to Chapter 10 on terrorism and mass violence.

Dr. Roberts gives special thanks and gratitude to colleagues and old friends who have influenced and increased my knowledge based over the past three decades. Specifically, Ann Wolhert Burgess DNSc, Professor of Psychiatric Nursing at Boston College for useful suggestions with chapter 4 on crisis intervention and chapter 6 on Intimate Partner Violence; and Karen Knox, PhD, Associate Professor of Social Word at Texas State University in San Antonio for useful suggestions with chapter 11 on school violence.

1

Victims of Violent Crime: An Introduction

SCOPE OF THE PROBLEM

In 2002 the Federal Bureau of Investigation's (FBI) Uniform Crime Report (UCR) estimated that one Crime Index offense was committed every 2.7 seconds in the United States. Over the past two decades, violent crime has become one of the most serious domestic problems in the United States. The United States has the highest violent crime rate of any industrialized nation, and crime in the United States accounts for more deaths, injuries, and loss of property than all natural disasters combined. Approximately 13 million people (nearly 5% of the U.S. population) are victims of crime every year. Approximately one and a half million are victims of violent crime. From 2004 to 2005, the rate of violent crime was estimated at 469.2 violent offenses per 100,000 inhabitants (US Department of Justice, 2005). Statistics provided in *Crime in the United States, 2005,* include

- An estimated 1,417,745 violent crimes occurred nationwide in 2006.
- There were an estimated 473.5 violent crimes per 100,000 inhabitants.
- When data for 2006 and 2005 were compared, the estimated volume of violent crime increased 1.9%. The five-year trend (2006

compared with 2002) indicated that violent crime decreased by
0.4%. For the 10 year trend (2006 compared with 1997) violent
crime fell 13.3%.

- Aggravated assault accounted for the majority of violent crimes,
  60.7%. Robbery accounted for 31.6% and forcible rape accounted
  for 6.5%. Murder, the least committed violent offense, made up
  1.2% of violent crimes in 2006.
- In 2006, firearms were used in 67.9% of the nation's murders,
  in 42.2% of the robbery offenses, and in 21.9% of the aggravated assaults. (Weapon data are not collected for forcible rape
  offenses.)
- An estimated 17,034 persons were murdered nationwide in 2006,
  an increase of 1.8% from the 2005 estimate.
- Murder constituted 1.2% of the overall estimated number of violent crimes in 2006.
- There were an estimated 5.7 murders per 100,000 inhabitants.
- In 2006, an estimated 90.6% of the murders occurring in the
  nation were within Metropolitan Statistical Areas.
- In 2006, there were an estimated 92,455 forcible rapes reported
  to law enforcement.

Experiencing a criminal victimization, be it violent or nonviolent,
is among one of the most stressful human experiences. Consequently,
ensuring quality of life for victims of crime is a major challenge facing
policy makers and mental health providers.

HISTORICAL PERSPECTIVE ON VICTIMOLOGY

The scientific study of victimology can be traced back to the 1940s and
1950s and stems from theories of crime. Mendelsohn began to explore
the field of victimology by creating "typologies." Mendelsohn is one of
the first theorists whose focal point was the victim. He took into account
the victim–offender relationship, but concentrated on the victim's role.
He posited that there was a personal relationship between the victim and
offender, and he offered several classifications of victims:

- the completely innocent victim (i.e., a child or unconscious victim)
- the victim with minor guilt (i.e., a woman who induces a miscarriage and dies as a result)

- the victim who is as guilty as the offender (i.e., assisting others with a crime)
- the victim more guilty than the offender (i.e., individuals who provoke others to commit a crime)
- the most guilty victim (i.e., when a perpetrator acts aggressively and is killed by another person acting in self-defense)
- the imaginary victim (i.e., mentally ill individuals who believe they are victims, such as acting on paranoia)

Likewise, Hans von Hentig's (1948) theory of victimization utilized classes of victims but extended to psychological types of victims. His general classes consisted of: the young, the female, the old, the mentally defective (mentally disordered, substance and alcohol abusers), and immigrants, minorities, and dull normals (indicates those individuals who are easy victims due to feelings of helplessness in a foreign land). Von Hentig's psychological types included

- the depressed
- the acquisitive (an individual with an excessive desire for gain)
- the lonesome and heartbroken
- the tormentor (when a child is abused for years and kills the abuser when the child grows up)
- the blocked, exempted, and fighting (an individual who is enmeshed in a bad situation and becomes immobile)
- the activating sufferer (when a victim is transformed into a perpetrator)

He concluded that crimes happened to certain individuals and that those individuals were responsible for the crime, not the offender.

Wolfgang conducted the first large-scale investigation on victim-precipitation and murder. Both parties (victim and perpetrator) were viewed as "mutual participants" in the homicide. Over 25% of all homicides studied involved a victim that initiated the violent act—was first to use force. Several victim precipitation factors were identified (prior relationship, argument, alcohol consumption by victim). Wolfgang (1958) developed theories of victimization and also perceived the victim as a major player in the crime event, often at the exclusion of the offender's responsibility. These perspectives are based on the old point of view of blaming the victim.

These historical perspectives of victimization perpetuate a victim-blaming approach to understanding the phenomenon of crime, the offender, and the victim. Although the victims' movement has generated a move toward a victim-centered approach and away from the victim-blaming approach, theoretical foundations have not fully adopted this premise. From a victim-centered and strengths perspective, as opposed to a victim-blaming perspective, the victim has often encountered a terrible situation with a bad outcome, over which the victim is angry and sad, but might still feel proud about how he or she handled himself or herself. If we approach this victim from a victim-theoretical perspective, we would worsen an already difficult situation by imposing value judgments and placing responsibility and blame on the victim, resulting in higher levels of distress.

VICTIM PROGRAMS, LEGISLATION, AND FUNDING

In response to the growing increase in violence in the 1980s, President Ronald Reagan announced in 1981 that he would create a Task Force on Victims of Crime. The President signed an executive order on April 23, 1982, promising to make a "swift, serious, and substantive effort to study what could be done to help crime victims" (President's Task Force on Victims of Crime, 1982, p. 2). Additionally, the work of the American Psychological Association's Task Force on Crime Victims (1984) and the Attorney General's Task Force on Family Violence (1984) increased the awareness of the psychological and emotional impact of crime on victims and on indirect crime victims (family, friends, and relatives of the victim). As a result of these efforts, both criminal justice and mental health professionals began observing and responding to the needs of crime victims. "Violent crimes, like homicide, rape and physical assault touch the lives of millions of Americans each year and produce persistent emotional effects which can last for years" (Kilpatrick, Saunders, Veronen, Best, & Von, 1987, p. 3).

Victim's Assistance is mandated under the Victims of Crime Act of 1984, as amended. The mission of the Victims of Crime Act (VOCA) Program is to enhance and expand direct services to victims of crime, with special emphasis placed on victims of domestic violence, child abuse, and sexual assault. The program administers grants that provide funding support and technical assistance to approximately 63 community-based public or private agencies in the states that offer a range of services including crisis intervention, counseling, guidance, legal advocacy, transportation to court or to shelters, and referrals. According to federal guidelines, priority is given to eligible crime victims assistance programs providing direct services to victims of

- rape or sexual assault
- spousal abuse
- child abuse

Priority is also given to previously underserved victims of (violent) crime (survivors of homicide victims, elderly victims of abuse or neglect, victims of drunk drivers, adult survivors of child sexual assault or incest, or other violent crimes that are being neglected or not being served adequately).

The Victims of Crime Act of 1984 (VOCA) created the Crime Victims Fund, which is a major funding source for victim services throughout the nation. Millions of dollars have been deposited into the Fund annually from criminal fines, forfeited bail bonds, penalties, and special assessments collected by U.S. Attorneys' Offices, federal U.S. courts, and the Federal Bureau of Prisons. To date, Fund dollars have always come from offenders convicted of federal crimes, not from taxpayers. Previous legislation expanded the sources from which Fund deposits may come. Passed in October 2001, the Uniting and Strengthening America by Providing Appropriate Tools Required to Intercept and Obstruct Terrorism Act (USA PATRIOT Act) provided authority for the deposit of gifts, bequests, or donations from private entities into the Fund beginning in fiscal year (FY) 2002.

When the Fund was authorized in 1984, a cap was placed on how much could be deposited into it for the first 8 years. The amount of money deposited into the Fund has fluctuated from year to year. Lifting of the cap in 1993 allowed for the deposit of all criminal fines, forfeited bail bonds, penalties, and special assessments authorized by VOCA to support crime victim program activities. In FY 2000, Congress reinstated the cap on the Fund. Under this scheme, the actual amount of funding available for programs authorized by VOCA is determined each year during the appropriations process.

For the past three decades, victims of crime have joined together in a national crime victims' movement, whose focus is to change the ways in which the criminal justice system perceives victims. This movement is evidenced by the development of organizations such as

- National Organization of Victims Assistance—NOVA's mission is to promote rights and services for victims of crime and crisis everywhere.

- Mothers Against Drunk Driving—MADD believes it's possible for our nation to eliminate the tragedy of drunk driving and prevent underage drinking and is committed to serving drunk driving victims and survivors.

- Office for Victims of Crime—The Office for Victims of Crime (OVC) was established by the 1984 Victims of Crime Act (VOCA) to oversee diverse programs that benefit victims of crime. OVC provides substantial funding to state victim assistance and compensation programs—the lifeline services that help victims to heal. (Roberts, 1990) The agency supports trainings designed to educate criminal justice and allied professionals regarding the rights and needs of crime victims. OVC also sponsors an annual event in April to commemorate National Crime Victims Rights Week (NCVRW). OVC is one of five bureaus and four offices with grant-making authority within the Office of Justice Programs, U.S. Department of Justice.

- Parents of Murdered Children—POMC® provides the ongoing emotional support needed to help parents and other survivors facilitate the reconstruction of a "new life" and to promote a healthy resolution. Not only does POMC help survivors deal with their acute grief, but it also helps them with the criminal justice system. The staff of the National Headquarters of POMC will assist any survivor and, if possible, will link that survivor with others in the same vicinity who have survived their loved one's murder. In addition, the staff is available to provide individual assistance, support, and advocacy. The staff will help interested parents or immediate family members form a chapter of POMC in their community. POMC will provide training to professionals in such fields as law enforcement, mental health, social work, community services, law, criminal justice, medicine, education, religion, the media, and mortuary science who are interested in learning more about survivors of homicide victims and the aftermath of murder.

One result of the movement's efforts is that all 50 states and the federal government have passed important legal protections for victims of violent crime, and more than half of the states have amended their constitutions to guarantee rights for victims. However, these state constitutional rights are limited and are often overridden by the offenders' federal constitutional rights. One goal of the victims' movement is to see the rights of victims elevated to the same status as the rights of the accused. Several bills passed by the U.S. Congress over the past 20 years to promote the rights of victims include: the Victims' Bill of Rights of 1990, the 1994 Violent Crime Control and Law Enforcement Act, and the Justice for Victims of Terrorism Act of 1996. Most recently, the U.S. Congress passed the Victims' Rights Clarification Act of 1997. This bill included the right of victims to observe the trial; and to further allow victims the opportunity to provide the court with a victim impact statement at the sentencing phase of the trial. One example of such rights being implemented was in the Oklahoma City bombing trial, in which the victims of the bombing of the Alfred P. Murrah Federal Building (April 19, 1995) were allowed to observe the trial of Timothy McVeigh, one of the accused bombers.

Another bill introduced to the U.S. legislature in September 1998 was the Crime Victims Assistance Act. This act includes the following rights:

- the right to be heard on the issue of pretrial detention
- the right to be heard on plea bargains
- the right to a speedy trial
- the right to be present in the courtroom throughout the proceedings
- the right to give a statement at sentencing
- the right to be heard on probation revocation
- the right to be notified of a defendant's escape or release.

To date, there are in excess of 15 constitutional rights for offenders and no constitutional rights for victims of crime. In April 2002, President George W. Bush stated that "The Feinstein-Kyl Amendment was written with care, and strikes a proper balance. Our legal system properly protects the rights of the accused in the Constitution, but it does not provide similar protection for the rights of victims, and that must change. The protection of victims' rights is one of those rare instances when amending the Constitution is the right thing to do. And the Feinstein-Kyl Crime Victims' Rights Amendment is the right way to do it. There have been many initiatives, yet for all the new initiatives, victims have gotten far less than promised, as rights have often not been enforced."

Although there is a plethora of literature on the financial, psychological, medical, and emotional costs of victimization (Green, Streeter, & Pomeroy,

2005; Klaus, 1994; Rothbaum, Foa, Riggs, Murdock, & Walsh, 1992), which led to the Victims Bill of Rights, there is a dearth of literature on whether or not victims are being informed of these rights. Furthermore, the relationships among victims being informed of those rights, victims receiving services, and the impact of these rights on victims' emotional responses to crime have not been examined thoroughly.

In light of the lack of data examining the relationship between the impact of crime and victims' rights, researchers at the University of Texas at Austin, in collaboration with the Crime Victims Institute of the Office of the Attorney General in Texas, undertook the first statewide survey of victims that focused on these areas of research. The purpose of the study was to understand the impact of crime on victims and to determine whether victims were being informed of their rights. It was found that an integral component of victim services is the provision of information. In view of the growing national interest in this area, issues relating to the provision of services to crime victims deserve special consideration.

The study found that approximately 14% of the individuals were informed of their rights. It further found that those individuals who were informed of their rights and who received services experienced lower levels of impact than those victims who were neither informed of their rights nor received services. The authors found that the fragmentation of services provided and the lack of consistency in informing victims of rights were intrinsic in the criminal justice system. It was concluded that this fragmentation and lack of information could lead to increased levels of impact of crime on victims; however, these were not identified as the foremost concerns of those in the criminal justice system.

Thompson, Norris, and Ruback (1996) conducted a study exploring the experiences of homicide survivors (family members of the murdered), including the criminal justice system and activities therein. The authors also found that fragmented services provided by the criminal justice system increased levels of distress, which could in turn lead to long-term emotional difficulties. They found that fragmented services often lead to the victims' loss of control, lack of social support, and fear, resulting in increased levels of low self-esteem, depression, and complicated grief. Therefore, services provided within the criminal justice system can impact the recovery of victims.

COSTS: TANGIBLE AND HUMAN COSTS
OF VICTIMIZATION

The impact of crime on victims includes the emotional, financial, medical, physical, and social consequences of the crime. Society incurs many costs as a result of criminal acts. A 2003 report by the Centers for Disease Control and Prevention calculated the annual health-related costs of rape, physical assault, stalking, and homicide by intimate partners to exceed $5.8 billion each year (Centers for Disease Control and Prevention [CDC], 2003). Victims incur costs associated with stolen property, medical care, and wages lost as well as the costs of the pain and suffering experienced. These costs are often passed on to society at large through taxes and insurance costs.

The financial costs can be broken down into tangible and intangible costs of crime. Estimating the intangible costs (pain and suffering), the total cost of crime for fatal crime is approximately $93 billion; the cost of rape and sexual assault is approximately $127 billion; the cost of robbery and attempted robbery with injury is $11 billion; the cost of assault or attempted assault is $93 billion; and the cost of burglary or attempted burglary is $9 billion annually (National Institute of Justice [NIJ], 1996).

Regarding physical costs, 28% of rape victims report incurring physical injury (National Victim Center and Crime Victims Research & Treatment Center, 1992). It is estimated that the average tangible cost to a victim of rape is $52,058, whereas the average cost to a victim of assault or robbery is $12,594. In Los Angeles, $53 million was spent in hospitals on gunshot wounds of victims of crime.

The average costs for psychological injury are calculated based on the medical expenses incurred, such as emergency room medical costs for a gunshot wound. However, this does not take into account the pain and suffering that result that are not medically treated (fear of injury or death). Cohen (1998) has identified three main components in the cost of crime to victims: (1) direct monetary out-of-pocket costs; (2) pain, suffering, and fear of injury; and (3) risk of death.

There is a paucity of research on the cost of mental health care and the use of mental health care by victims of crime. It is estimated that between 3.1 and 4.7 million individuals received mental health care in 1997 as a result of crime, and victims comprise approximately 25% of the client population utilizing mental health care (Cohen,

1998). The National Crime Victims Survey addresses issues regarding physical and medical expenses, but it does not address the mental health costs of victims (Freedy, Resnick, Kilpatrick, Dansky, & Tidwell, 1994).

Research findings indicate that individuals are at higher risk of developing emotional and physical problems when they have been victims of violence (Resnick, 1997). Resnick found that physical injuries as a result of crime may lead to heart attacks, fractures, sexually transmitted diseases, chronic infection, and systemic disorders. Violence can often result in an impairment of physical functioning and may result in an increased use of unhealthy behaviors (smoking, drinking, lack of sleep). The medical costs of treatment of victims are 2.5 times as great as that of nonvictims (Resnick, 1997).

EMOTIONAL, PHYSICAL, FINANCIAL, AND SPIRITUAL IMPACT

Through research and media attention, both social scientists and the general public have begun to realize the emotional and psychological effects of crime on victims (Roberts, 1990; Green et al., 2005). In a study by Kilpatrick, Edwards, and Seymour (1992) examining posttraumatic stress disorder (PTSD) in rape victims and in the general population, 31% of the rape victims were found to have posttraumatic stress disorder, whereas only 5% of the women in the study who were not victims of a crime experienced PTSD symptoms. In a similar vein, 30% of the rape victims experienced major depression, whereas only 10% of the women who were not victims experienced major depression.

Victims of violent and nonviolent crime often experience emotional turmoil following the crime. Bard and Sangrey (1986) state:

> They may have trouble understanding their own intense feelings—waves of guilt or shame or rage or fear. Victims may be unable to handle uncertainty, frustration, unfamiliar situations, and rude strangers as well as other sources of anxiety outside of themselves. In this state of heightened vulnerability, they must cope not only with their everyday lives but also [with] a whole new set of problems created by the victimization. Ironically, victims have to deal with these new difficulties at precisely the time when they are least well equipped to do so. (p. 106)

Numerous studies have shown that victims of rape suffer from psychological and emotional difficulties including depression, anxiety, and PTSD. Green et al. (2005) found that individual differences of victims prior to the crime event could not account for individual differences in the effects of crime. They found similar psychological distress across victim types. Rando (1993) suggested that factors such as violence, suddenness, unexpectedness, and randomness of the violent crime, coupled with the anger of the victim, may place victims at risk for complicated grief. Shock, disbelief, numbness, changes in appetite or sleeping patterns, difficulty concentrating, confusion, anger, fear, and anxiety are all symptoms of complicated grief (Redmond, 1989). Complicated grief reactions may persist for many years and include experiencing and re-experiencing feelings of loss, anger, self-blame, guilt, and isolation. Complicated grief may become major depression if not treated properly, and it may result in PTSD. Victims of violent crime may suffer undiagnosed PTSD for many years, at great cost to their health and to the health care system (Kilpatrick & Falsetti, 1994). Resick (1988) found that lifetime prevalence of PTSD was significantly higher among victims of violent crime (25.8%) than among those who were victims of other traumatic events (9.4%).

Among the traumatic losses that may occur when one is the victim of a crime is a crisis in faith and a questioning of spirituality (Green & Pomeroy, 2007). In the death of a child, parents can become angry and question why an innocent child was taken. A woman who is the victim of a rape may question her faith in a higher power as a protector. There are feelings of betrayal, as can be seen by the response of a religious woman who faithfully said the rosary to protect her and her family in the midst of danger. Her husband was murdered, and now she finds it difficult to say the rosary as she feels betrayed by God. Victims who have lost a loved one may find it difficult to return to church without reliving the funeral (Johnson, 1997).

Another issue for victims may be that their rabbi, priest, or other religious leader, in an effort to provide support, tells them about the importance and necessity of forgiveness. These types of statements can be very distressing and can lead to the development of anger and rage. Janoff-Bulman (1992) states that people often operate on the basis of the underlying assumptions about the way the world is and why things happen. She further explained that when these assumptions are challenged, as they often are following a crime, the victim is left with no sense of control, often resulting in anger and rage. There is a paucity of research surrounding the spiritual effects on victims of crime. However, victims universally expressed a need for support from organized religious institutions.

There is an increasing amount of diversity in the United States, and victims' service providers recognize the need for culturally specific responses to the needs of victims of crime. Ogawa (1990) states: "The effectiveness of counseling for minority victims of crime can only derive from the cultural appropriateness of the treatment being offered. There must be a correspondence between how the victim identifies the most important aspects of a crime's impact and how these are addressed" (p. 253). Several issues should be considered: the role of the family, community values, gender roles, death perceptions and attitudes, migration and immigration experiences, religious and spiritual beliefs, education and employment, language, and level of assimilation (National Organization for Victims Assistance, 1998). African Americans represent the largest group of individuals to be victims of crime. They tend to have strong family ties and, as such, address issues within the family more often (Whitaker, 1990). Many Latinos do not speak English and have suffered oppression as immigrants. Furthermore, Catholicism is their predominant religion, and some of their cultural traits are extended family, silence, and avoidance of eye contact (Bastian, 1990). Asian Americans are usually taught to be task-oriented and therefore the therapy sessions should occur over a brief time period with specific tasks and concrete goals (Ogawa, 1990). While these are generalizations regarding minority cultures, it is important for service providers to become culturally competent and aware of social diversity in the provision of services to victims of crime.

SYSTEMS THEORETICAL FRAMEWORK

There are many deleterious effects that the impact of crime can have on its victims. In an attempt to move away from the victim-blaming perspective, this handbook will use systems theory, the holistic notion of examining the client in his or her environment. Coping, crisis, and attribution theories utilized under the metatheory of systems theory provide a good framework for victim-centered intervention (Green et al., 2005). It pertains to those victims who may be adequately coping with the stressful situation but may also need information and support in order to reduce the psychological distress and increase the overall well-being that they are experiencing at the time.

Systems Theory

Systems theory emphasizes the interconnections of events and the bidirectionality of effects between organism and environment. A systems theory perspective views human development from a person-in-environment context, emphasizing the principle that all growth and development take place within the context of relationships.

The basic assumption of systems theory focuses on homeostasis. A crime event causes a change in homeostasis and often results in disequilibrium. The victim's focus at this point is to regain equilibrium. The victim attempts to accomplish this through appraising the situation and choosing coping strategies. General systems theory finds its roots in the works of Von Bertalanffy (1968). Although his scientific study was based in physical science, he drew many of systems theory's concepts from philosophy, psychology, and neurophysiology. One of the first social workers to implement systems theory in practice was Carol Meyer (1970). She used systems theory within a transactional framework. From her perspective, the environmental system and personal system of victims of violent crime need to be taken into account in the victimization equation, and support systems (formal and informal) need to be investigated. The theory postulates that some forms of coping may be affected by the personal systems and the environmental systems (i.e., age, gender, and ethnicity) and that these systems account for certain appraisals in particular ways. It should also be recognized that coping and appraisal, especially when emotion-focused, are often so closely related that it is difficult to separate them.

Stress and Coping

"When a person faces an obstacle to important life goals, for a time, insurmountable through the use of customary methods of problem solving, a period of disorganization ensues, a period of upset, during which many abortive attempts at a solution are made" (Collins, 1978, p. 14).

An unexpected crime event often causes disequilibrium. If disequilibrium occurs, as described earlier, tension and discomfort are felt, resulting in feelings of anger, fear, anxiety, and depression. Coping is typically defined as "efforts to manage demands that tax or exceed our resources" (Folkman, 1997, p. 1107). In a stressful life situation such as when a crime occurs, an individual's emotional health may depend on the coping strategies used. Stress and coping theories posit that three factors determine the state of balance: (1) perception of the event; (2) available situational support; and (3) coping mechanisms (Collins, 1978).

Folkman and Lazarus (1988) have identified perception as a key in understanding the stress process. The victim's perception of the event and his or her ensuing assessment are necessary components to understanding the stress-coping process. Situational support includes formal and informal social support, emotional support, and tangible support. Social support has been shown to have strong positive effects on positive outcomes of stressful situations (Green & Pomeroy, 2007). In the stress buffer model (Cassel, 1976; Cobb, 1976), those individuals with strong social support are affected in a more favorable way than those with weak social support.

A cognitive paradigm is widely used in analyzing emotions within the stress-coping continuum. The basic assumption is that a stressful situation is interpreted or appraised by individuals, which results in their emotional experience (Berkowitz, 1993). Lazarus and Folkman (1984) define coping as "constantly changing cognitive and behavioral efforts to manage specific external and/or internal demands that are appraised as taxing or exceeding the resources of the person" (p. 1108). Their transactional model of coping includes problem-focused and emotion-focused functions and asserts that an individual's beliefs and appraisals play a key role in the coping process and recovery. Emotion-focused coping relates to activities aimed at controlling the emotional impact of the event, such as feelings of fear, anger, and sadness (Winkel & Vrij, 1995). The main issue with emotion-focused coping is how to manage these emotions and thus limit the negative psychological distress levels. Emotion-focused responses are aimed at regulating emotional distress. The problem-focused responses are aimed at altering person-environment relationships.

In a study conducted by Strentz and Auebach (1988), emotion-focused and problem-focused coping strategies were evaluated regarding the degree to which captivity was perceived as stressful. They found that individuals with emotion-focused strategies reported lower levels of anxiety and emotional distress levels. They further found that individuals with external locus of control used more emotion-focused coping. However, those individuals with external locus of control who used problem-focused coping strategies responded the most poorly on all of their measures.

Several researchers identify a coping model that expands on Lazarus and Folkman's transactional model (Green et al., 2005; Billings & Moos,

1981; Endler & Parker, 1990; Norwack, 1989). They posit that in addition to problem-focused and emotion-focused there are avoidance strategies. Endler and Parker (1990) divide avoidance into two components: social diversion (seeking out others) and distraction (engaging in an alternative task). From their perspective, avoidance (social diversion) is directly linked to social support. Social support, such as emotional, tangible, formal, informal, and informational support, has been widely established to decrease stress.

Most stress and coping theories focus on the "unidirectional causal pattern in which emotion affects coping both by motivating it and impeding it" (Folkman, 1997, p. 1108). In an attempt to understand the complex nature of the coping process, Susan Folkman conducted a longitudinal study of caregivers of men who are infected with AIDS and examined both positive and negative psychological states as a result of certain coping strategies. She demonstrated how distress, social support, and coping interface in the stress process by recognizing both individual and environmental factors. She further adds a cognitive appraisal component, and considers costs and benefits in the overall distress process. Her findings resulted in a proposed modification to the original Lazarus and Folkman transaction coping theory to include positive outcomes. These results support the research indicating that particular coping strategies have been shown to either assist or impede the mental and physical health status and recovery of victims (Endler & Parker, 1990).

CRISIS AND ATTRIBUTION THEORIES: HOW VICTIMS EXPERIENCE THEIR VICTIMIZATION

Crisis Theory

Crisis theory has its roots in stress theory, psychodynamic theory, and learning theory (Roberts, 2005). For some time, it has been debated as to whether crisis theory is indeed a theory, or whether it is rather a model or intervention. This book takes a theoretical approach that may translate into crisis intervention for victims. In order to understand the basis upon which this book considers crisis theory as a theory, crisis and theory must be defined. First, Roberts (2005) defines crisis as

1. perceiving a precipitating event as being meaningful and threatening

2. appearing unable to modify or lessen the impact of stressful events with the traditional coping methods
3. experiencing increased fear, tension, and/or confusion
4. exhibiting a high level of subjective discomfort
5. proceeding rapidly to an active state of crisis—a state of disequilibrium

Second, theory is defined as:

> A set of interrelated constructs (concepts), definitions, and propositions that present a systematic view of phenomena by specifying relations among variables, with the purpose of explaining and predicting the phenomena. (Kerlinger, 1986, p. 9)

Turner (1996) states the following with regard to using theory in practice intervention:

> When the practitioner looks at theory, the goal is to develop and refine an intellectual structure by which the complex array of facts encountered in practice can be understood, so that the nature of the intervention can be deduced and the effects of such intervention predicted. The clinician's principal interest is in the utility of theory: What can it tell me about the situation that will permit me to act effectively? (p. 4)

Crisis theory offers a framework to understand a victim's response to a crime. The basic assumption of crisis theory asserts that when a crisis occurs, people respond with a fairly predictable physical and emotional pattern (Roberts, 2005). The intensity and manifestation of this pattern may vary from individual to individual. The initial physical response includes the inability to move accompanied by emotional responses of numbness, denial, and disbelief. This stage typically ends rapidly and results in a fight-or-flight response. In preparation for danger, the body accelerates heartbeat, adrenaline begins pumping into the system, and emotions begin to burst forth, including fear, anger and rage, confusion, and so forth. After some time, the exhausted body rests, and the mind begins the process of emotional restructuring (Turner, 1996).

The victim of a violent crime often enters a crisis following the crime event. The initial state of the victim is that of disequilibrium. The actual state of active disequilibrium is time limited, typically lasting from 4–6 weeks (Turner, 1996).

In addition to the disequilibrium experienced, loss is often the result of a crisis situation. People live their lives on certain assumptions, which provide a grounding to help them make sense of the world around them. When a crime occurs, these assumptions are shattered (Janoff-Bulman, 1979). These losses may include the loss of a sense of control, loss of trust in God, loss of a sense of fairness, loss of security, guilt, and a sense of helplessness. A victim whose family member has been murdered may feel responsible for not protecting the victim, may question his or her faith, and may have lost the safety of his or her own home. The appraisal of these losses results in certain coping responses, which in turn either impede or assist in the recovery process of victims, which is directly linked to the following stress and coping model. Choice of coping strategy is expected to influence the emotional outcome of the victim. Individuals choosing a problem-focused coping strategy attempt to regain their equilibrium by problem solving, seeking direct information, and taking direct action, and often regaining a sense of control and equilibrium to their life (Green et al., 2005). From this perspective, victims may emerge from a crisis with new coping skills, stronger social support, and stronger well-being.

Attribution Theory

Attribution theory asserts that individuals make cognitive appraisals of a stressful situation in both positive and negative ways. These appraisals are based on the individual's assertion that they can understand, predict, and control circumstances, and they result in the victim's assignment of responsibility for solving or helping with problems that have arisen from the crime event. Thus, there are internal and external attributions of the cause of the victim's current problems and concerns. Attribution style is often considered as a regulating factor for problem-focused or emotion-focused coping with criminal victimization (Perloff, 1983; Peterson, Semmel, Abramson, Metalsky, & Seligman, 1982).

There are two conflicting models reflected in the literature. The Janoff-Bulman model (1979) asserts that more successful coping processes are characterized by internal attributions. This model posits that internal attribution works to increase the victim's sense of control and thus decreases the victim's sense of fear, resulting in more successful coping. Janoff-Bulman and Frieze (1983) state the following:

> Interestingly, self-blame can be functional following victimization, particularly if it involves attributions of one's behavior rather than one's enduring

personality characteristics. Behavioral self blame involves attributions to a controllable and modifiable source, and thus provides the victim with a belief in the future ability to avoid re-victimization. Victims can maintain a belief in personal control over future misfortunes. Characterological attributions are associated with depression and helplessness. Behavioral self blame, then, can help a victim re-establish not only a view of the world as orderly and comprehensible, but also a view of oneself as relatively invulnerable. (p. 54)

Conversely, the Abramson, Metalsky, and Alloy (1989) model asserts that internal attributions are damaging. This model posits that by utilizing external attributions for crimes, people will guard their self-esteem. They further assert that positive self-esteem enhances adjustment. In an attempt to understand these two opposing models, Winkel and Vrij (1993) examined the relation between external behavior and character attributions and several fear responses of burglary victims. Their results did not suggest that external attributers adjusted best, but rather suggested that they were least successful using the emotion-focused coping style. Victims with external attributions experienced higher levels of fear. Their study did, however, support the Janoff-Bulman model. Those victims with internal attributions, and as Janoff-Bulman specifically asserts, those with behavior attributions, were more successful in coping.

Most of the literature on internal attributions has focused on post-rape adjustment (Katz & Burt, 1988; McCaul, Veltum, Boyechko, & Crawford, 1990). Little research could be found dealing with internal attribution in various violent and nonviolent crime victim samples.

In this book, attribution refers to explanation of and perceptions about the cause of the crime and the cause of the experiences within the criminal justice system that potentially revictimizes the victim. The importance of cognition is easily seen when similar crimes result in differing interpretations from various victims. Victims of crime have significantly different experiences in the initial aftermath of the crime event (Green & Pomeroy, 2007). Victims may learn to attribute greater personal control over their behaviors and see possibilities for them to be change agents in their individual case and in the victims' movement. Self-efficacy is embedded within this perspective in Bandura's (1977) learning theory. Bandura states: "Expectations of personal efficacy determine whether coping behavior will be initiated, how much effort will be expended, and how long it will be sustained in the face of obstacles and aversive experiences" (p.191). In this sense, self-efficacy is a mediating variable to be considered in the change process and recovery for victims. Additionally, attribution theory is utilized in the victimization coping process to explain seeking social support networks.

SUMMARY OF THEORETICAL FRAMEWORK

The main function of coping strategies is to provide psychosocial adaptation in crisis situations (Green et al., 2005; Green & Pomeroy, 2007; Lazarus & Folkman, 1984; Moos & Schafer, 1993). Victims of crime encounter many challenges to their existing repertoire of coping strategies and equilibrium of self. Individuals often emerge from crisis or stressful situations with new coping strategies resulting in better subjective well-being. It is assumed that the individual chooses specific coping strategies based on the crime event and the ensuing appraisal and initial levels of distress (Green et al., 2005).

In essence, there are two ways of viewing the coping process from an interindividual and intraindividual approach to coping (Endler & Parker, 1990; Endler, Parker & Summerfeldt, 1993). The interindividual perspective involves the identification of basic coping styles used by individuals across stressful situations. From the intraindividual perspective, one is interested in specific situations that are stressful and "assumes that individuals have a repertoire of coping options available to them from which they can build what they believe to be the most effective strategy, depending on the nature of the situation" (Cox & Ferguson, 1991, p. 20).

Conceptual and theoretical approaches to the victimization process are particularly relevant to victim service providers. In summary, these four theories can delineate a definite model for approach to the victimization process. Systems theory takes into account both individuals and environmental factors and the interaction between the two. The overarching systems theoretical framework draws from the transactional stress and coping model and attribution model. Coping theory exemplifies the relationship of coping and social support in the transactional process by taking into consideration the individual and the environmental perspectives. Attribution theory demonstrates the help-seeking behavior and choices of coping strategies and possible negative effects of the social support systems. Finally, the framework combines the previously mentioned theories with crisis theory, which recognizes the immediate crisis stage in the future development of either positive or negative appraisals. It is from this theoretical framework that this book approaches an examination of interventions with a fuller understanding of the victimization recovery process.

2 Grief and Loss Reactions and Theories

"There can be no knowledge without emotion. We may be aware of a truth, yet until we have felt its force, it is not ours. To the cognition of the brain must be added the experience of the soul." *—Arnold Bennett (1867–1931)*

OVERVIEW, DEFINITIONS, AND COMMON GRIEF REACTIONS

No amount of knowledge can prepare us for being victims of a violent crime. Grief is the most intense and enduring emotion we can experience as a result of the victimization. There is no quick fix, no shortcut. An ancient African saying is "there is no way out of the desert except through it." Knowledge of the grief process gives us a generalized map of the terrain that must be covered. Each victim will take a different route, and each will choose his or her own landmarks. Each victim will travel at his or her own unique speed and will navigate using the tools provided by culture, experience, and faith. In the end, victims will be forever changed by their journey. Knowledge helps us avoid the major pitfalls of grief. Knowledge of what is known of grief assures victims that they have not lost all sense of sanity. When victims find themselves feeling befuddled in a mist-shrouded swamp they can say, "It's okay. This, too, is part of my journey. Others have gone this way before me, and I will survive. I am human."

While several theories of victimization have been developed in an attempt to understand the victim's role in the crime event, none of the theories of victimization attempts to understand the impact and outcome of the crime event on the victims. Numerous studies have shown that victims of rape suffer from psychological and emotional difficulties including depression, anxiety, and posttraumatic stress disorder (PTSD). Norris and Kaniasty (1991) found that individual differences of victims prior to the crime event could not account for individual differences in the effects of crime. They found similar psychological distress in victims across the board. Rando (1993) suggested that factors such as violence, suddenness, unexpectedness, and randomness of the violent crime, coupled with the anger of the victim, may place victims at risk for complicated grief. Shock, disbelief, numbness, changes in appetite or sleeping patterns, difficulty concentrating, confusion, anger, fear, and anxiety are all symptoms of complicated grief (Redmond, 1989). Complicated grief reactions may persist for many years and include experiencing and reexperiencing feelings of loss, anger, self-blame, guilt, and isolation. Complicated grief may become major depression if not treated properly and often results in PTSD. Victims of violent crime may suffer undiagnosed PTSD for many years, at great cost to their health and the health care system (Kilpatrick & Falsetti, 1994). Resnick (1987) found that lifetime prevalence of PTSD was significantly higher among victims of violent crime (25.8%) than among those who were victims of other traumatic events (9.4%).

Among the traumatic losses that may occur when one is the victim of a crime are a crisis of faith and a questioning of spirituality. In the death of a child, parents can become angry and question why an innocent child was taken. A woman who is the victim of a rape may question her faith in a higher power as a protector. There are feelings of betrayal, as can be seen by the response of a religious woman who faithfully said the rosary to protect her family and herself in the midst of danger. Her husband was murdered, and now she finds it difficult to say the rosary since she feels betrayed by God. Victims who have lost a loved one often find it difficult to return to church without reliving the funeral (Johnson, 1997).

Another issue for victims may be that their rabbi, priest, or other religious leader, in an effort to provide support, tells them about the importance and necessity of "forgiveness." These types of statements can be very distressing and lead to the development of anger and rage. Janoff-Bulman (1992) stated that people often operate on the basis of underlying assumptions about the way the world is and why things happen. She further explained that when these assumptions are challenged, as they often are following a crime, the victim is left with a sense of having no control, and anger and rage often result. There is a paucity of research surrounding the spiritual effects on victims of crime. However, victims universally expressed a need for support from organized religious institutions.

Thompson, Norris, and Ruback (1996) conducted a study exploring the experiences of homicide survivors (family members of the murdered), including experiences with the criminal justice system and activities therein. The authors found that fragmented services provided by the criminal justice system increased levels of distress, which could lead to long-term emotional difficulties. They found that fragmented services often led to the victims' loss of control, lack of social support, and fear, resulting in increased levels of low self-esteem, depression, and complicated grief. Therefore, services provided within the criminal justice system can impact the recovery of a victim (Amick-McMullan, et al., 1989).

There remains confusion about the experience of victims and the severity and clinical significance of the recovery process reported by clinicians and victims. The sudden and unanticipated criminal act is a catalyst to the trauma and grief that is experienced. Psychological consequences of crime are not limited to a few days or weeks after the crime. Evidence is mounting that criminal victimization can be an extremely stressful event, leaving many victims with significant levels of psychological distress (Atkeson et al., 1982; Kilpatrick et al., 1985). The presence of such distress implies that many victims would benefit from professional mental health services (Norris et al., 1990).

Trauma destroys cognitive schemas regarding safety and self-efficacy (van der Kolk & van der Hart, 1989). Trauma represents an insult or injury to the structure of one's personality (Everly & Lating, 2004). As human beings, we require and create assumptions about ourselves, others, and the world in general. These beliefs can be thought of as "assumptive worldviews" (Janoff-Bulman, 1992). According to Janoff-Bulman, there are five core worldviews:

1. the belief in a just and fair world
2. the belief that some people can be trusted
3. the belief in self as a good, self-efficacious person
4. the need for safety
5. the belief in some order to life such as religion or spirituality

Janoff-Bulman asserts that psychological trauma is the result of a violation of one or more of the core assumptive worldviews. Some examples of these violations are injustice, betrayal, guilt, lack of safety, lack of meaning, and being affected by events that one cannot understand. As will be seen in Chapter 4 on child abuse, children are more vulnerable to these types of violations, because they have fewer coping strategies and their worldviews are more prominent. When children encounter these violations, the result can be arrested normal development. They can also develop maladaptive coping strategies such as self-blame.

The remainder of this chapter describes several theories of dealing with a loss of one's assumptive world. These are theories of grief and loss that have typically been applied to death and dying, but that must be recognized in the context of any violent crime to be able to understand and assist victims of crime. Every crime victim encounters a loss in her or his assumptive world and therefore must grieve that loss. The main thrust behind all these theories is a basic understanding that the grieving process and how a victim experiences it are directly related to the relationship of the victim to whatever is lost (i.e., loss of safety; loss of belief that humans are, at their core, basically kind and good). Throughout this chapter, the term "death" will refer to loss, not just to death.

Most crime victims achieve some significant recovery sometime between one and three months (1–3 months) after the crime. During this time period, they are shocked, surprised, and terrified about what has happened to them. They often have feelings of unreality, thinking, "This can't be happening to me." Many will also report having periods of rapid heart rate and hyperventilation. Such physiological and emotional reactions are normal "flight or fight" responses that occur in dangerous situations.

In the days, weeks, and the first two or three months after the crime, most violent crime victims continue to have high levels of fear, anxiety, and generalized distress. This distress disrupts their ability to concentrate and to perform simple mental activities that require concentration. They are preoccupied with the crime (e.g., they think about it a great deal of the time; they talk about it; they have flashbacks and bad dreams about it). They are often concerned about their safety from attack and about the safety of their family members. They are concerned that other people will not believe them or will think that they were to blame for what happened. Many victims also experience negative changes in their precrime beliefs that the world is a safe place where you can trust other people and where people can get the things they deserve out of life.

Long-term psychological trauma also takes on various forms. The DSM-IV diagnosis of PTSD refers to a characteristic set of symptoms that develop after exposure to an extreme stressor. Experiencing sexual assault, physical attack, robbery, mugging, or kidnapping; observing the serious injury or death of another person as a result of a violent assault; and learning about the violent personal assault on or death of a family member or close friend are specifically mentioned in the DSM-IV as types of stressors that are capable of producing PTSD. When exposed to these stressor events, the person's response must (according to the DSM-IV) involve intense fear, helplessness, or horror. Characteristic symptoms of PTSD include

1. persistent reexperiencing of the event (e.g., distressing dreams, distressing recollections, flashbacks, or emotional or physiological reactions when exposed to something that resembles the traumatic event)
2. persistent avoidance of things associated with the traumatic event or reduced ability to be close to other people and have loving feelings
3. persistent symptoms of increased arousal (e.g., sleep difficulties, outbursts of anger, difficulty concentrating, being constantly on guard, extreme startle response)
4. duration of at least one month of symptoms
5. clinically significant distress or impairment in social, occupational, or other important areas of functioning

The lifetime prevalence of PTSD was significantly higher among crime victims than among victims of other traumatic events (25.8% vs. 9.4%). Rates of PTSD appear to be higher among victims who report crimes to the criminal justice system than among nonreporting victims. There is also evidence that many crime victims with PTSD do not spontaneously recover without treatment, and that some crime victims have PTSD years after they were victimized. Long-term, crime-related psychological trauma is not limited to PTSD. Compared to people without a history of criminal victimization, people with criminal victimization have been found to have significantly higher rates of major depression, thoughts of suicide, alcohol and drug problems, panic disorders, agoraphobia, and obsessive compulsive disorders. In addition to these mental disorders and mental health problems, violent crime often results in profound changes in other aspects of the victim's life. Many victims experience problems in their relationships with family and friends. Among the relationship problems they can suffer is difficulty in sexual relations with their partners.

Victims of any types of violent crime experience profound losses and a sense of grief. These losses include the loss of self, loss of the belief in a just world, loss of spiritual belief, and loss of relationships. It is important to understand the grief process and how to help victims through the recovery process by allowing them to grieve their individual loss in their unique ways. Grieving these losses is paramount to moving successfully through any part of the recovery process. Grief is the physical, emotional, somatic, cognitive, and spiritual response to actual or threatened loss of a person, thing, or place to which we are emotionally attached. We grieve because we are biologically willed to attach. Some common grief responses are

- numbness
- shock
- anger
- anxiety
- loneliness
- fatigue
- yearning
- relief
- tightness in the chest
- shortness of breath
- lack of energy
- panic attack–like symptoms
- disbelief
- confusion
- sense of presence

GRIEF WORK, STAGES AND PHASES

Several theories about grief have been proposed. Sigmund Freud began with the concept of having to do "grief work." That is, a specific job should be finished before the next job begins. Stages-of-grief theories abound. The following are snapshots of some of these theories provide by Mental Health Net.

Teresa Rando

Teresa Rando (1993) surmised that if one or more circumstances surrounding the loss contributed to the experience being traumatic, the factors were present for a high risk of complicated mourning. Because there is no warning, the suddenness of the crime attacks the victim's sensibilities. With this trauma, the victim is presented with the task of working through his or her interpretation of how difficult or horrid the crime event was. If this imagery combines with feelings of guilt, and the victim's view that the crime was somehow preventable, several elements can arise that complicate the grieving process. As Rando identified eleven issues inherent in sudden and unanticipated death, she noted the reoccurring theme of the intense reactions experienced by victims. There is no singular emotion that takes precedence over another—all emotions are amplified. It is as if a hurricane's force captures a person and spins him or her into a wild array of human emotions, with no release until the fury dissipates. A person is able to survive this turbulence, but typically not without emotional if not physical injury. It is this injury that can have a dramatic impact on the individual working through the grief process. "When emotional injury has taken place, the body begins a process as natural as the healing of the physical wound" (Colegrove, Bloomfield, & McWilliams, 1976, p. 1). A person may need validation, regardless of the crime, along with supportive guidance so that his or her lament will eventually be transformed. Rando also has contributed a model of the grief process that she observed people to experience while adjusting to significant loss. She called her model the "Six R's":

- **Recognize** the loss: First, people must experience their loss and understand that it has happened.
- **React**: People react emotionally to their loss.
- **Recollect** and **Reexperience**: People may review memories of their lost relationship (events that occurred, places visited together, or day-to-day moments that were experienced together).
- **Relinquish**: People begin to put their loss behind them, realizing and accepting that the world has truly changed, and that there is no turning back.
- **Readjust**: People begin the process of returning to daily life, and the loss starts to feel less acute and sharp.
- **Reinvest**: Ultimately, people reenter the world, forming new relationships and commitments. They accept the changes that have occurred and move past them.

Robert Neimeyer

Although different in approach and in the ordering of stages, all of these models of the grief process share common similarities. They all understand grief to involve an often painful emotional adjustment that necessarily takes time and cannot be hurried along. This much appears to be universally true, although each person's grief experience will be unique. Currier, Holland, and Neimeyer (2006) found that the survivor's subjective interpretation of the loss is more influential in explaining the ensuing grief response. Neimeyer offers a new approach to grief theory that places the central emphasis on sense making and the struggle to reconstruct a personal world of meaning that has been challenged by loss (Gillies & Neimeyer, 2006; Neimeyer & Anderson, 2002). Currier Holland, and Neimeyer (2006) propose a constructivist conceptualization of loss/bereavement in which:

1. Individuals bring a set of existing beliefs about themselves and the world to the loss experience.
2. The experience of loss can violate or fracture these basic assumptions.
3. Restoration entails a struggle to adapt one's personal world of meaning to "make sense" of the loss, with less "normative" or violent losses being more challenging to comprehend.
4. Complications in grieving result when the individual is unable to "make sense" of the loss within the context of his or her current system of meaning.

Currier, Holland, and Neimeyer (2006) support a model of bereavement whereby the complicated grief (CG) that follows violent loss is conceptualized as coming from one's inability to make sense of the experience. By way of illustration, Robert Neimeyer offers the following poem:

Breakfast at the Retreat

To the survivors of Victims to Victory,
and their quest to find grace beyond the homicide
bereavement that is their common bond

The clean round tables gather the women
like open palms, call them together
for the morning meal.

Night's grasp still holds them
in silence, like the still-fresh graves
that hold their husbands, their babies,
their lives.

To strengthen themselves
to tell the story again,
suture the wounds in group,
they take their plates,
find their place,
feel the always-empty chair
for each seat filled.

A woman with moist eyes
and a blue tattoo of her daughter
on her forearm lifts the white jar,
pours sugar on her grits, forks in
the scrambled egg.

It's a Black thing, her Aunt Ethel explains,
a way to have something sweet
when your life is poor.

Bowlby and Parkes

The conceptual framework of the attachment theory (the bonds that are formed early in life with parental figures and derived from the need to feel safe and secure) and of human information processing (the process used to filter out or let through unwanted information) have been combined to explain loss and bereavement. According to Bowlby and Parkes's model, the bereavement process can be divided into four phases that survivors (family, friends, colleagues) of a loss may experience:

1. Shock and Numbness: During this initial phase, survivors have difficulty processing the information of the loss; they are stunned and numb.
2. Yearning and Searching: In this phase, there is a combination of intense separation anxiety and disregard or denial of the reality of the loss. This engenders a desire to search for and recover the lost person. Failure of this search leads to repeated frustration and disappointment.
3. Disorganization and Despair: Individuals often report being depressed and have difficulty planning future activities. These

individuals are easily distracted and have difficulty concentrating and focusing.

4. Reorganization: This phase overlaps to some degree with the third phase.

The phases adjust to allow existing internalized, representational figures of safety and security to be reshaped.

Elisabeth Kübler-Ross

Probably the most famous formulation of the stages of grief was developed by Dr. Elisabeth Kübler-Ross in her book, *On Death and Dying*. Kübler-Ross actually wrote about the stages that dying people tend to go through as they come to terms with the realization that they will soon be dead (see Table 2.1). However, her stages have since been borrowed by the larger grief community as a means of describing the grief process more generally. Coming to terms with dying is certainly a loss experience and an occasion for grief, so there is merit to this borrowing and reason to become familiar with Kübler-Ross's stages. Again, not everyone will experience all of these stages, or, if all are experienced, they will not necessarily occur in this particular order.

Kübler-Ross's first stage is Denial. In this stage, grieving people are unable or unwilling to accept that the loss has taken (or will shortly take) place. People can feel as though they are experiencing a bad dream, that the loss is unreal, and that they are waiting to "wake up," as though from a dream, expecting that things will be normal. After people have passed through the denial and accepted that the loss has occurred (or will shortly occur), they may begin to feel Anger at the loss and the unfairness of it. They may become angry at the person who has been lost (or is dying). In the next stage, Bargaining, people beg their "higher power" to undo the loss, saying things along the lines of "I'll change if you bring her (or him) back to me." This phase usually involves promises of better behavior or significant life change that will be made in exchange for the reversal of the loss.

Once it becomes clear that Anger and Bargaining are not going to reverse the loss, people may then sink into the Depression stage, where they confront the inevitability and reality of the loss and their own helplessness to change it. During this period, grieving people may cry, experience sleep or eating habit changes, or withdraw from other relationships and activities while they process the loss they have sustained. People may

Table 2.1

GRIEF'S BLUEPRINT

Let this circle represent a stage, phase, or piece of work. It can be denial, shock, anger, resolution, confusion, numbness, a behavior, or whatever you are feeling right now.

Add a second circle and let it overlap the first. Give it another name. Perhaps what you were feeling yesterday, last week, or one hour ago.

Continue adding circles that overlap and represent emotions, physical sensations, cognition, or behaviors that belong to you.

This is Grief's Blueprint. You may feel secure and at peace one moment, and then find yourself in the paralyzing center of all the overlapping elements of grief the next. It's okay. It's human.

also blame themselves for having caused or in some way contributed to their loss, whether or not this is justified. Finally (if all goes according to Kübler-Ross's plan), people enter a stage of Acceptance, where they have processed their initial grief emotions, are able to accept that the loss has occurred and cannot be undone, and are once again able to plan for their futures and reengage in daily life.

Which Theory Is Right?

The Rev. Howard R. Gorle offers the following analogy: Grief or bereavement theories are the generalized maps discussed earlier. Each theory is an attempt by a caring investigator to understand and guide us through our pain. However, humans are unique and cannot be forced into particular patterns of behavior. Individuals travel through grief at their own speed using their own appropriate routes.

SUMMARY

Regardless of practice settings, you will encounter clients who are coping with life trauma, violence, impeding illnesses, death, grief, and bereavement. Victim service providers should be trained to implement early intervention strategies in an effort to avoid or reduce an exacerbation of the crime event. A proficient practitioner would assess the losses the client has experienced and would provide support. The practitioner should explore any client history of mental health treatment or psychological distress, and attempt to differentiate between depression and the grief reactions related to the crime event.

The goals of grief counseling as outlined by Kenneth Doka include

- helping the victim to actualize and accept the loss, most often by helping him or her talk about the loss and the circumstances surrounding it
- helping the victim to identify and to express feelings related to the loss (e.g., anger, guilt, anxiety, helplessness, sadness)
- helping the bereaved to live without the deceased and to make independent decisions
- helping the bereaved to withdraw emotionally from the deceased and to begin new relationships
- providing support and time to focus on grieving at critical times such as birthdays and anniversaries
- "normalizing" appropriate grieving and explaining the range of individual differences in this process
- providing support in an ongoing manner, usually not on a time-limited basis (as with grief therapy)
- helping the bereaved to understand his or her coping behavior and style
- identifying problematic coping mechanisms and making referrals for professional grief therapy

Victim service providers play a unique role in the recovery and healing process experienced by victims of crime for a number of reasons. The overall focus is to promote self-sufficiency of victims through empowerment and advocacy. A set of core values should be present that focus on service, social justice, dignity and worth of the victim, importance of human relationships, integrity, and competence.

Loss is the state of being deprived, and grief is the natural response to loss. Grief is the victim's way of trying to process a crime event that affects the victim on multiple levels. When working with victims of violent crime, it is important to remember the following:

- You cannot take away the pain from the victim. Do not let your own sense of helplessness prevent you from reaching out; expect to have to tolerate unpredictable reactions.

- Recognize the critical value of your presence (Being vs. Doing). Be sure to view and understand the loss(es) nonjudgmentally and from the victim's unique perspective.
- Let genuine concern and caring show. Do not let your own needs determine how the victim's loss should be experienced; do not attempt to minimize the situation.

3

Stress and Coping Model for Victims of Crime

In 2005, U.S. residents age 12 or older experienced approximately 23 million crimes, according to findings from the National Crime Victimization Survey. Because of the increase in the number of crimes and the violent nature of those crimes, growing numbers of men and women are faced with having to adapt to the mental, physical, and emotional consequences associated with being a victim of a crime. Understanding the role of stress and coping is vital to practitioners involved with victims of crime. The first thing that must be understood is what stress is. There are several approaches to considering stress. One approach is to focus on the environment: stress as a stimulus (stressor). The second is to focus on the reaction to stress: stress as a response (distress). The third is to focus on the relationship between the victim and the environment: stress as an interaction (coping).

Victims of crime have encountered obvious stressors. The ensuing result is either acute stress (experiencing a sudden, typically short-lived, threatening event) or chronic stress (experiencing an ongoing environmental demand such as interacting with the criminal justice system or changing daily activities as a result of victimization). Lazarus and Folkman's (1984) cognitive model of stress includes these considerations:

- Primary appraisal—Is there a potential threat?
- Outcome—Is it irrelevant, good, or stressful?

- If stressful, evaluate further:
  - Harm or loss—how much damage has already occurred?
  - Threat—what is the expectation for future harms?
  - Challenge—what are the opportunities to achieve growth?
- Secondary appraisal—Do I have the resources to deal effectively with this challenge or stressor?
- Coping possibilities—Will I be able to manage the discrepancy between the demands of the situation and the available resources?
  - Coping includes the ongoing process of appraisal and reappraisal and is not static.
  - Coping can alter the stress problem or regulate the emotional response.

APPRAISAL

The level of threat or harm that the victims feel largely affects the psychological trauma they experience (Sales, Baum, & Shore, 1984; Wilson, Smith, & Johnson, 1985). Although a criminal act often produces stress, victims differ in their sensitivity toward, interpretations of, and reactions to the crime event. One person may respond to a sexual assault with anger, another with depression, and another with guilt; another may feel challenged or threatened for days or weeks after the crime. Even in the most devastating of circumstances, individuals will respond in a myriad of ways. Benner, Roskies, and Lazarus (1980) found that survivors of the Nazi concentration camps differed in responses and choice of coping strategies. Although coping refers to "what a person thinks or does to try to manage an emotional encounter, appraisal is an evaluation of what might be thought or done in that encounter" (Lazarus, 1991, p. 113). In an attempt to understand effective coping processes, the researcher must understand the cognitive processes that intervene between the crime event and the victim's adaptation. Ekehammer (1974) summarized the implication of appraisal in the coping process this way: " the person is a function of the situation, but also, and more importantly . . . the situation is a function of the person through the person's (a) cognitive construction of the situation and (b) active selection and modification of the situation" (p. 105).

There are two types of appraisal: primary and secondary. Appraisal can be defined as "an evaluative process that determines why and to what extent a particular transaction or series of transactions between the person and the environment is stressful" (Lazarus & Folkman, 1984, p. 19). The primary appraisal includes the conscious assessment of the crime to determine whether it is harm, a loss, a threat, or a challenge. The secondary appraisal occurs when the victim begins to question what he or she can do to influence the situation at hand and, in so doing, assesses potential resources to use in problem solving.

Appraisal is not information processing; rather, it is evaluative, focused on determining meaning, and intervenes between the crime event and the immediate stress response. It is through appraisal processes that the victim evaluates the significance of the crime on his or her well-being. Clinical implications from this intraindividual perspective posit that cognitive restructuring, behavior modification, biofeedback, and relaxation techniques would enhance the coping mechanisms and lead to a positive adaptation.

SOCIAL SUPPORT

Research supports the role of social support in stress resistance (Cohen & McKay, 1984; Thoits, 1985). Oatleley and Bolton (1985) suggest that social support functions as a deterrent in the experience of depression. A number of other studies demonstrate social support as enhancing well-being and deterring distress (e.g., Cohen & Wills, 1985; Hobfall & Lerman, 1988; Karasek, Triantis, & Chaudhry, 1982). There has been an increasing recognition of the role of coping in relation to social support. From a coping theory perspective, social support is one variable to be considered in the individual's appraisal of the event, in the immediate stress response, and in the general well-being of the victim.

Social support has been conceptualized as "those activities that enhance a person's sense of competence through receiving material and cognitive help as well as emotional comfort" (Hobfall & Vaux, 1993, p. 7). Studies of social support (Antonucci, 1985; Deimling & Harel, 1984) suggest that social support is a major factor in physical and psychological well-being. Lazarus and Folkman (1984) and Gore (1980) also propose that social support may have an indirect effect on well-being by improving effective coping strategies or cognitive and behavior-based problem-solving strategies. Social support is an important factor that may buffer against the ill effects of the crime event on the victim.

Social support has also been established as being linked to the handling of stressful situations (Bolger & Eckenrode, 1991; House, Umberson, & Landis, 1988). Several cross-sectional and longitudinal studies have shown a positive association between social support, recovery from depression, and protection from adverse effects of stress (Antonucci, 1985; Harel & Deimling, 1984; Koenig, Westlund, George, Hughes, Blazer, & Hybels, 1993). Kahn and Antonucci (1993) suggest that adults with strong supportive relationships are able to cope better with the stresses of their environment.

Situational determinants of the need for social support are of specific relevance to this volume. Theorists in social support hold that individuals require a medium to high intensity of support when they are caregivers to the terminally ill as well as at critical points in the illness (Folkman, 1998; Lazarus & Folkman, 1986). It stands to reason that this would hold true for any individual in a crisis situation.

Social support is an important coping resource for persons experiencing stressful life changes (Cohen & Wills, 1985). Additionally, Hansen et al. (1995) found that social support plays a vital role in victim recovery from crime-related psychological trauma. Kaniasty and Norris (1994) found that support from friends, family, and community assists in recovery. As a result of a crime, victims often experience a restricted social life (Nadelson, Notman, Zackson, & Gornick, 1982). Cutrona and Russell (1990) classify emotional support as most beneficial to victims since it fosters feelings of acceptance and comfort at a time when victims often feel isolated. Material and tangible support have been shown to have a positive effect in the recovery process. Social support is considered an asset in providing necessary resources that the victimization experience depletes (Hobfall, Freedy, Geller, & Lane, 1990). Hobfall and Vaux (1993) conceptualized social support as "those activities that enhance a person's sense of competence through receiving material and cognitive help as well as emotional comfort" (p. 686). Social exchange theorists emphasize the dual nature—supportive behavior and unsupportive behavior—of social ties (Homans, 1974; Thibaut & Kelley, 1959). Hall and Wellman (1985) found that many problems stem from or are exacerbated by unsupportive behavior of others. Victims often feel that the criminal justice system is unsupportive; thus, it revictimizes the individual, and the psychological consequences are exacerbated.

Social support has been shown to have a positive relationship with victims seeking professional help. Steinmetz (1984) found that victims with fewer social support networks are more likely to seek professional help. Conversely, other studies have found that responsive social networks actually enhance and facilitate higher use of services by encouraging the victim to find needed care (Frieze, Hymer, & Greenberg, 1987; Gourash, 1978; Horowitz, 1977). Several studies indicate the positive effect that social support has on the posttrauma recovery of victims of crime (Burgess & Holstrom, 1974; Ellis, Atkeson, & Calhoun, 1981; Moss, Frank, & Anderson, 1990). Other studies indicate that stressful events are less likely to adversely affect persons with strong social support. For victims of crime, social support is seen to foster acceptance and comfort (Kraus, 1986).

Lazarus and Folkman (1984) state: "Social support provides vital resources which the individual can and must draw upon to flourish. That people gain sustenance and support from social relationships has been known intuitively for a long time, and should be in a sense obvious" (p. 243). The victim is often left isolated from his or her family and society and is often shunned or stigmatized by both. The development of social support networks is crucial in the recovery process of any victim. As a result, social support has important implications for therapeutic change (Mallinckrodt, 1989).

Social workers have a long tradition of concern for the client's environment as an important factor in healing and in promoting optimal functioning. Social support upholds the belief in a systems perspective, upon which social work is based. Systematic ways to assess the influences of the environment or the support of social networks are tantamount to proper assistance. Research that uses person-in-environment variables will lead to an accumulation of knowledge answering the question, "What types of social networks are most useful for victims in terms of what particular issues under what environmental conditions?"

The stress-buffer model has been depicted most often in research (Cutrona & Russell, 1990). From this perspective, stress affects individuals with weak social supports more adversely than it does those individuals with strong social support (Cassel, 1976; Cobb, 1976). Which types of social support are most beneficial to a victim's well-being? In order to answer this question, two domains (perceived social support and received/enacted social support) must be explored. While some research clearly documents that perceived social support functions as a buffer, there is limited research examining the role of received social support (Cohen & Wills, 1985; Kessler & McCleod, 1985). However, there is little agreement as to the definition of perceived support (Bruhn, 1991).

It has been well established that social support is a multidimensional construct, and as such, it is difficult to capture a universally accepted definition (Barrera, 1986). Researchers investigating victimization have not thoroughly explored the potentially important influence of all of the social support dimensions (Pearlin, 1985).

Perceived and Received Social Support

While the term *received social support* refers to the helping behaviors that are actually provided, *perceived social support* refers to the belief that one is held in high esteem and loved by family and friends and that those individuals would be there for support if needed (Norris & Kaniasty, 1996). These two forms of support are shown to be independent domains within the literature. There is a paucity of research examining the mediating effect of received support on well-being.

One component that has been identified universally is the concept of the subjective appraisal of support, or perceived support. Perceived social support consists of the individual's appraisal of being connected to and loved by others. This definition implies that if one feels connected, then one also perceives that the social support will be readily available when needed. A variety of social support networks may influence the well-being of a victim since the impact may affect the victim in a myriad of ways. Kaniasty and Norris (1994) found that perceived social support was more effective in the buffering process for victims of crime than received support was. Additionally, Sarason, Sarason, and Shearin (1986) suggest that social support should be considered as an individual difference variable.

The role of social support in stress resistance is well documented (Cohen & McKay, 1984; Cohen & Willis, 1985). However, little research exists that examines the role of social support in the coping process of victims. Coping research from the transactional model defines social support as those resources victims "draw on in order to cope" (Lazarus & Folkman, 1984, p.158). Holohan and Moos (1994) propose a coping-process model where social support directly and indirectly affects adaptation.

As researchers have begun to examine the role of social support, it has become evident that receiving support may not always have positive effects on the emotional outcome (e.g., Coyne, Wortman, & Lehman, 1988). Although receiving help may not always have a positive influence on well-being, the reception of help might be affected by the meaning tied to it in the form of perceived support. In resolving problems, victims may be assisted by the knowledge that friends and family are readily available and willing to help if needed.

The complex process and nature of social support should not be underestimated. In an attempt to understand how perceived social support and received social support are related, Kaniasty and Norris (1997) undertook an investigation of a social support deterioration model. This model posits that stress would "threaten the perceived availability of support but that when support was adequately mobilized, the otherwise deleterious impact of stress on perceived support would be suppressed" (p. 4). The underlying assumption of this model is that this relationship would eventually uphold the notion that perceived support benefits the victims' emotional outcome in part through activation of such support. Although received support may play an important role in shaping perceived support, perceived support may also determine whether or not those support systems are mobilized. As a result of research on social support, much of the research community has called for further analysis of perceived and received social support and the role they play in the victimization process (e.g., Barrera, 1986; Cohen, 1992; Eckenrode & Wethington, 1990).

Formal Social Support

Crime victims attempt to cope with the crime emotionally and physically, in part through the use of formal support systems. While there has recently been a proliferation of services for victims of crime, there is a dearth of research on the effects of these services. Johnson (1997) conducted a longitudinal study examining the effects of professional help on the emotional adaptation of victims following a crime event, and on the frequency with which victims seek professional help. Johnson found that the majority of victims do seek professional help of some sort (e.g., financial, medical, mental health). The results of this study regarding the effectiveness of this help were inconclusive.

In another study, Friedman, Bischoff, Davis, and Person (1990) investigated the problems that victims face and the extent to which formal and informal support systems were used. The results of their study indicate that crime universally disrupted victims' lives. This disruption manifested itself in psychological problems such as anxiety, shame, loss of sleep, and fear, as well as financial problems. They found that the majority of victims did receive support from their informal support networks but underused the formal support networks available. They attributed this underuse, in part, to lack of knowledge that the formal support systems existed. They concluded that victim assistance programs should be based locally and should be comprehensive in nature.

Victims of crime inevitably encounter the criminal justice system. Previous research suggests that victims are often revictimized by the criminal justice system (Elias, 1984; Thompson & Norris, 1992). Few studies have attempted to assess the impact of formal support systems on victims of crime.

Social Support as a Mediator and a Moderator

Social support as a mediator of stress has received much attention in coping research (Cohen & McKay, 1984; Cohen & Wills, 1985). Lazarus and Folkman (1984) stated that social support is the support system upon which individuals "draw on in order to cope" (p. 158). They further maintain the idea that social support "precedes and influences coping" (p.158). According to traditional coping theory, the coping process would follow this path: the event occurs, and then social support moderates the coping mechanism, which, in turn, results in the emotional outcome. However, what has not been established is whether perceived social support existed prior to the event and, therefore, functions as a moderator. Once the crime occurs, the victim experiences distress, and then the received social support mediates this distress response and the emotional outcome. Research examining the mediating and moderating effects of perceived and received social support could broaden our conceptual understanding of the coping process.

COPING

In the past few decades, *coping* has become a term that has received considerable interest in the behavioral sciences (e.g., Billings & Moos, 1981; Heppner, 1988; Lazarus & Folkman, 1984; Pearlin & Schooler, 1978). According to Folkman, Lazarus, Dunkel-Schetter, Delongis, and Gruen (1986), the emotional consequences resulting from a crime and the coping strategy chosen to deal with this crime depend on how well the chosen strategies match the situational demands. For example, if the situation resulting from the crime is perceived by the victim as somewhat controllable, he or she would be more likely to have positive emotional outcomes using a problem-focused coping strategy as opposed to an avoidance-oriented strategy (Valentiner, Holohan, & Moos, 1994). Holohan and Moos (1990) further state that coping strategies become increasingly important as the stressful situation increases in severity. Therefore, in order to understand the recovery process for victims of crime, it may be helpful to understand the relationship between the type of crime committed and the coping strategy used.

Coping refers to those conscious or unconscious thoughts and actions that provide the means of dealing with a stressful event (Stone, Helder, & Schneider, 1988). Lazarus and Folkman's (1984) theory defines coping as the "constantly changing cognitive and behavioral efforts to manage specific external and/or internal demands that are appraised as taxing or exceeding the resources of the person" (p. 141). In an attempt to "manage demands," one may avoid, tolerate, accept, or minimize the stress. Both mental and physical health can be affected by coping strategies (Clark & Hovanitz, 1989; Endler & Parker, 1990). There is a plethora of research supporting the role that coping strategy plays in the well-being of people in stressful situations (e.g., Endler, 1988; Miller, Brody, & Summerton, 1988; Nezu, Nezu, Saraydarian, Kalmar, & Ronan, 1986). However, there is inconclusive evidence as to the role of coping in mediating initial distress and producing well-being. The current volume defines coping as "constantly changing cognitive and behavioral efforts to manage specific external and/or internal demands that are appraised as taxing or exceeding the resources of the victim" (Lazarus & Folkman, 1984, p. 141). Since coping is determined by the relationship between the victim and the victim's environment, it is transactional in nature and has three dimensions: emotion focused, problem focused, and avoidance oriented.

Coping as Mediator

Coping theory posits that coping behaviors affect mental health outcomes. However, it is suggested that distress often increases coping efforts (e.g., Haan, 1969; Miller, 1987; Moos & Schafer, 1993), and that coping processes in turn reduce distress. When viewed in this manner, coping functions as a mediator between a negative event and distress (Folkman & Lazarus, 1988). Mediator variables should not be confused with moderator variables. Mediating variables are generated in the encounter, and they affect the relationship between the antecedent variable and the emotion outcome. Moderating variables exist prior to the event and include factors such as age, gender, and ethnicity. From the transactional perspective, coping is viewed as a mediator (i.e., the coping strategy is generated by the crime event and affects the emotion outcome of the victim) (Folkman & Lazarus, 1988). The majority of research on coping has been an examination of those mediating effects of coping on distress. The question remains as to whether coping is a response to the initial stress reaction or a result of the appraisal of the stressful event. In an attempt to overcome this limitation in current research, studies must look at both functions of coping and causality.

One area largely neglected in coping research is the "co-occurrence of positive and negative psychological states throughout enduring and profoundly stressful circumstance" (Folkman, 1997). In an attempt to overcome this limitation, Folkman (1997) looked at coping processes that are associated with positive psychological states for caregiving partners of men with AIDS. Folkman concluded that a modification to the transaction coping theory should be made to include the co-occurrence of positive and negative psychological states. What remains to be explored is whether coping is a mediator of the initial stress response and the well-being of victims of crime. The analysis in the current volume attempts to identify this direction of causality.

Coping Dimensions

As stated earlier, victims of crime often experience psychological distress in response to a crime. Lazarus and Folkman (1984, 1987) developed a process-oriented model differentiating between emotion-focused coping and problem-focused coping. *Emotion-focused coping* relates to those coping behaviors aimed at managing these emotions or regulating the emotional distress. Emotion-focused coping strategies focus on some aspect of the stressful situation and are generally considered to be maladaptive. *Problem-focused coping* refers to those cognitive efforts used to regulate the stress. Defining the problem and generating, evaluating, and implementing solutions are all considered indicative of a problem-focused approach to coping. This approach involves "short circuiting the negative emotions through behaviors that modify the stressor or minimize its impact" (Strentz & Auerbach, 1988, p. 653). According to this definition, problem-focused coping is goal oriented (Folkman, 1997). Folkman (1997) found that problem-focused coping is more likely to contribute to positive emotional outcomes, in part because the individual has a sense of control in the problem-solving process.

Avoidance-oriented coping refers to efforts to direct attention away from the stress. This approach to coping is characterized by denial (Meneghan, 1989). Billings and Moos (1981) found that depressive symptoms were more often associated with avoidance-oriented coping strategies than with emotion-focused or problem-focused coping strategies. Similarly, Wirtz and Harrel (1987) found that victims using avoidance-oriented coping demonstrated higher levels of distress, resulting in a longer recovery process. In contrast to emotion-focused coping, with the focal point being on some aspect of the stressful situation, victims using the avoidance dimension of coping distance themselves from or avoid the stressful situation.

In summary, problem-focused coping strategies attempt to resolve or minimize the stressor; emotion-focused coping strategies involve conscious behaviors related to affect regulation; and avoidance-oriented coping strategies rely on activities that divert or distract the victim (Endler & Parker, 1990). While problem-focused, emotion-focused, and avoidance-oriented coping are unique approaches, the literature reviewed does not provide a way of identifying the specific effect of each strategy. Further research is needed to examine the most effective coping strategies with positive emotional outcomes, thus providing a clear basis for intervention and treatment. In an attempt to overcome this limitation in research, Strentz and Auerbach (1988) conducted a study simulating abduction followed by 4 days of captivity. There were three groups: one with preparation in emotion-focused coping, one with preparation in problem-focused coping, and a control group with no preparation. The researchers found that participants typically used the coping strategy in which they had been oriented. The practice implication for this finding would be enhanced if it were known which strategy actually improved well-being. We need a fuller understanding of the relationship of coping to distress and social support. Collins, Taylor, and Skokan (1990) summarize the importance of understanding the coping process in the following manner:

> Because victimizing events produce many problems and disruptions, different aspects of the event are likely to be amenable to different strategies of coping. A repertoire of responses may allow individuals to take maximum advantage of each situation to facilitate positive perceptions and experience. (p. 280)

WELL-BEING

The main focus of conventional coping theories has been on the management of stress (Folkman, 1997). Folkman (1997) has recently modified transaction coping theory to include the occurrence of both distress and positive adaptation. She postulates that stressful encounters eventually result in adaptation, and that research needs to take into account this variable for consideration.

The term *well-being* includes concepts such as life satisfaction, absence of feelings of anger or guilt, physical health, emotional health, happiness, lack of anxiety, lack of depression, spiritual health, and control over one's situation (George & Gwyther, 1986; Parkes & Pillisuk, 1991). Well-being is a useful and appropriate outcome measure for several reasons: it can be used when comparing types of crime victims and nonvictims, and more importantly, the well-being scales do not force the victim to look solely at the negative effects of the crime.

Ory et al. (1985) define well-being as the impact of the changes in cognition and behavior, subsequent need for care, and the ability to cope. This definition recognizes that behavioral and cognitive changes do not have the same impact on all individuals. Spiritual well-being has been demonstrated as a significant factor in coping with traumatic events (Baumeister, 1991; Idler, 1995; McIntosh, Silver, & Wortman, 1993). Traumatic events may trigger changes in or questioning of one's religious belief and faith. However, there has been little research about the role that spiritual faith plays in the recovery from or adaptation of a traumatic event. Kennedy (1999) conducted a study examining the extent to which women experiencing sexual assault report a change in the role of faith. The results of the study indicate a significant increase ($p < .0001$) in the role that spirituality played in the aftermath of a sexual assault.

Much of the literature on well-being documents studies that have been conducted with chronically and terminally ill populations. Well-being is often referred to in this body of literature as "quality of life." There are many findings from the well-being literature describing studies with other populations that can translate into the victim population. DeHaes and Knippenberg (1985) stated that research on quality of life (well-being) can be meaningful in several ways: it can provide insight into (victim) reactions, and it can enhance the methods by which supportive care can be promoted and organized (p. 809). Most authors include physical, psychosocial, and spiritual well-being (Ferrell & Dow, 1993).

Polinsky (1994) used physical, psychological, and social functioning as specifically related to treatment concerns of cancer patients. There are several domains that well-being or quality of life researchers have developed for studying the impact of the illness on a population.

The following summarizes the mental, physical, and spiritual components of well-being. Feelings of shock, depression, isolation, being emotionally overwhelmed, distrust, anger, and anxiety are often manifestations of a crime's impact on victims. Research studies summarized by Kilpatrick, Edwards, and Seymour (1992) identified a range of problems associated with victimization, including medical complications, financial difficulties, anxiety, depression, posttraumatic stress, and loneliness. These problems can greatly impact the victim's sense of well-being. Social workers may advocate for victims experiencing these problems by continually interacting with the criminal justice system and victim assistance programs.

Spiritual beliefs can aid victims in the acceptance of the crime and assist victims with coping. A sense of spirituality can often help with guilt and blame that the victim imposes on himself or herself. Having spiritual beliefs can readily facilitate adapting to possible outcomes of the criminal justice process. As victims look for the meaning of life, a sense of spirituality can lead to a regrouping of resources; priorities can change, and a renewed personal commitment to living a productive and content life can occur.

Well-being is a multidimensional framework with specific domains. The well-being in each domain is readily affected by change within another domain. Examining the well-being framework of a victim will allow social workers to fully understand potentially positive dynamics associated with the recovery process.

DISTRESS

Victimization is a stressful event resulting in significant levels of psychological distress (Atkeson, Calhoun, Resick, & Ellis, 1982; Burman et al., 1988; Cook, Smith, & Harrell, 1987; Frieze, Hymer, & Greenberg, 1987; Kilpatrick et al., 1985). Exposure to such stress often carries a risk of depression, anxiety, and posttraumatic stress. Additionally, victims of crime are affected by the crime event and by subsequent contact with the criminal justice system in a myriad of ways. Unique challenges exist for victims of crime because of the uncertain nature of the criminal justice process. Before social workers can give support to victims of crime, they must be able to assess and understand the immediate reaction to the crime by the victim. As Bard and Sangrey (1986) indicate,

> [Victims] may have trouble understanding their own intense feelings—waves of guilt or shame or rage or fear. Victims may be unable to handle uncertainty, frustration, unfamiliar situations, and rude strangers as well as other sources of anxiety outside of themselves. In this state of heightened vulnerability, they must cope not only with their everyday lives but also with a whole new set of problems created by the victimization. Ironically, victims have to deal with these new difficulties at precisely the time when they are least well equipped to do so. (p.106)

A study of 105 violent crime victims, 227 property crime victims, and 190 nonvictims found the symptomatology of anxiety, depression, somatization, hostility, and fear prevalent in all victims, with the victims of violent crime demonstrating higher levels of distress than the victims of nonviolent crime. Studies have consistently shown that the effects of crime are pervasive and deleterious to the victims' emotional health (e.g., Davis & Friedman, 1985; Kilpatrick et al., 1985; Lurigio & Resick, 1990; Kaniasty & Norris, 1994; Witrz & Harrel, 1987).

Previous research indicates psychological problems are the primary result of being victimized by a crime. Norris and Kaniasty (1991) found that violent crime has a direct effect on psychological distress. Bard and Sangrey (1979) posited that even victims of nonviolent crimes could experience emotionally deleterious effects resulting from the loss of control and a weakening of a belief in an orderly and just world.

While the negative effects of stressful situations are clearly documented in research, the stress-and-coping process remains unclear. In an attempt to gain an understanding of this process, both distress and well-being need to be examined. In the current volume, distress is defined as the manifestation of depression, posttraumatic stress, anger, and/or anxiety. Literature on each of these components of distress will be reviewed in the sections that follow.

Depression

One area of the victim's mental health that is particularly salient in understanding his or her responses to a crime event is the amount of depression exhibited. As Kilpatrick (1983) pointed out, virtually all victims of violent crime experience some level of depression. What accounts for the ability of some victims to cope effectively with the crime event while maintaining their own mental health, while others become overwhelmed and experience depression? Depression is a mental health problem for which there are effective interventions that can assist in the improvement of the victim's well-being.

Christensen (1981) found that increases in stressful life events are associated with an increase in levels of depression and anger. Depression has been cited as a manifestation of anger turned inward, or anger that is suppressed (Alexander & French, 1984). Clay, Anderson, & Dixon (1993) conducted a study that supported these assumptions and further found that people who direct their anger outward experience significantly lower levels of depression.

The relationship between coping and depression has received increasing interest in empirical research (Endler & Parker, 1990). Several research studies demonstrated the association of emotion-focused coping and depression (Holohan & Moos, 1992; Stanton, Danoff-Burg, Cameron, & Ellis, 1994). While victims of violent crime demonstrate higher levels of depression, property crime victims have also been shown to exhibit depressive symptoms (Cook, Smith, & Harrel, 1987; Lurigio, 1987). Violent crime, in particular, leads to more negative schemas resulting in long-lasting depression (Janoff-Bulman, 1992; Roth & Newman, 1991). In a study conducted on elderly bereaved spouses, Prigerson et al. (1997) found that symptoms of complicated grief are distinct from depressive symptomatology, while both appeared to be associated with long-lasting functional impairment.

Kaniasty and Norris (1994) found that symptoms of depression initially were exhibited immediately following the crime as well as 3, 9, and 15 months after the crime. Atkeson et al. (1982) obtained measures of depression at 2 weeks and at 1, 2, 4, 8, and 12 months after rape. They further found that victims of rape had significantly higher depression than did nonvictims for the first 4 months. Homicide survivors (family and loved ones of the homicide victim) have been shown to have depression manifested by shock, disbelief, numbness, changes in appetite, sleeping difficulties, heightened anxiety, and phobic reactions (Redmond, 1989). Tasks of grieving should be a focus of intervention in an attempt to alleviate depressive symptomatology. Frank, Turner, and Duffy (1979) found that 50% of rape victims were moderately to severely depressed following a sexual assault. Kilpatrick (1987) found that lifetime rates of depression were approximately 80% for women who had been sexually assaulted.

Depressed individuals have been shown to use emotional and avoidance coping strategies more often than problem-focused coping strategies (Zeidner & Saklofske, 1996). The relationship between coping and depression is complex. Endler and Parker (1994) suggest the need for further research in examining the tendency of individuals to employ certain coping strategies, and in the coping strategy's relationship to the ensuing emotional responses.

Posttraumatic Stress Disorder

The most prevalent classification of psychological injury in crime victims' cases is posttraumatic stress disorder (PTSD) (Sabbagh, 1995). A study by Irwin, Falsetti, Lydriad, Ballenger, and Brener (1996) found high rates (80%) for PTSD among victims. Rothbaum, Foa, Riggs, Murdock, & Walsh (1992) found that 90% of rape victims met criteria for PTSD within 2 weeks of the rape. They further found that 50% continued to meet criteria for PTSD 3 months following the rape. Victims of any violent crime are often affected by traumatic grief reactions, which can ultimately manifest into depression and PTSD if not treated (Kilpatrick, Saunders, Veronen, Best, & Von, 1987). While traumatic grief is not measured in the current study, it is an important variable in understanding posttraumatic stress, which is a variable measured in this study. For example, the sudden, traumatic death of a loved one is often the impetus for a traumatic grief reaction and hence PTSD.

Traumatic grief is an aspect of human behavior that accompanies loss. The classic study of grief reactions was written by Erich Lindemann, who observed and treated both victims and survivors following the tragic Cocoanut Grove nightclub fire that took place in Boston in the 1940s. According to Lindemann (1944), grief is a definite syndrome with somatic and psychological symptomatology, although the medical definition may not recognize it as such. Frequently, however, traumatic grief may find its fullest expression following a traumatic criminal act. Its effects may strike the victims at any moment following the crime, be it immediately or months and perhaps years later.

In a study of reactions of victims of rape, Riggs, Dancu, Gershuny, Greenber, and Foa (1992) found that initial anger, depression, anxiety, and rape-related fear were prevalent in all victims but at higher degrees in victims with PTSD. Prigerson et al. (1997) examined the effect of symptoms of traumatic grief on subsequent mental and physical health. They found that bereaved individuals were at a higher degree of risk for poor health outcomes when the subjects scored high on the traumatic grief scale.

Being a victim of violent crime does not mean that a survivor will develop PTSD, but if a victim is not afforded the opportunity to work through the crisis and begin the recovery process, the surviving victim's chances of developing PTSD are strongly increased. Many victims continue to reexperience the event and crisis reactions over long periods of time, and these reactions can be triggered by specific events (National Organization for Victim Assistance, 1992). Victims are often revictimized by the criminal justice system, the media, the hospital and emergency room, victim service providers, and victim compensation and social service workers.

A 1987 National Institute of Justice study found that 28% of all crime victims developed crime-related PTSD. Saunders, Kilpatrick, Resnick, and Tidwell (1989) found high levels of PTSD (51%) among victims who had high exposure to the criminal justice system. A study by Irwin, et al. (1996) found high rates of PTSD and other psychiatric diagnoses among victims of violent crime. Further empirical evidence for this relationship has been provided by Falsetti, Resnick, Dansky, Lydriad, and Kilpatrick (1995). PTSD has been considered a result of complicated grief and bereavement-related depression (Prigerson et al., 1997). They identified seven factors that constituted complicated grief that should be considered in the provision of services to ameliorate PTSD symptoms: searching, yearning, preoccupation, crying, disbelief, feeling stunned, and lack of acceptance.

PTSD affects from 9% to 15% of the general population and close to 50% of women who have been raped (Rothbaum et al., 1992). In a study comparing the level of PTSD between victims of rape and victims of other violent crime, Riggs et al. (1992) found similar symptoms with the symptoms of other violent crimes decreasing over time. Kilpatrick et al. (1987) found that 57% of women who had experienced rape suffered from PTSD. An average of 34% of victims of violent crimes was found to have experienced PTSD.

Valentiner, Foa, Riggs, and Gershuny (1996) found PTSD symptomatology to be a normative response to assault in a study of 215 female assault victims who were assessed within 2 weeks of the crime event. Freeman, Shaffer, and Smith (1996) found significant symptoms of depression, anxiety, posttraumatic stress, and psychosocial impairment in a study of 15 children following the murder of a sibling. There is a plethora of literature supporting the association of posttraumatic stress with conditions reported by adult family member survivors of homicide (Amick-McMullan, Kilpatrick, & Resnick, 1991; Amick-McMullan, Kilpatrick, Veronen, & Smith, 1989; Burgess & Holstrom, 1974; Freeman et al., 1996; Getzel & Masters, 1984; Vargas, Loa, & Hodde-Vargas, 1989).

Brewin, Andrews, Rose, and Kirk (1999) found that victims of violent crime who were interviewed within 1 month of the event exhibited acute stress disorder (19%) and posttraumatic stress disorder (20%) symptomatology. Additionally, in a study of trauma survivors, Shalev et al. (1996) found that 25% of the survivors developed PTSD. They further found that the severity of the trauma was not indicative of the PTSD symptoms manifested. As can be seen from these studies, it is important to identify those individuals who are at risk of developing PTSD.

Resnick, Kilpatrick, Dansky, Saunders, and Best (1993) found significantly higher rates of PTSD in victims of crime than in victims of other traumatic events (25.8% vs. 9.4%). Kilpatrick and Resnick (1991) further found that PTSD is more prevalent among those victims who reported the crime to the criminal justice system than those victims who did not report the crime. This could be a result of the revictimization that victims often feel when interacting with the criminal justice system, thus exacerbating the symptoms and responses of PTSD. Saunders et al. (1989) found that PTSD levels were higher among victims and families with exposure to the criminal justice system.

Working with crime victims suffering from psychological trauma requires extraordinary patience, understanding, and sensitivity. For many victims, the emotional responses become long-term and debilitating. Nightmares, fear, avoidance, and feelings of unreality are indicative of PTSD, and recovery is only a long-term hope given the current knowledge of PTSD.

Anger

While there is an absence of extant literature on victims' anger, it has begun to receive attention within the victim literature. Anger reflects a pattern of emotional distress that is associated with depression, anxiety, and posttraumatic stress (Deffenbacher, 1992). Research further suggests that anger indirectly influences coping style and emotional outcome, in part by eroding social support (Houston & Vavak, 1991; Siegel, 1992). Because anger is an emotion that occurs frequently in conflict-laden interactions (Averill, 1982), the nature of anger and its effects are critical issues in relation to successful recovery for victims of crime. Victims tend to demonstrate feelings of vulnerability, frustration, injustice, and anger (Rando, 1993). The importance of anger can be seen in the relationship of anger and levels of distress. Anger has been defined in terms of the ensuing aggressive behavior displayed by an individual (Berkowitz, 1962). Through the victim's interpretation and judgment of the crime event and situation, a victim may feel anger or hatred toward the offender and the situation (Garofalo, 1997).

Research suggests that anger is a factor in domestic violence (e.g., Leonard & Blane, 1992; Maiuro, Cahn, Vitaliano, Wagner, & Zegree, 1988; Pan, Neidig, & O'Leary, 1994). Anger is also often the result of bias-related crimes: "From the victim's point of view, the purpose of hate/bias crimes adds to the extra dimensions of fear" (Coleman, Gaboury, Murray, & Seymour, 1999, p. 21.1–9), and fear often leads to anger. Anger has been reported to increase the amount of depression and PTSD experienced by victims (Novaco, Hamada, Gross, & Smith, 1997; Resick, 1988).

Research has further indicated that there is a relationship between anger and stressful life situations in predicting depression (Nezu, Nezu, & Perri, 1989; Nezu & Ronan, 1988; Reynolds & Gilbert, 1991) and posttraumatic stress (Carroll, Rueger, Foy, & Donahoe, 1985). Anger has been observed repeatedly in victims of violent crime (Kilpatrick, Best, & Veronen, 1984; Yassen & Glass, 1984). A question that victims often ask is, "Why me?" If the crime is blamed on someone or something, the emotion experienced is anger, guilt, shame, or disgust (Goldberger & Brenitz, 1993).

Spielberger (1996) adapted a state trait theory of anger. *State anger* refers to the situational and transitory emotional factors, whereas *trait anger* is posited to be a broader personality dimension. When examining the emotional outcome of a crime event, state anger offers the most meaningful attempt to understand distress. State anger is considered to be experienced along a continuum of emotions ranging from no anger to extreme anger (Deffenbacher et al., 1996).

Anxiety

The core relational theme of anxiety is in facing an existential threat (e.g., Averill, 1988). Many crime victims describe experiencing high levels of anxiety (Kilpatrick & Falsetti, 1994; Kilpatrick, Veronen, & Resick, 1979). There are physiological anxiety symptoms (rapid heart rate, hyperventilation) and cognitive anxiety symptoms (fear of crime, helplessness). These reactions are often considered "fight-or-flight" responses and have direct impact on coping strategies. An example of this can be seen in the following:

> The disruptive effects of high levels of stress in circumstances requiring immediate productive activity are illustrated by the thoughtless action taken by a law enforcement agent during the race riot in Detroit in 1967 . . . A white National Guardsman believed that his own life was in immediate danger from snipers when he heard shots nearby after having been summoned by a night-watchman to investigate looting. Instead of taking cover and watching to see what was going on, he promptly decided to shoot to kill when he caught sight of a black man holding a pistol. The victim turned out to be the night-watchman, who had shot his pistol into the air to scare off the looters. (Janis & Mann, 1977, p. 61)

Additionally, anxiety often results in the victim questioning his or her belief that the world is a safe place where people get what they deserve out of life (e.g., Janoff-Bulman & Frieze, 1983). Victims often exhibit high levels of fear, anxiety, and distress for months following the crime event (Norris & Kaniasty, 1994). The felt anxiety often disrupts victims' ability to concentrate or work because they may be preoccupied with the crime. Victims are often concerned about their safety from future attacks on themselves or their family (Kilpatrick, Veronen, & Resick, 1979).

The association between anxiety and depression has been demonstrated repeatedly in research (Clark, 1989; Gotlib & Cane, 1989). Several studies demonstrate the difficulty in differentiating between depression and anxiety (Blumberg & Hokanson, 1983; Gotlib & Robinson, 1982; Hollon & Kendall, 1980). However, Burns and Eidelson (1998) investigated whether or not these two variables could be loaded on a single factor. Patients (n = 483) from a clinic in Philadelphia ranging in age from 15 to 80 were administered structured interviews using the Beck Depression Inventory, the Burns Anxiety Schedule, and the SCL-90 (Derogatis, 1974). The researchers found that symptoms of anxiety and depression could not be adequately represented by a single factor. Additionally, Endler, Cox, Parker, and Bagby (1992) found that both state and trait anxiety could be reliably differentiated from depression.

There are some adaptive qualities of anxiety. Barow (1991) states that "it is a future-oriented mood state where one is ready or prepared to cope with upcoming negative events" (p. 235). However, in the research on victims of crime, the distinction of the role of anxiety, separate from other levels of distress, has not been examined.

SUMMARY

Currently, there is no generally accepted paradigm that specifies the pattern of psychological correlates with coping strategies and levels of stress. Understanding the patterns of psychological correlates and how victims cope will inform the development of interventions designed to ameliorate the negative impact of crime and focus on successful coping strategies for crime victims. Uncovering dynamic relationships within the stress-and-coping process of crime victims may lead to more effective interventions with more successful adaptations. We must examine the multidimensional construct of social support and the discovery of social support networks' effect on the recovery process for victims of crime. Certain individual characteristics, appraisal choices, social support systems, and coping strategies can ameliorate distress and emotional outcomes, and help victims successfully respond to crime events.

One of the key recommendations of the 1982 President's Task Force on Victims of Crime stated that "the mental health community should work with public agencies, victim compensation boards and private insurers to make the psychological treatment readily available to crime victims and their families" (p. 2). The goal of this book is to begin the process of understanding one of the most serious problems in our time, enabling us to attain a first step in finding more humane and effective ways to assist the thousands of crime victims in the country.

4 Crisis Intervention

HISTORY

Historically, the roots of crisis intervention can be traced back to the aftermath of the Cocoanut Grove Nightclub fire on November 28, 1942, in Boston. At that time, 493 people died when flames ignited and rapidly spread through the crowded nightclub. Dr. Erich Lindemann, a community psychiatrist affiliated with Massachusetts General Hospital and Harvard Medical School, assessed and treated 101 survivors and close relatives of the victims of this tragic fire. Lindemann observed grief that seemed to be acute at onset, lasted for a brief time period, and followed a predictable sequence of stages. Lindemann further believed that preventive clinical interventions prevented psychopathology. In 1948, Lindemann established the first community mental health clinic for bereaved disaster victims and their families. It was known as the Wellesley Human Relations Service. Lindemann is best known as the founder of preventive crisis psychiatry, also known as crisis intervention.

Following Lindemann's lead, Morton Bard and Katherine Ellison firmly believe that crisis intervention is very relevant to police response toward crime victims, especially victims of forcible rape (Bard & Ellison, 1974). During the late 1960s, Bard and associates trained 18 New York City Police Department (NYPD) officers in family crisis intervention so that they could intervene more effectively in all family disturbance calls (now called domestic violence) in West Harlem.

Caplan (1964) eloquently summarized the four stages of a crisis:

1. There is an initial rise of tension from the impact of an external event, which results in problem-solving responses.
2. Any lack of success of these problem-solving responses, plus the continued impact of the stimulus event, further increases tension and feelings of upset.
3. As the tension increases, other problem-solving resources are mobilized. At this point, the crisis may be averted by any of the following: reduction in the external threat, success of new coping strategies, redefinition of the problem, or the giving up of tightly held goals that are unobtainable.
4. If none of these tension-averting events occurs, however, the tension mounts to a breaking point, resulting in severe emotional disorganization.

Dr. Bernard Bloom (1963) was the first clinical researcher to identify and isolate five common, specific variables of the crisis state. He had eight expert judges identify which variables depicted crisis situations in a series of case histories: (1) knowledge or lack of knowledge of a precipitating event; (2) rapidity of onset of reaction; (3) awareness or lack of awareness of personal, inner discomfort; (4) evidence of behavioral disorganization; and (5) rapidity of resolution. The results of the analysis indicated that two variables predominate: knowledge of a precipitating event, and slow resolution of between 1 and 2 months.

PRACTICE MODELS

Several systematic practice models have been used over the years in crisis intervention work. These crisis intervention models build upon the work of Caplan (1964), Golan (1978), Parad (1965), Roberts (1991), and Roberts and Dziegielewski (1995). Each of these practice models includes efforts to minimize and resolve immediate problems, emotional conflicts, and distress experienced through a minimum number of contacts between the victim and the intervener. Crisis-oriented treatment is by nature time limited and goal directed. This stands in stark contrast to traditional psychotherapeutic approaches, which may take years to complete.

Crisis intervention programs have changed dramatically since the late 1940s and 1950s, when the first crisis clinics were opened in Boston; Elmhurst, NY; and Los Angeles. Currently, hundreds of thousands of individuals experiencing acute crisis episodes telephone or walk into health, mental health, and family counseling facilities throughout the United States and Canada every day. Professional interest in crisis intervention, crisis management, crisis response teams, disaster mental health, and emergency management has grown tremendously since the horrific terrorist bombings of the World Trade Center and the Pentagon on September 11, 2001. "Crisis-inducing events and situations can often be critical turning points in a person's life. They can serve as a challenge and opportunity for rapid problem resolution and growth, or as a debilitating event leading to sudden disequilibrium, failed coping, and dysfunctional behavior patterns" (Roberts, 2005, p. xx). Many crises are triggered by an unpredictable, overwhelming, fear-inducing, or life-threatening event, such as acute cardiac arrest, psychiatric emergency, attempted murder, drug overdose, motor vehicle crash, child custody battle, turbulent divorce, domestic violence incident, aggravated assault, rape, or communitywide disaster (Roberts, 2005).

Crisis, trauma, disaster, critical incident, and emergency are words with which we have become all too familiar during the past decades. The terms used and the understanding of their meanings have changed over the years. This chapter provides a historical perspective and a current-practice guideline for the identification and management of crisis.

In examining issues of crisis, there are two primary paths that describe crisis experiences. One path relates to an individual's turning point or critical stage that exceeds internal resources to address whatever issues are being faced by the person. Another path is produced by a disaster or crisis-inducing event that functions as a trigger when it short-circuits the individual's coping mechanisms. Whatever the trigger episode is, individuals experiencing crisis events struggle to cope and attain a previously experienced level of composure and balance in their lives. Therefore a crisis is

an acute disruption of psychological homeostasis in which one's usual coping mechanisms fail and there exists evidence of distress and functional impairment[; t]he subjective reaction to a stressful life experience that compromises the individual's stability and ability to cope or function. (Roberts, 2005, p. 779)

The main cause of a crisis is an intensely stressful, traumatic, or hazardous event, accompanied by two other conditions: (1) the individual's perception of the event as the cause of considerable upset and/or disruption, and (2) the individual's inability to resolve the disruption through previously used coping methods. The presence of these two factors combine with the event to create "an upset in the steady state of the individual experiencing the crisis" (Roberts, 2005). While all crises are unique to the affected individuals, there are similar components within crisis episodes. Crisis episodes usually comprise five components: a hazardous or traumatic event, a vulnerable state, a precipitating factor, an active crisis state, and the resolution of the crisis (Roberts, 2005).

Crisis interveners should "adopt a role which is active and directive without taking problem ownership" from the individual experiencing the crisis (Fairchild, 1986, p. 6). Skilled crisis interveners consistently demonstrate characteristics of hopefulness and acceptance as they undertake efforts to communicate with persons experiencing intense emotional turmoil or threatening situations. At the same time clinicians are assuring the individual that she or he can survive this incident, they are also helping the individual resolve what may appear to be insurmountable problems in regaining physical, emotional, and social equilibrium in her or his life.

Recognition of the psychological, traumatic, and mental health impact of violent crimes has increased dramatically in recent years throughout the world. We live in an era in which violent crimes—domestic violence, rape, armed robbery, aggravated assault, violence in schools and the workplace, terrorist bombings, bioterrorism threats, sniper or drive-by shootings, and attempted murder—result in millions of situational and acute crisis episodes for children, youths, adults, and families. Every day, throughout the world, millions of people are affected by potentially crisis-inducing violent victimizations that they are not able to resolve on their own. They need immediate help from mental health professionals, crisis intervention workers, and/or their families.

Many people have existing resources, inner strengths and social supports to rely on in the aftermath of victimization. However, many more crime victims are poor, physically ill, or suffering from mental disorders, which makes them considerably more vulnerable to short-term crisis and long-term PTSD in the aftermath of serious crimes. For example, mental health problems are considerably worsened when a crime victim has a pre-existing serious mental illness (e.g. schizophrenia, bipolar disorder I and II, schizo-affective disorder, personality disorder, obsessive compulsive disorder, and/or major depression). The prevalence of mental health problems in American society is mind-boggling. Over 42,000 adults are diagnosed with affective disorders (bipolar, major depression, dysthymia) each day of the year. Over 55,000 adults are diagnosed with anxiety disorders such as phobias, panic disorders and obsessive compulsive disorders each day of the year. (Roberts, 2005)

In the early part of the twenty-first century, the Federal Bureau of Investigation (FBI) reported a significant increase in threats of terrorism throughout the nation, particularly related to chemical, biological, radiological, and nuclear terrorism. The homicide rate in the United States is the highest of all countries except for Colombia and South Africa. Cyber crime and cyber stalking are costing businesses millions of dollars in computer and network damages and are producing fear and physiological trauma in millions of cyber-stalking victims. Domestic violence is prevalent throughout the United States, with an estimated 8.7 million cases annually. More specifically, every nine seconds, somewhere in the United States, a woman is assaulted by her intimate partner or former partner (Roberts & Roberts, 2005).

All of these situations, events, and crimes can produce acute crisis episodes and posttraumatic stress disorder (PTSD). Therefore, it is critically important for all mental health and criminal justice professionals to provide early responses in the form of crisis intervention and trauma treatment.

A crisis or traumatic event can change people's lives forever. Crisis intervention can lead to early resolution of acute stress disorders or crisis episodes, while providing a turning point so that the individual is strengthened by the experience. A crisis or traumatic event can provide a danger or warning signal, a challenge, or an opportunity to sharply reduce emotional pain and vulnerability. The ultimate goal of crisis intervention is to bolster an individual's current coping methods or help the individual reestablish coping and problem-solving abilities, while helping individuals take concrete steps toward managing their feelings and developing action plans. Crisis intervention can reinforce strengths and protective factors for individuals who feel somewhat overwhelmed by a traumatic event; in addition, it aims to reduce lethality and potentially harmful situations, and provides referral linkages to community agencies. Each person's perceptions and perspective in the aftermath of a violent crime are critical factors in determining whether or not an incident will escalate into an acute crisis episode. Specifically, two people could experience the same potentially trauma-inducing event; one will cope in a positive way and experience a minimum amount of stress, while the other person may fall apart and become dysfunctional because of inadequate coping skills and a lack of crisis counseling (Roberts, 2005).

Throughout the United States, Canada, and England, crisis counselors, victim advocates, clinical social workers, psychiatric nurses, psychologists, and emergency services personnel are working collaboratively to provide a new vision and clinical insights into crisis intervention and protocols for crisis response teams. Crisis intervention has become the most widely used, time-limited treatment modality in the world. As a result of the crisis intervention and critical incident stress management movement, millions of persons in crisis situations have been helped in a cost-efficient and timely manner (Roberts, 2005). However, many victim advocates throughout the United States and Canada are only receiving minimal training in crisis intervention and time-limited treatment modalities. The following sections examine innovations, best practices, and evidence-based crisis intervention strategies used with crime victims.

EVIDENCE-BASED PRACTICE NEEDS

Adopting evidence-based practices requires a volume of scientifically sound research that has been tested in ways that allow for the practices to be applied reliably in new communities.

Currently, the base of solid empirical research evidence on crisis intervention with crime victims is still in an early developmental state. Given the highly individualized nature of crime victimization, there is considerable skepticism in some circles that practices can, or even should, be delivered with consistency. Others argue with conviction that services proven effective in rigorous studies should be replicated with fidelity in order to reap the benefits of the services as demonstrated by research.

Crisis theory has its roots in stress theory, psychodynamic theory, and learning theory. In order to understand the basis of crisis intervention and critical incident debriefing, crisis theory must be defined. First, *crisis* is defined as "a specific set of temporary circumstances that result in a state of upset and disequilibrium" (Wallace, 1998, p. 132). Second, *theory* is defined as a set of interrelated constructs (concepts), definitions and propositions that present a systematic view of phenomena by specifying relations among variables with the purpose of explaining and predicting phenomena. (Kerlinger, 1986, p. 9)

Turner (1996) states the following with regard to using theory in practice intervention:

When the practitioner looks at theory, the goal is to develop and refine an intellectual structure by which the complex array of facts encountered in practice can be understood, so that the nature of the intervention can be deduced and the effects of such intervention predicated. The clinician's principal interest is in the utility of the theory: What can it tell me about the situation that will permit me to act differently? (p. 4)

From this perspective, crisis theory offers a framework to understand a victim's response to crime. The basic assumption of crisis theory asserts that when a crisis occurs, people respond in a fairly predictable physical and emotional pattern. The intensity and manifestation of this pattern may vary from individual to individual. The initial physical response includes the inability to move, accompanied by emotional responses of numbness, denial, and disbelief. This stage typically ends rapidly and results in a fight-or-flight response. In preparation for danger, the body accelerates the heartbeat; adrenaline begins pumping into the system; and emotions such as fear, anger, rage, and confusion begin to burst forth. After some time, the exhausted body rests, and the mind, begins the process of emotional restructuring (Turner, 1996).

The victim of a crime often enters a crisis following the crime event. The initial state of the victim is that of disequilibrium. In addition to the disequilibrium experienced, a sense of loss is often the result of a crisis situation. People live their lives on certain assumptions that provide a grounding to help them make sense of the world around them. When a crime occurs, these assumptions may be shattered. These losses may include the loss of a sense of control, loss of trust in a higher being, loss of a sense of fairness, and loss of security—as well as guilt and a sense of helplessness. A victim whose family member has been murdered may feel responsible for not protecting the one who was killed, may question his or her faith, and may have lost a sense of safety at home. The critical response to the crisis is affected by the victim's appraisal of the losses; this appraisal results in certain coping responses, which in turn either impede or assist in the recovery process (Green & Pomeroy, 2007). The coping strategy is expected to influence the emotion of the victims. Individuals may attempt to gain their equilibrium by problem solving, seeking direct information, or taking direct action, often recreating a sense of control. From this perspective, victims may emerge from a crisis with new coping skills, stronger social support, and stronger well-being.

Early psychological intervention can reduce the harmful psychological and emotional effects of crime victimization. Identifying those individuals most at risk for higher levels of distress and reduced levels of well-being will guide practitioners' clinical interventions (Green, Streeter, & Pomeroy, 2005). While some practitioners assume that people have relatively stable preferences for coping styles, the implications from Green et al. (2005) emphasize that a person's choice among alternative coping processes is based on his or her appraisal of the situation. Appreciating the existence of choice making by the victim is tantamount to understanding the critical need for treatment immediately following the crime event in order for a positive adaptation to the recovery process to occur. Crisis intervention may help victims gain a sense of control over daily activities and understand reactions such as depression, anger, and anxiety, both of which may enhance their coping. Educating social workers about coping tasks as well as disentangling the recovery process will enable practitioners to assess and treat victims of crime more effectively.

If victims are to recover from the victimization event, it is crucial that they are provided with the proper support during the initial impact. Every victim's experience is different, and therefore the recovery process is unique to the individual. If victims have difficulty rebuilding or finding new equilibrium, they may suffer from long-term crisis reactions or PTSD. Victims who suffer from long-term crisis reactions can be thrown back into the initial crisis reaction when "triggers" to the event occur. Treatment to minimize long-term crisis reactions is similar to that used for PTSD, which has three principal components: (1) processing and coming to terms with the horrifying, overwhelming experience, (2) controlling and mastering physiological and biological stress reactions, and (3) reestablishing secure social connections and interpersonal efficacy. Crisis intervention, critical incident stress management, and critical incident stress debriefing are approaches used to reduce the severity of a victim's crisis.

As stated earlier in the chapter, "crisis" encounters involve a myriad of intense and turbulent emotions. There is no way to predict which victims will experience crisis, when the crisis onset will occur, or how severe the intensity or duration will be. For these reasons, the sooner crisis intervention is offered, the better. There is a conviction among practitioners that on-scene crisis intervention, when the victim is in the early stages of distress, may prove to potentially prevent or reduce the crisis symptoms of the victim (NOVA, 2001). For example, when the Alfred P. Murrah Federal Building in Oklahoma City was bombed on April 19, 1995, federal authorities immediately recognized the bombing's traumatic impact on surviving victims, family members, rescue workers, allied professionals, and the community-at-large. By the end of that day, the federal Office for Victims of Crime (OVC) had placed a nine-member crisis intervention team on the ground to work with victims and people responding to the disaster.

GUIDELINES FOR PRACTICE

Guidelines for practice need to be rooted in theoretical foundations of transactional intrapersonal coping theory coupled with crisis theory. Practitioners need to be aware of the theoretical underpinning from which they practice and recognize that recovery from criminal victimization is not congruent with "normal" change. Crisis theory is a model that provides the conceptual framework for crisis intervention with crime victims. Clinicians cognizant of incremental changes in victims will continually assess the progress of the individual victim. In response to crises, individuals strive to maintain their equilibrium by using familiar coping mechanisms. Crisis intervention is time limited, and the goal is to reduce the individual's feelings of distress, helplessness, and isolation; activate social resources; and support effective coping. This is accomplished through the use of education, listening, validation, normalization, reassurance, acceptance, advocacy, and finding resource linkages. Immediately following the trauma, the crisis intervener's emphasis should be on self-regulation and rebuilding. This means the reestablishment of a sense of security and predictability, and active engagement in adaptive action.

It is imperative that crisis workers have a step-by-step crisis assessment and intervention model in mind in order to guide them in rapidly responding to the mental health needs of crime victims. A comprehensive and structured model allows the relatively new as well as the experienced crisis clinician to be mindful of maintaining the fine line that allows for a response that is active and directive enough but does not take problem ownership away from the client. In addition, a crisis intervention model provides a blueprint or roadmap that can suggest steps for how the crisis worker can intentionally meet the client where he or she is at, assess level of risk, mobilize client support systems and community resources, and move strategically to stabilize the individual and improve social functioning.

While there is not one single model of crisis intervention (Jacobson, Strickler, & Mosley, 1968), there are generally agreed-upon principles used to alleviate distress in victims and restore equilibrium. Crisis intervention involves three components: (1) the crisis itself, or the perception of an unmanageable situation; (2) the individual or group in crisis; and (3) the helper, or mental health worker, who provides aid. Crisis intervention requires that the person experiencing the crisis receive timely and skillful support to help cope with his or her situation before future physical or emotional deterioration occurs. Roberts's (2005) Seven-Stage Crisis Intervention Model (R-SSCIM) can facilitate effective intervention with crime victims by emphasizing rapidly assessing the victim's problem and resources, collaborating on goal selection and attainment, finding alternative coping methods, developing a working alliance, and building upon the client's strengths. This model has as its goals to (1) mitigate the impact of the event (lower tension), (2) facilitate normal recovery processes, and (3) restore the individual to adaptive function. The basic principles of this seven-stage model are

1. Simplicity: people respond to the simple not to the complex when in crisis.
2. Brevity: acting within minutes or during the first hour can be critical in most cases.
3. Innovation: creativity enhances the management of new situations.
4. Pragmatism: suggestions must be practical if they are to work.
5. Proximity: the most effective contacts are closest to operational zones.
6. Immediacy: the state of crisis demands rapid intervention.
7. Expectancy: the crisis worker sets up expectations of a reasonable, positive outcome.

Roberts's Seven-Stage Crisis Intervention Model (R-SSCIM)

The R-SSCIM (Roberts, 1991 and 2005) (see Figure 6.1) identifies and discusses seven critical stages through which clients typically pass on the road to crisis stabilization, resolution, and mastery. It is important to be aware that stages one and two often take place simultaneously, and stages three and four sometimes overlap.

Stages of the R-SSCIM

Stage 1: Rapidly Plan and Conduct a Crisis Assessment. Psychosocial assessment and determination of the level of danger require an immediate assessment of a victim-survivor's current situation. Successful early intervention is often based on the crisis counselor's ability to respond in a nonjudgmental and sensitive manner when completing an accurate assessment, and while beginning to establish rapport. The therapeutic goal of the intervention during the initial crisis assessment is for the crisis worker to facilitate the restoration of equilibrium in favor of stability and well-being. The severely traumatized or profoundly depressed person will easily find reasons to express intense anxiety, sadness, and fear, but may need help in identifying reasons for living and/or specific levels of fear. We now will apply the case illustration of James to R-SSCIM:

- Assess lethality by asking the father whether James is currently taking any medication.
- If yes, how long has James been taking it, who prescribed it, and are there any other medications that James is using?
- Ask James's father what specifically caused him to bring his son into the center now. Was there a triggering or precipitating incident?
- Obtain background information quickly from the father, and then speak to James alone.
- Assess the presence of suicidal or homicidal thoughts, substance abuse history, and preexisting mental disorders.
- Ask about the frequency of thoughts about suicide, whether there is a specific plan or method for carrying it out, whether any preparations have been made, and whether the client has talked to others about suicidal thoughts.
- Investigate social support networks and follow through with procedures to ensure James's safety (e.g., removal of medications or potentially dangerous items referred to in his suicide plan).
- Listen for unexpected pieces of the client's story and reflect these parts back through mirroring of feelings and paraphrasing.
- Ask James how his distress has affected his thoughts of being a failure as a protective older brother.
- Assess James's sense of helplessness and hopelessness.

Stage 2: Establish Rapport and a Therapeutic Relationship.
Stages 1 and 2 often occur simultaneously. It is very important for the crisis worker to introduce himself or herself to the individual and speak in a calm and neutral manner.

- Do your best to make a psychological connection with the person in a precrisis or acute crisis situation.
- Be nonjudgmental, listen actively, and demonstrate empathy to help establish rapport and put the person at ease.
- Establish a bridge, bond, or connection by asking James what sports or music he likes:
  - "Are you playing in any sport now?"
  - "Do you have a favorite team?"
  - "Do you have a favorite recording artist?"
- Understand that many adolescents are impulsive and impatient, may have escape fantasies, and may be very sensitive and temperamental. As a result, do not lecture, preach, or moralize. Make concise statements, be caring, display keen interest, and do not make disparaging or insulting statements of any kind.

Stage 3: Identify the Major Problem, Including Crisis Precipitants or Triggering Incidents.
Stages 3 and 4 sometimes take place simultaneously.

- Ask questions to determine the final straw or precipitating event that led James into his current situation.
- Focus on the problem or problems, and prioritize the worst problem.
- Listen carefully for symptoms and clues regarding suicidal thoughts and intent.
- Make a direct inquiry about suicidal plans and pay attention to examples of nonverbal gestures or communication (e.g., diaries, poems, journals, school essays, paintings, or drawings).
- Since most adolescent suicides are impulsive and unplanned, determine whether the youth had easy access to a lethal weapon or drugs (including sleeping pills, methamphetamines, or barbiturates).

Stage 4: Deal With Feelings and Emotions, and Provide Support.

- Deal with the client's immediate feelings or fears.
- Allow the client to tell his or her story and explain his or her feelings.

- Use active listening skills (e.g., paraphrasing, reflection of feelings, summarizing, reassurance, compliments, advice giving, reframing, and probes).
- Normalize the client's experiences.
- Identify and validate the client's emotions.
- Examine the client's past coping methods.
- Encourage the client to vent mental and physical feelings.

Stage 5: Explore Possible Alternatives.
First, reestablish balance and homeostasis, also known as equilibrium.

- Ask James what has helped in the past: for example, what has he done to cope with earlier situations? Through assessing inner resources, the discovery process develops as a collaborative experience that looks at the pros and cons of his current perceived helpless and hopeless situation. When the client is able to view the situation logically, his sense of hopelessness decreases.
- Integrate solution-based therapy (e.g., use a question such as "If you had a dream, and you woke up with absolutely no mental health problems, what would it be like?").
- Ask James about his hobbies, birthday celebrations, sports successes, academic successes, vacations, or other similar topics.
- Mutually explore and suggest new coping options and alternatives.
- Jog James's memories so he can verbalize the last time everything seemed to be going well, and when he was in a good mood. Help the client find untapped resources. If appropriate, it may be helpful to mention that you have specialized in helping young people and have helped hundreds of other teens in crisis.
- Provide James with a specific phone number of a therapist who has extensive experience working with young crime victims, and a plan to follow with that therapist. The therapist needs to be someone who is willing and able to work with challenging and difficult adolescents in crisis. This person also should have extensive clinical experience with crime victims so he or she can provide James with an open-door return policy, whether he needs a new appointment 1 month or 1 year after the victimization.

Stage 6: Develop and Formulate an Action Plan.

- Assist James in realistically understanding what happened and what led to the crisis.
- Help James understand specific meanings (e.g., how the event conflicts with expectations, life goals, and beliefs).
- Restore cognitive functioning through implementation of an action plan.
- Help James focus on why a specific event led to a crisis state.
- Develop and formulate with James what he can do to master the experience effectively.
- Restructure, rebuild, and replace irrational beliefs and erroneous cognitions with rational beliefs and realistic cognitions.
- Formulate how James can cope with similar events if they occur in the future.

Stage 7: Follow Up With Phone Call, In-Person Appointment for Booster Session, or Home Visit.

- Let James know he can call you, and give him your beeper number or cell phone pager. Let him know that the beeper is for an emergency.
- Depending on your assessment at the exit interview session, schedule a follow-up with the therapist to whom James is being referred so that there is a team approach. Follow-up may include a booster session with the therapist scheduled for 3 days, 1 week, or 30 days later.

Applying the Seven Stages

To fully use the seven stages, the crisis intervener initially must make use of active focusing techniques to obtain a thorough assessment and develop rapport with the client. The clinician should assess potential suicidal or homicidal risk. The first hour may be spent assessing the immediate crisis situation circumstances. Accurate assessment of the precipitating event and the resulting crisis is critical to ensuring the victim's safety from a psychological and physical perspective. The victim may have suppressed some feelings, such as depression or anger, and recognition of these feelings will allow for a reduction in the tension caused by these emotions. It is important to seek information that will identify the victim's strengths and coping skills, thus enabling an exploration of what the victim is feeling and how he or she may have successfully coped in the past.

The minimum goal of crisis intervention is the individual's psychological resolution of the immediate crisis and restoration to precrime functioning. Planning and implantation of a therapeutic intervention do not bring about major changes, but are meant to restore the victim to his or her precrisis level of equilibrium.

Critical Incident Stress Management

Another model of crisis intervention is Critical Incident Stress Management (CISM) (Everly & Mitchell, 1999), which is an integrated, multifaceted, systematic approach designed to manage and alleviate reactions to traumatic events (Mitchell & Everly, 1997). Everly, Flannery, Eyler, and Mitchell (2001) strongly argue that CISM may be considered an empirically validated clinical intervention. Manzi (1995) found that use of CISM produced significant decreases in cognitive, physical, emotional, and behavioral stress symptom patterns. Multicomponent CISM, also referred to as group crisis intervention, consists of a minimum of three sessions, including precrisis training (e.g., stress inoculation), individual or group crisis intervention right after the traumatic event, and postevent crisis counseling 1 month later. Roberts and Everly (2006) conducted an exploratory meta-analysis of CISM and found high average effect sizes (average 1.545), demonstrating that adults in acute crisis or with trauma symptoms as well as abusive families in acute crisis can be helped.

We conclude that intensive, home-based crisis intervention with families as well as multicomponent CISM are effective interventions (Everly, Lating, and Mitchell, 2000; Roberts and Everly, 2006). We identify the following seven core components:

1. precrisis preparation
2. one-on-one crisis intervention counseling or psychological support throughout the full range of the crisis spectrum (identified as the most widely used of the CISM interventions)
3. disaster or large-scale interventions as well as school and community support programs, including demobilizations, informational briefings, and town meetings
4. Critical Incident Stress Debriefing (CISD), which refers to the International Critical Incident Stress Foundation (ICISF) model (Mitchell & Everly, 1996)

5. three-phase defusing to assess, triage, and mitigate acute symptoms
6. family crisis intervention
7. follow-up and referral

Critical Incident Stress Debriefing

An additional model of group crisis intervention developed by Mitchell (1988) and referred to above is the Critical Incident Stress Debriefing (CISD). Critical incident stress debriefing can be a valuable tool following a crime event. Research on the effectiveness of applied critical incident debriefing techniques has demonstrated that individuals who are provided CISD within a 24- to 72-hour period after the initial critical incident sometimes experience fewer short-term and long-term crisis reactions or less psychological trauma (Mitchell, 1988; Young, 1994). Campfield and Hills (2001) found that the decline in PTSD symptoms was significantly greater for victims who were provided CISD. The victims were assessed at 2 days, 4 days, and 2 weeks. Amir, Weil, Kaplan, Tocker, and Wirzum (1998) found that CISD that included a debriefing 2 days after and then once a week for 6 weeks following a terrorist attack resulted in a decrease of traumatic stress symptoms. Critical incident debriefing, coupled with CISM, can consist of multiple crisis intervention components and is a tool for prevention of PTSD and acute stress disorder, among others.

Forms of time-limited critical incident interventions have been developed for use with primary and secondary victims and are widely used in numerous countries. CISD uses a structured, small-group format to facilitate discussion of the crime event. Most approaches to CISM incorporate one or more aspects of Roberts's seven-stage model. Participants are encouraged to describe the traumatic events, including specifics of what occurred, their thoughts, and their feelings. Emotional responses are considered in detail, and victims are then reassured that their responses are normal. Victims are prepared for future emotional reactions and advised how to deal with them.

There is substantial controversy regarding the effectiveness of CISM versus CISD. Richards (2001) found that comprehensive CISM was far more effective than CISD when evaluating participants in follow-up. Hiley-Young and Gerrity (1994) state that "we recognize that CISD procedures may help some disaster victims. We are concerned, however, that an unreasonable expectation of CISD usefulness may be developing among field practitioners" (p. 17). In a review of the literature, Dyregov (1998) found that multicomponent CISM is indeed effective and contends that the debate regarding debriefing may be political as well as scientific. Everly, Flannery, and Mitchell (2000) found evidence of the clinical utility of CISM.

Requirements for Intervention

Deal With Feelings and Emotions

It is nearly impossible to comprehend the vast array of emotional responses to a violent crime. Most victims will experience difficulty putting into words their experiences of fear, grief, loss, and anger, to name a few. There are times when parallel activities are more calming and serve as an effective vehicle for examining strong, reactive emotions. For example, listening to music, reading, drawing, and storytelling are all methods to move the individual toward examining and addressing feelings and emotions. When a survivor is willing to discuss the situation, it is important to permit the individual to progress at his or her own speed. The intervener should not feel compelled to control the conversation or even to talk a lot. Rather, it is important to permit the conversation to emerge naturally. In these circumstances, there are specific actions to take—and not to take.

Do

- Remain calm.
- Offer respect and consider concerns for privacy.
- Offer support to assist with focusing on specific feelings or emotions.
- Reassure grieving individuals that what they are experiencing is understandable and acceptable.
- Provide information to orientate the individual to his or her surroundings.
- Let the person know he or she will most likely continue to experience waves of sadness, anger, fear, and loneliness.
- Offer support for continued expression of feelings of grief, depression, and fear, offering access to a variety of supports including other counselors, clergy, or peers.
- Ask for specific actions you can take to assist the person in processing feelings and emotions.

- Provide the person with selected readings or other resources to aid in coping.

Do Not

- Say you know how he or she feels.
- Divert the conversation to another topic.
- Suggest the disaster was meant to be.
- Say you need to grieve.
- Say you need to relax now.
- Say it's good that you are alive and survived this.
- Say it could be worse.
- Say everything happens according to a higher plan.
- Say that no individual is given more than he or she can bear.

Generate and Explore Alternatives

Most adults have a network of social and emotional resources. Spend time with the individual to determine what aspects of his or her life will serve as support for stabilization. Working toward the solution and building upon individual strengths is the foundation of disaster mental health. Each individual has an inherent skill set that can be applied to disaster response. It is important to frame this stage of intervention as examining knowledge that will bring forward opportunities to problem solve. Such problem-solving opportunities include but are not limited to

- practical problem-solving skills, more frequently referred to a common sense
- emotional capacity for understanding and acceptance
- establishment of realistic expectations for the recovery processes
- ability to comprehend and follow instructions
- ability to access potential support systems

It is the identification of alternative actions that serves as the first step in the rebuilding process. Until this point in the intervention, actions have been directed toward stabilization and restoration of cognitive functioning. At this point, the intervener begins to move the individual into the recovery process.

Generate an Action Plan

Providing access to relevant supports for emotional and physical well-being are key aspects. However, empowerment becomes the foundation for developing an action plan. As previously noted, most survivors are connected to other people not involved in the disaster. Assisting survivors to tap into their existing support networks is one key aspect that will assist with their disaster recovery. In this phase, it is important to note the needs list that has previously been generated. It is the role of the mental health response professional to facilitate linkages with collaborative services. While providing this information, the worker also discusses with the patient his or her treatment needs, preferences, and priorities. It is the responsibility of the intervener to do what is necessary to provide referral in response to the identified needs list in the least intrusive and restrictive manner. Examples of situations requiring immediate referral are

- acute medical needs
- acute mental health problems, such as a psychotic episode or pending substance withdrawal
- worsening of a preexisting medical, emotional, or behavioral problem
- identification of domestic violence, child, or elder abuse.

Additional linkages include but are not limited to

- emotional support
- social connection
- advice and information
- material assistance
- insurance assistance
- legal assistance
- family support
- disaster support
- financial support
- housing support

Establish a Follow-up Plan

Timing is critical to the establishment of follow-up services. Timing is also central to the concept of secondary prevention of acute stress disorder and PTSD as well as other negative consequences of violent crime. It is believed that early intervention is critical to the prevention of crime-related syndromes. Mental health consideration also should be given to the survivor's level of readiness. Because of the overwhelming nature of their needs, many survivors will be forced to pursue practical needs instead of mental health needs—finding housing, working through insurance claims, and addressing physical treatments and needs. Not all will be willing or able to address the emotions that discussing the trauma will bring forth. Additionally, survivors may not recognize the need for follow-up. They may not identify residual psychological symptoms generated by the crime.

To this end, it is probably important to present potential follow-up recipient opportunities. All survivors should be provided information that will do the following:

- assist in identifying and normalizing common reactions to the crime
- improve coping mechanisms
- identify significant symptoms associated with traumatic response to violent crime in self and others
- increase awareness and access to services

Follow-up content should consist of these components:

- rapid access to services
- recognition that recovery is a process requiring consistent action
- involvement of external sources in the recovery process
- survivor and family education and therapy
- follow-up screening physical and mental health

CONCLUSION

This chapter has examined many aspects of crisis intervention and the mental health needs of violent crime victims. It is intended to serve as an overview to assist human service workers and mental health professionals in framing the complexities of crisis intervention and the mental health response. We are aware that there is no possible way this or any other chapter could fully capture all the intricacies of an individual or group response to crisis or violent crime. Rather, it is our hope that this model will serve as a framework upon which other professionals will build by adding specific interventions designed to meet the needs of those experiencing traumatic life experiences.

5   Cases of Child Abuse

Child abuse and neglect can have devastating effects on children's intellectual, physical, social, and psychological development. Numerous studies have documented significant developmental problems in children who have been neglected by their caregivers. The effects of child sexual abuse may include fear, anxiety, depression, anger, hostility, inappropriate sexual behavior, poor self-esteem, substance abuse, and difficulty with close relationships. Effects of physical child abuse can include the immediate effects of bruises, burns, lacerations, and broken bones as well as longer-term effects such as brain damage, hemorrhages, and permanent disabilities. Physical trauma and abuse can also negatively affect children's physical, social, emotional, and cognitive development. Emotional abuse, also known as psychological maltreatment, can seriously interfere with a child's cognitive, emotional, psychological, or social development. The effects of emotional abuse may include insecurity, poor self-esteem, destructive behavior, withdrawal, poor development of basic skills, alcohol or drug abuse, suicide, difficulty forming relationships, and unstable job histories. Rycus and Hughes (in press) summarize with the following: "Child protective services may be the most difficult field of practice within the social work profession. Balancing the right of children to safety, permanence, and stability with parental rights to make family decisions is a fundamental responsibility of child protective services social worker."

Statistics provided by the Administration for Children and Families (2007) indicate that during 2005, an estimated 3.3 million referrals, involving the alleged maltreatment of approximately 6.0 million children, were made to child protective services (CPS) agencies. This increase of approximately 73,000 children who received an investigation during FFY 2005, as compared to FFY 2004, is largely to the result of including data from Alaska and Puerto Rico for FFY 2005. In that year, an estimated 3.6 million children in the 50 states, the District of Columbia, and Puerto Rico received investigations by CPS agencies.

- A majority (62.1%) of referrals were screened in for investigation or assessment by CPS agencies.
- Approximately one third (28.5%) of the reports included at least one child who was found to be a victim of abuse or neglect.
- A majority (60.3%) of the reports were found to be unsubstantiated; about one quarter (25.2%) of the reports were substantiated.

According to the National Child Abuse and Neglect Data System's most current report, *Child Maltreatment 2005*, of the approximately 899,000 child abuse and neglect victims in 2005, the largest percentage of perpetrators (79.4%) were parents, including birth parents, adoptive parents, and stepparents. Other relatives accounted for an additional 6.8%, residential staff for 0.2%, and day care providers for 0.6%. Unmarried partners of parents accounted for 3.8% of perpetrators, while foster parents accounted for 0.5%. In 2005, 57.8% of child abuse and neglect perpetrators were females, and 42.2% were males. For the most part, female perpetrators were younger than male perpetrators; of the women who were perpetrators, 45.3% of females were younger than 30 years of age as compared to 34.7% of males.

Data from the Administration of Children and Families (2007) regarding children confirmed as victims by CPS agencies in 2005 included these specifics:

- Children in the age group of birth to 3 years had the highest rate of victimization at 16.5 per 1,000 children of the same age group in the national population.
- More than half the victims (54.5%) were 7 years old or younger.

- More than half the child victims were girls (50.7%), and 47.3% were boys.
- Approximately one half of all victims were White (49.7%), 23.1% were African American, and 17.4% were Hispanic.

As in prior years, neglect was the most common form of child maltreatment. CPS investigations determined that

- Almost two thirds (62.8%) of victims had suffered neglect.
- More than 15% (16.6 %) of the victims had suffered physical abuse.
- Fewer than 10% (9.3%) of the victims had suffered sexual abuse.
- Fewer than 10% (7.1%) of the victims had suffered from emotional maltreatment.

Child fatalities are the most tragic consequence of maltreatment. Yet each year children die from abuse and neglect. During 2005, for example,

- An estimated 1,460 children died because of child abuse or neglect.
- The overall rate of child fatalities was 1.96 deaths per 100,000 children.
- More than 40% (42.2%) of child fatalities were attributed to neglect; physical abuse was also a major contributor to child fatalities.
- More than three quarters (76.6%) of the children who died because of child abuse and neglect were younger than 4 years old.
- Infant boys (younger than 1 year) had the highest rate of fatalities, at 17.3 deaths per 100,000 boys of the same age in the national population.
- Infant girls had a rate of 14.5 deaths per 100,000 girls of the same age in the national population.

Child abuse and neglect are defined by federal and state laws. The Child Abuse Prevention and Treatment Act (1988) (CAPTA) is the federal legislation that provides minimum standards that states must incorporate in their statutory definitions of child abuse and neglect. CAPTA defines "child abuse and neglect" as any recent act or failure to act on the part of a parent or caretaker, which results in death, serious physical or emotional harm, sexual abuse, or exploitation, or an act or failure to act which presents an imminent risk of serious harm. (http://www.acf.hhs.gov/programs/cb/laws_policies/cblaws/capta/index.htm)

The CAPTA definition of "sexual abuse" includes the following:

> The employment, use, persuasion, inducement, enticement, or coercion of any child to engage in, or assist any other person to engage in, any sexually explicit conduct or simulation of such conduct for the purpose of producing a visual depiction of such conduct; or the rape, and in cases of caretaker or interfamilial relationships, statutory rape, molestation, prostitution, or other form of sexual exploitation of children, or incest with children.

All states, the District of Columbia, American Samoa, Guam, the Northern Mariana Islands, Puerto Rico, and the Virgin Islands provide definitions of child abuse and neglect in statutes. As applied to reporting statutes, these definitions determine the grounds for state intervention in the protection of a child's well-being. States recognize the different types of abuse in their definitions, including physical abuse, neglect, sexual abuse, and emotional abuse. Some states also provide statute definitions for parental substance abuse or for abandonment as child abuse.

Accoring to the Child Welfare Information Gateway (2007), physical abuse is generally defined as any non-accidental physical injury to the child and can include striking, kicking, burning, or biting the child, or any action that results in a physical impairment of the child. In approximately 36 states and American Samoa, Guam, the Northern Mariana Islands, Puerto Rico, and the Virgin Islands, the definition of abuse also includes acts or circumstances that threaten the child with harm or create a substantial risk of harm to the child's health or welfare.

Neglect is frequently defined in terms of deprivation of adequate food, clothing, shelter, medical care, or supervision. Approximately 21 states and American Samoa, Puerto Rico, and the Virgin Islands include failure to educate the child as required by law in their definition of neglect. Seven states further define medical neglect as failing to provide any special medical treatment or mental health care needed by the child. In addition, four states define as medical neglect the withholding of medical treatment or nutrition from disabled infants with life-threatening conditions.

All states include sexual abuse in their definitions of child abuse. Some states refer in general terms to sexual abuse, while others specify various acts as sexual abuse. Sexual exploitation is an element of the definition of sexual abuse in most jurisdictions. Sexual exploitation includes allowing the child to engage in prostitution or in the production of child pornography.

All states and territories except Georgia and Washington include emotional maltreatment as part of their definitions of abuse or neglect. Approximately 22 states, the District of Columbia, the Northern Mariana Islands, and Puerto Rico provide specific definitions of emotional abuse or mental injury to a child. Typical language used in these definitions is "injury to the psychological capacity or emotional stability of the child as evidenced by an observable or substantial change in behavior, emotional response, or cognition," or as evidenced by "anxiety, depression, withdrawal, or aggressive behavior" (Child Welfare Information Gateway, 2007).

Many states now provide definitions for child abandonment in their reporting laws. Approximately 18 states and the District of Columbia include abandonment in their definition of abuse or neglect. Approximately 13 states, Guam, Puerto Rico, and the Virgin Islands provide separate definitions for establishing abandonment. In general, it is considered abandonment of the child when the parent's identity or whereabouts are unknown, the child has been left by the parent in circumstances in which the child suffers serious harm, or the parent has failed to maintain contact with the child or to provide reasonable support for a specified period of time.

The standards for what constitutes an abusive act vary among the states. Many states define abuse in terms of harm or threatened harm to a child's health or welfare. Other standards commonly seen include "acts or omissions," "recklessly fails or refuses to act," "willfully causes or permits," and "failure to provide." These standards guide mandatory reporters in deciding whether to make a report to child protective services.

A number of states provide exceptions in their reporting laws that exempt certain acts or omissions from their statutory definitions of child abuse and neglect. For instance, in 11 states and the District of Columbia, financial inability to provide for a child is exempted from the definition of neglect. In 14 states, the District of Columbia, American Samoa, and the Northern Mariana Islands, physical discipline of a child, as long as it is reasonable and causes no bodily injury to the child, is an exception to the definition of abuse.

The CAPTA amendments of 1996 added new provisions specifying that nothing in the Act be construed as establishing a federal requirement that a parent or legal guardian provide any medical service or treatment that is against the religious beliefs of the parent or legal guardian. At the state level, civil child abuse reporting laws may provide an exception to the definition of child abuse and neglect for parents who choose not to seek medical care for their children because of religious beliefs. Approximately 30 states, the District of Columbia, Puerto Rico, and Guam provide for such an exception. Three states specifically provide an exception for Christian Science treatment. However, 16 of the 30 states and Puerto Rico authorize the court to order medical treatment for the child when the child's condition warrants intervention. Five states require mandated reporters to report instances when a child is not receiving medical care so that an investigation can be made.

ASSESSMENT

Special Issues in Child Abuse Cases

In the course of child protective services interventions, safety and risk assessments are often conducted to determine how safe children are in their environments and the level of risk for future harm. Assessments also often include identification of families' strengths as well as the families' perceptions of their problems and strengths. Reports or referrals of possible child abuse and neglect are generally received by child protective services intake staff. Often, statewide, toll-free hotlines are used to receive calls. In some cases, reports are received by local police departments. Staff use criteria to decide whether a report should be accepted for investigation or assessment; these are often called screened-in reports. Reports that do not meet the criteria may be screened out and referred to other services.

Within the minimum standards set by CAPTA, each state is responsible for providing its own definitions of child abuse and neglect. Most states recognize four major types of maltreatment: neglect, physical abuse, sexual abuse, and emotional abuse. Although any of the forms of child maltreatment may be found separately, they often occur in combination. The examples provided below are for general information. Not all states' definitions will include all of the examples listed below, and individual states' definitions may cover additional situations not mentioned here.

Neglect is failure to provide for a child's basic needs. Neglect may be

- physical (i.e., failure to provide necessary food or shelter, or lack of appropriate supervision)
- medical (i.e., failure to provide necessary medical or mental health treatment)
- educational (i.e., failure to educate a child, or failure to attend to special education needs)
- emotional (i.e., paying little or no attention to a child's emotional needs, failing to provide psychological care, or permitting the child to use alcohol or drugs)

These situations do not always mean a child is neglected. Sometimes cultural values, the standards of care in the community, and poverty may be contributing factors, indicating the family is in need of information or assistance. When a family fails to use information and resources, and the child's health or safety is at risk, then child welfare intervention may be required.

Physical abuse is physical injury (ranging from minor bruises to severe fractures or death) as a result of punching, beating, kicking, biting, shaking, throwing, stabbing, choking, hitting (with a hand, stick, strap, or other object), burning, or otherwise harming a child. Such injury is considered abuse regardless of whether the caretaker intended to hurt the child.

Sexual abuse is defined by CAPTA as "the employment, use, persuasion, inducement, enticement, or coercion of any child to engage in, or assist any other person to engage in, any sexually explicit conduct or simulation of such conduct for the purpose of producing a visual depiction of such conduct; or the rape, and in cases of caretaker or inter-familial relationships, statutory rape, molestation, prostitution, or other form of sexual exploitation of children, or incest with children."

Emotional abuse is a pattern of behavior that impairs a child's emotional development or sense of self-worth. This may include constant criticism, threats, or rejection, as well as the withholding of love, support, or guidance. Emotional abuse is often difficult to prove; therefore, CPS may not be able to intervene without evidence of harm to the child. Emotional abuse is almost always present when other forms are identified.

Risk Factors

Research findings suggest that there are a number of characteristics of sexually abusive experiences that are predictive of additional mental health and social problems (Lipovsky, 2002):

- more intrusive sexual behavior, particularly sexual penetration
- concomitant physical injury
- concomitant physical violence
- cognitive appraisal of life threat or serious injury
- psychological abuse
- closer relationship to the offender
- longer duration of abuse incidents
- higher frequency of abuse incidents
- less maternal support
- less sibling support
- less community support
- gender (male victims seem to have greater difficulties)
- multiple perpetrators
- disturbed family relationships and family conflict

Assessment of Children, Parent/Caregiver-Child and Other Familial Relationships

It is difficult to make a general statement regarding the treatment needs of child victims of abuse or neglect since, as noted above, the effects of such experiences, the contexts in which these experiences occur, and the nature of each family's response to disclosure are so varied. The timing of the assessment in relation to when the disclosure occurred may also affect the child's immediate treatment needs. In addition, children may have difficulty expressing their concerns, fears, or questions directly to a professional. Young children may lack the ability to communicate clearly about their emotional responses. Older children may be mistrusting of professionals. Finally, parents may be poor reporters of their children's reactions. That is, an abuse offender may have a motivation to minimize the child's emotional reactions. A neglectful parent may have a psychiatric impairment that would also distort perceptions of the child. It is important to assess the situation from multiple perspectives, including both the child and the parent in the assessment process.

Having said all of this, it is recommended that a child be seen by a qualified mental health professional for a clinical assessment following disclosure or discovery of abuse/neglect. Note that a clinical assessment differs from a forensic assessment. The goal of the clinical assessment is to identify treatment needs, strengths, and deficits rather than to determine whether or not abuse occurred. A thorough clinical assessment addresses multiple areas of child functioning as well as the child's family situation prior to and following disclosure. The results of the assessment provide information regarding the child's need for treatment. Although some children's need for treatment will be painfully obvious, even to a layperson (e.g., excessive aggression towards peers), many children's reactions will be more subtle (e.g., depression, posttraumatic stress disorder [PTSD]) and identifiable only through a professional evaluation. Given that the effects of child maltreatment can vary widely, it is essential that the treatment process begin with a thorough assessment of the child's current situation regarding the following target areas.

- abuse-related information
- characteristics of the abuse
- type of response to the child's disclosure
- type of legal involvement expected
- current living situation
- cognitions/attributions about abuse
- behavioral functioning
- sexualized behavior
- aggression
- withdrawal
- self-destructive behavior
- substance abuse
- suicidal thoughts/behaviors
- emotional functioning
- depression
- anxiety
- fear
- anger
- trauma-specific symptoms
- social functioning
- peer involvement
- social skills
- school achievement and behavior

The current functioning of the supportive caregiver(s) is assessed as well in order to determine specific treatment needs that may impact the child's functioning.

- caregiver functioning
- level of support
- level of supervision
- trauma history
- cognitions/attributions regarding child's abuse experiences
- substance abuse
- emotional functioning
- cognitive functioning
- future abuse/neglect potential
- parenting and social skills
- level of familial and community support

The first step in helping abused or neglected children is learning to recognize the signs of child abuse and neglect. The presence of a single sign does not prove child abuse is occurring in a family; however, when these signs appear repeatedly or in combination, you should take a closer look at the situation and consider the possibility of child abuse.
The following signs may signal the presence of child abuse or neglect:

- The child
    - shows sudden changes in behavior or school performance
    - has not received help for physical or medical problems brought to the parents' attention
    - has learning problems (or difficulty concentrating) that cannot be attributed to specific physical or psychological causes
    - is always watchful, as though preparing for something bad to happen
    - lacks adult supervision
    - is overly compliant, passive, or withdrawn
    - comes to school or other activities early, stays late, and does not want to go home

- The parent
    - shows little concern for the child
    - denies the existence of—or blames the child for—the child's problems in school or at home

- asks teachers or other caretakers to use harsh physical discipline if the child misbehaves
- sees the child as entirely bad, worthless, or burdensome
- demands a level of physical or academic performance the child cannot achieve
- looks primarily to the child for care, attention, and satisfaction of emotional needs

- The parent and the child
  - rarely touch or look at each other
  - consider their relationship entirely negative
  - state that they do not like each other

The following are some signs often associated with the specific types of child abuse and neglect: physical abuse, neglect, sexual abuse, and emotional abuse. It is important to note, however, these types of abuse are more typically found in combination than alone. A physically abused child, for example, is often emotionally abused as well, and a sexually abused child also may be neglected.

Consider the possibility of physical abuse when the child

- has unexplained burns, bites, bruises, broken bones, or black eyes
- has fading bruises or other marks noticeable after an absence from school
- seems frightened of the parents, and protests or cries when it is time to go home
- shrinks at the approach of adults
- reports injury by a parent or another adult caregiver

Consider the possibility of physical abuse when the parent or other adult caregiver

- offers conflicting, unconvincing, or no explanation for the child's injury
- describes the child as "evil," or in some other very negative way
- uses harsh physical discipline with the child
- has a history of abuse as a child

Consider the possibility of neglect when the child

- is frequently absent from school
- begs or steals food or money

- lacks needed medical or dental care, immunizations, or glasses
- is consistently dirty and has severe body odor
- lacks sufficient clothing for the weather
- abuses alcohol or other drugs
- states that there is no one at home to provide care

Consider the possibility of neglect when the parent or other adult caregiver

- appears to be indifferent to the child
- seems apathetic or depressed
- behaves irrationally or in a bizarre manner
- is abusing alcohol or other drugs

Consider the possibility of sexual abuse when the child

- has difficulty walking or sitting
- suddenly refuses to change for gym or participate in physical activities
- reports nightmares or bed wetting
- experiences a sudden change in appetite
- demonstrates bizarre, sophisticated, or unusual sexual knowledge or behavior
- becomes pregnant or contracts a venereal disease, particularly if under age 14
- runs away
- reports sexual abuse by a parent or another adult caregiver

Consider the possibility of sexual abuse when the parent or other adult caregiver

- is unduly protective of the child or severely limits the child's contact with other children, especially those of the opposite sex
- is secretive and isolated
- is jealous or controlling with family members

Consider the possibility of emotional maltreatment when the child

- shows extremes in behavior, such as overly compliant or demanding behavior, extreme passivity, or aggression

■ is either inappropriately adult (parenting other children, for example) or inappropriately infantile (frequent rocking or head banging, for example)
■ is delayed in physical or emotional development
■ has attempted suicide
■ reports a lack of attachment to the parent

Consider the possibility of emotional maltreatment when the parent or other adult caregiver

■ constantly blames, belittles, or berates the child
■ is unconcerned about the child and refuses to consider offers of help for the child's problems
■ overtly rejects the child

Use of Standardized Measures

The *Beck Youth Inventories of Emotional and Social Impairment* (2005) are five self-report measures that may be used separately or in any combination to assess a child's experience of depression, anxiety, anger, disruptive behavior, and self-concept. National norms, based on a stratified standardization sample, are provided as well as comparisons with scores obtained by a clinical outpatient sample and a sample of children qualifying for special education. The original *Beck Youth Inventories* were intended for use with children between the ages of 7 and 14; the second edition of the *Inventories* has been normed for children and adolescents up to age 18. The inventories are easy to administer and brief (approximately 5–10 minutes each). Each inventory contains 20 statements about thoughts, feelings, or behaviors associated with emotional and social impairment in youth. Children respond to each item by indicating how frequently the statement is true for them. The items are written at the second-grade level and are easy to understand; however, the inventories may be administered orally if necessary. A brief introduction to each inventory follows.

■ Beck Depression Inventory for Youth (BDI-Y). In line with the depression criteria of the American Psychiatric Association's *DSM-IV-TR* (2000), this inventory is designed to identify symptoms of depression in children. It includes items that reflect children's negative thoughts about themselves, their lives, and their future; feelings of sadness; and physiological indications of depression.

■ Beck Anxiety Inventory for Youth (BAI-Y). The items in this inventory reflect children's fears (e.g., about school, getting hurt, health), worrying, and physiological symptoms associated with anxiety.

■ Beck Anger Inventory for Youth (BANI-Y). Items include perceptions of mistreatment, negative thoughts about others, feelings of anger, and physiological arousal.

■ Beck Disruptive Behavior Inventory for Youth (BDBI-Y). Behaviors and attitudes associated with conduct disorder and oppositional defiant disorder are addressed in the inventory.

■ Beck Self-Concept Inventory for Youth (BSCI-Y). This inventory addresses self-perceptions such as attitudes about competence, potency, and positive self-worth.

The Child Abuse Potential (CAP) Inventory was designed primarily as a screening tool for the detection of physical child abuse by protective services workers in their investigations of reported child abuse cases. The CAP Inventory is a 160-item, reliable, valid, and objective self-report screening instrument that can assist protective services workers in making case decisions. It contains 10 scales. The primary clinical scale (Abuse) can be divided into six factor scales: Distress, Rigidity, Unhappiness, Problems with Child and Self, Problems with Family, and Problems with Others. In addition, the CAP Inventory contains three validity scales: Lie, Random Response, and Inconsistency. The CAP Inventory is appropriate for use as a preliminary screening tool in cases where a group of high-risk patients has been identified, and the professional wants to screen this identified population quickly to identify a subgroup of individuals most likely to be at risk for physical child abuse. Intervention/treatment programs have successfully used the CAP Inventory at pre- and posttreatment and on a follow-up basis to assist in program evaluation.

The Parenting Profile Assessment (PPA) by Anderson was developed to evaluate the potential of parents to be abusive or non-abusive. Anderson's aim was to develop an instrument that is easily implemented by nurses in the clinical setting. In the most recent research using the PPA, Cronbach's Alpha reliability coefficient was .75. The instrument demonstrated a sensitivity of 95.8% and specificity of 98.6%, indicating a validity estimate of 97.18% (Anderson, 2000).

Summary of Assessment

If a child displays any of the signs and symptoms of traumatic stress, the child should be evaluated. A therapist who has experience working with children who have been sexually abused can determine whether the child needs help. Some children will not need any help at all, and many will need some help. Some may just need a therapist to provide information so they can understand more about what has happened to them.

When assessing and evaluating children, look for symptoms of traumatic stress, depression, or anxiety. Try to find out if they have any unrealistic beliefs or ideas about the event (called cognitive distortions). For example, it is common for children to blame themselves for the abuse, or to feel they could have prevented it. It is important to explore these kinds of "distorted" ideas because they can continue to cause problems in a child's life. You should also look for any signs the child is having difficulty in school or life because of the abuse.

TREATMENT: ISSUES AND INTERVENTIONS

Overview: General Principles of Treatment

Descriptions of treatment for child sexual abuse, physical abuse, and neglect have been reported separately within the literature, with much more attention paid to treatment of child sexual abuse. In fact, there are relatively few studies or reports dealing with individual treatment of the physically abused or neglected child. In practice, however, treatment programs often address these individual needs of children.

General Issues for Treatment

First and foremost, it is important that the child be safe from potential harm from the offender as well as from nonbelieving or unsupportive family members. In addition to the ethical issues involved in treating a child within an unsafe environment, treatment of abuse-related problems is not likely to be effective if the child is living in such conditions. The targets for treatment are determined to a large degree by the child's presenting symptomatology and are defined following the initial assessment. There are, however, certain overriding goals that should guide the treatment process. Treatment should be directive and focused on the abuse or trauma itself. Treatment approaches include these:

1. Help and encourage the child to talk and think about the abuse/ neglect without embarrassment or significant anxiety.
2. Help the child to modulate and express feelings about the abuse.
3. Reduce the intensity and frequency of behavioral and emotional symptoms.
4. Clarify and change distorted, inaccurate, or unhealthy thinking patterns that might negatively affect the child's view of self and others.
5. Help the child develop healthier attachments.
6. Strengthen the child's coping skills.
7. Enhance social skills.
8. Educate the child regarding self-protective strategies.

An additional goal, accomplished specifically through group therapy, is to reduce the child's sense of isolation or stigma through exposure to other victims of abuse. Group treatment for victims of child physical abuse can have positive effects but may also be associated with increased behavior problems. Therefore, the therapist should be cautious and monitor group participants' behavior closely.

Treatment Strategies

Strategies for treating the abused child are varied and are used as appropriate to the child's presenting problems. Recommended treatment approaches include cognitive-behavioral strategies, graduated exposure to aspects of the abusive experience, relaxation training, education regarding the abuse process and effects of abuse, skills training, supportive strategies, teaching of self-protective strategies, behavioral strategies/parent training, and clarification of responsibility/blame and offender's behavior.

Strategies for treating abuse victims have received some scientific support, including those derived from a cognitive behavioral perspective that focuses on the abuse itself. Cognitive behavioral strategies typically address the child's thinking patterns, affective response, and behavioral reactions to the abuse. In particular, the child's attributions of blame and responsibility for the abuse should be addressed. That is, the child should be helped to recognize that it is adults rather than children who are responsible for healthy parent-child interactions. Gradual exposure, or discussion of abuse experiences, helps to reduce the child's anxiety and embarrassment, and provides opportunities to modify inaccurate or self-defeating thinking processes. Relaxation training further addresses the child's fear or anxiety triggered by abuse-related cues and can facilitate more effective affect regulation. Educational approaches facilitate clarification of misperceptions developed in response to the abuse. Skills training is used to teach the child coping strategies to manage negative emotions and to improve social/interpersonal functioning. Supportive techniques also are required, as the child may be coping with nonsupportive family members, upcoming court proceedings, or negative reactions from peers.

Education in the use of self-protective strategies is important for minimizing the likelihood that the child will be abused or neglected again. It is important to establish a safety plan within the home, delineate danger cues, and identify support persons in the child's environment to decrease the secrecy within previously abusive or neglectful families. This, in turn, is expected to minimize the risk of repeated abuse.

Age-Related Issues

The treatment approach should be appropriate to the age of the child. For example, a 4-year-old child should not be expected to come into a therapist or counselor's office, sit on a couch, and recount the details of his or her abuse. The therapist can use a variety of play techniques to encourage the young child to communicate about abuse. Many cognitive behavioral strategies used with adolescents and adults can be modified or simplified for use with young children. For example, there are numerous scripts for relaxation training that are humorous and engage the child in the therapeutic process. Puppets and drawings are useful as well for helping children tell about their experiences, learn strategies for coping with negative emotions, and behave in a more organized and directed manner.

In contrast, older children and adolescents are more able to communicate their thoughts and feelings about their abuse experiences directly. It is recommended, however, that the therapist be flexible in method of approach. Drawings, therapeutic stories, and therapeutic games can be very helpful for engaging children of all ages.

Treatment Duration

There are no clear guidelines regarding the length of treatment for the abused or neglected child, although most studies of treatment effectiveness have examined short-term interventions. Clinical experience suggests that while some children can resolve their negative reactions to the abuse in a relatively brief period (often between 12 and 16 sessions), many will require more extended treatment. Typically, treatment length will be determined by the nature of the child's social, behavioral, or emotional difficulties. That is, the child who is experiencing a wide array of problems of a serious nature is likely to require more intensive treatment over a longer period of time. In addition, the quality of support that the child is receiving from the nonoffending caregiver or other family members will affect treatment length. Since child problems are typically more significant if there is no support coming from the nonoffending caregiver, treatment of the child whose nonoffending parent is disbelieving or nonsupportive is likely to be more extensive than that of a child who has the support of a nonoffending parent.

Family Involvement in Treatment

Children should not be treated in isolation without intervention in their family and/or current living situation. Thus, many in the field recognize the importance of incorporating family members, particularly parents or primary caregivers, into treatment addressing abuse and neglect. The goal of family work is to reduce the risk of recurring abuse, increase safety, and promote healthy growth and development for all family members. Family approaches address the needs of all family members while also targeting the interactions between them. However, it is difficult to specify the precise structure of therapeutic work addressing family issues. The specific approach with the family will vary depending upon the child's living context and the level of acknowledgement of abuse by offender(s) and nonoffending caregiver(s). For example, the approach for a child who has been placed in foster care because of parent-child abuse and lack of a supportive nonoffending caregiver will address different issues than that for the child who is receiving support from a nonoffending caregiver or whose abusive parent is acknowledging abuse and is committed to treatment. Family work is not indicated if the child is in out-of-home placement and there are no plans for reunification.

Treatment involving the entire family that has family reunification as a goal is generally of a much longer duration than individual treatment of the child. Initial stages involve the child, offender, and nonoffending caregiver in individual treatment, allowing each member to address first individual issues related to the development and outcomes of the abuse. In addition, marital work is recommended to address relational issues between the child's caregivers prior to any reunification efforts. If early work with caregivers is successful, family therapy may ensue. Therapeutic interventions with caregivers typically begin with individual sessions addressing the abuse itself as well as the specific needs of family members. These stages of treatment encourage assumption of responsibility by the offender and nonoffending caregiver(s). An alleged perpetrator who is denying having abused the child or a nonoffending parent who does not believe that abuse has occurred cannot fully benefit from abuse-specific treatment. Therefore, initial treatment efforts focus on reducing denial. If such efforts fail, family treatment is contraindicated.

If the offender is acknowledging having abused or neglected the child, then he or she can engage in abuse-specific treatment that addresses faulty thinking patterns, behavioral actions, emotional responses, and physiologic reactions. Sexual abuse offenders will attack their sexual arousal to children, thought patterns that allow them to justify perpetrating sexual abuse, and the behavioral repertoire that led up to abuse. Physical abuse offenders will learn strategies for managing anger, parenting skills, and nonphysical means of discipline. Caregivers who are neglectful will receive assistance in securing basic goods and resources, will learn parenting strategies, and will be taught skills that facilitate independent management of the children's and family's needs.

In the treatment of all forms of abuse, it is important to address attributions of blame. Invariably, child abuse/neglect offenders minimize their own responsibility for the abuse/neglect and project blame on other family members, most often the victim. The abuse clarification process, which addresses such attributions, should be included in treatment if at all possible. Abuse clarification involves an acknowledging offender who has proceeded through treatment to a sufficient degree to be able to clarify the nature of the abuse, assume responsibility for the abuse, demonstrate empathy for the child's responses to the abuse, and begin to participate in the development of a family safety plan. The abuse clarification process is addressed in the offender's individual or group treatment and is ongoing, often for many months before an abuse clarification session is possible. The abuse clarification session provides the opportunity for the offender to read a letter written to the child victim that focuses on the offender's assumption of responsibility, empathy for the child, and commitment to developing the family safety plan. This session is likely to occur some months after the abuse is disclosed, allowing the offender sufficient opportunity to engage in and progress in his or her own treatment. Ideally, at least one supportive adult should be included in the treatment process.

Several programs around the country have targeted noncaregiver parents in their approach to treating child sexual abuse, and have found success with such an approach. Treatment with nonoffending caregivers must also be built on a foundation of acknowledgement that abuse has occurred. In most cases, where nonoffending caregivers believe and support the child, family work addresses the caregiver's individual needs. Early treatment strategies must address denial if it is present.

Treatment of the nonoffending caregiver(s) addresses his or her emotional responses to the abuse and individual mental health needs. In addition, treatment focuses on the caregiver's responses to the child's abuse, education regarding the child's symptoms, and assistance for developing strategies to reduce these symptoms. It is recommended that the nonoffending parent be involved in an abuse protection clarification. This process is similar to the abuse clarification conducted with the offender. The protection clarification involves clarification of the abuse, commitment to protection of the child, and participation in the development of a family safety plan. The protection clarification may be initiated relatively early in treatment, especially if the nonoffending parent believes and supports the child from the time of disclosure.

Long-term family resolution of parent-child abuse is a lifelong process and involves changing many aspects of family functioning. Some type of resolution must occur in all cases, regardless of whether the child or offender has been removed from the home. Resolution may take the form of helping a child adjust to permanent foster care and cope with a nonsupportive family; alternatively, it may involve reunification of the family following the successful completion of individual/group treatment, the clarification process, and family therapy that addresses a safety plan and alteration of family members' rigid patterns of thinking and behaving. If reunification becomes a therapeutic goal, certain preconditions must exist:

- offender acknowledgment of abuse
- offender assumption of responsibility for the abuse

- offender awareness of offending pattern and commitment to change
- offender demonstration of willingness to participate in safety plan
- nonoffending caregiver assumption of responsibility of safety for the child
- nonoffending caregiver demonstration of willingness to participate in safety plan

Family-Centered Practice

Family-centered practice is a way of working with families, both formally and informally, across service systems to enhance their capacity to care for and protect their children. It focuses on the needs and welfare of children within the context of their families and communities. Family-centered practice recognizes the strengths of family relationships and builds on these strengths to achieve optimal outcomes. Family is defined broadly to include birth, blended, kinship, foster, and adoptive families.

Family-centered practice includes a range of strategies, including advocating for improved conditions for families, supporting the improved conditions, stabilizing those in crisis, reunifying those who are separated, building new families, and connecting families to the resources that will sustain them in the future.

Family-centered practice is based upon these core values:

- The best place for children to grow up is in families.
- Providing services that engage, involve, strengthen, and support families is the most effective approach to ensuring children's safety, permanency, and well-being.

Family-centered practice is characterized by mutual trust, respect, honesty, and open communication between parents and service providers. Families are active participants in the development of policy, program design, and evaluation, and they are active decision makers in selecting services for themselves and their children. Family and child assessment is strengths based and solution focused. Services are community based and build upon informal supports and resources. These practice elements can be incorporated into the work of diverse systems, including child welfare, early childhood development, the courts, and other community-based systems of care.

Key components of family-centered practice include

- working with the family unit to ensure the safety and well-being of all family members
- strengthening the capacity of families to function effectively
- engaging, empowering, and partnering with families throughout the decision- and goal-making processes
- providing individualized, culturally responsive, flexible, and relevant services for each family
- linking families with collaborative, comprehensive, culturally relevant, community-based networks of supports and services

Family-centered, community-based principles are at the heart of a number of practice approaches being implemented across program areas and service systems. These approaches are used at different points in the helping process for purposes of assessment, case planning, and decision making, and to address identified needs and concerns. Some have been developed to address a specific population, such as substance-involved families or families of prisoners.

Family Group Decision-Making Approaches

Family group decision making is a generic term that includes a number of approaches in which family members are brought together to make decisions about how to care for their children and develop a plan for services. Different names used for this type of intervention include *family team conferencing, family team meetings, family group conferencing, family team decision making, family unity meetings,* and *team decision making.* These approaches differ in various aspects, but most consist of several phases and employ a trained facilitator or coordinator.

Neighborhood-Based Foster Care

Family-centered, neighborhood-based foster care approaches, based on the principles of strengths-focused, neighborhood-based, culturally sensitive care for children and their families, can be neighbor to neighbor, neighbor to family, or family to family. These approaches focus primarily on innovations in the provision of foster care services, building on the support of community collaborations and networks for families. These child welfare reform initiatives have been incorporated into the child welfare practice of state and local jurisdictions throughout the country.

Alternative Response

Traditionally, child welfare agencies have responded to allegations of child abuse and neglect by investigating the report, determining whether maltreatment has occurred and whether the child is at risk, and putting an appropriate intervention in place. Many states and localities are moving to a more family-centered approach called *alternative response, differential response,* or *multiple responses.* In these models, the focus is on assessing the strengths and needs of the family and child while ensuring the child's safety, usually without requiring a determination regarding maltreatment. Families may receive services through diversion to community agencies.

Shared Family Care

In shared family care (SFC), parent(s) and children are placed together in the home of a host family who is trained to mentor and support the parents as they develop skills and supports necessary to care for their children independently. SFC can be used to prevent out-of-home placement, to provide a safe environment for the reunification of a family that has been separated, or to help parents consider other permanency options, including relinquishment of parental rights.

Family Mediation

Family mediation, also known as alternative dispute resolution, collaborative negotiation, conflict resolution, or conflict intervention, is increasingly used in making child protection, child placement, and permanency decisions for children. This model contrasts with the traditional adversarial, rights-based decision-making process. In the family mediation collaborative model, court- and community-based mediators work with families to resolve child abuse and neglect cases, expedite permanency planning, and develop postpermanency plans for ongoing birth-family involvement in the lives of their children. The process emphasizes the needs of the child, family empowerment, and cooperation between families and professionals.

Trauma-Focused Cognitive Behavioral Therapy

Trauma-focused cognitive behavioral therapy is a structured treatment that takes place over as short a period as 12 weeks. A child and (whenever possible) the child's parent or supportive caregiver participate. The treatment begins with *education*. The therapist shares information with the child and caregiver about common reactions and symptoms that may result from sexual abuse. This helps children understand that their reactions and feelings are normal, and that treatment can help them. It helps nonabusing parents accept that the abuse was not their fault or the child's fault. It is common for parents to react to their child's abuse by becoming either too permissive or too protective. The therapist helps them maintain normal routines, household rules, and expectations. If the perpetrator has been one of the parents, the whole structure of the family may have changed, and the remaining parent needs support to be consistent and keep family life as secure as possible.

Another step in the treatment, called *affect regulation and relaxation*, helps the child identify his or her negative feelings, such as anxiety, jumpiness, and sadness, which can occur after a trauma. The therapist gives the child techniques to modulate these feelings and to soothe himself or herself. This is important so that the child does not begin to withdraw from life to avoid having these feelings. Another part of the treatment helps children analyze the connections between their thoughts, feelings, and behaviors. Children who have been sexually abused often feel bad about themselves. They may blame themselves or believe that nothing good will ever happen to them again. We begin by helping children examine their thoughts about everyday events. We then move into exploring their thoughts, beliefs, and feelings about the abuse.

Another part of the therapy is overcoming *learned fears*. This means unlearning the connection a child has made between the abuse, negative feelings about it, and *trauma reminders*—other memories and events that have been associated with the experience. Desensitization may be necessary when a child continues to have intense reactions to particular things, places, people, or situations that remind him or her of the trauma. To avoid reactions to these trauma reminders, a child may limit his or her experiences. For example, a child may avoid going into the basement of the house if that is where the abuse occurred, because he or she associates the basement with negative feelings about the abuse. Reactions to trauma reminders may also generalize. A child may begin by being afraid to go into the particular basement where the abuse took place, and gradually become afraid of going into any basement, and then into any room that is downstairs or that in any way resembles a basement. In the case of a child afraid to go into any basement, our treatment would help the child overcome the fear of basements by having the child gradually imagine being in a basement without feeling upset. In some cases, the therapist might actually go into the basement with the child to be sure he or she can tolerate the experience.

One of the most significant parts of the treatment is the *trauma narrative*. The clinician helps the child tell a coherent account of what happened, how it felt, and what it meant. By putting memories in order, the child no longer feels haunted by them. The therapist helps identify and correct the child's distorted ideas and beliefs about the abuse. For example, an adolescent was in treatment for abuse that had occurred when she was 5 years old and the perpetrator was 15. She was still blaming herself for "letting" the abuse occur. By creating the trauma narrative, she realized she had been blaming herself for something she had not had the power to prevent. By telling the story to her therapist, she corrected her own false understanding. The mother had also felt confused about who was to blame. By sharing this story with her mother in a joint therapy session, the daughter helped her mother understand what really had happened. The therapy healed not only the young woman but the mother-daughter relationship as well.

Additional Treatment Approaches

The many treatment strategies and approaches go beyond the scope of this chapter; however, the following are brief descriptions of additional empirically based treatment approaches.

Dyadic developmental psychotherapy (DDP) is a family-centered treatment approach to strengthen attachment and resolve trauma. At its core is the use of a safe setting where a child can begin to explore, resolve, and integrate a wide range of memories, emotions, and current experiences that are frightening, shameful, avoided, or denied. The therapist and parents/caregiver work to be sensitive to the child and maintain an attitude of PACE (playfulness, acceptance, curiosity, and empathy).

Narrative attachment family therapy helps children develop beliefs about themselves and the world based on their early experiences with caregivers. Children with negative experiences form negative beliefs, such as "I'm bad," "I don't deserve love," or "I can't be safe." This belief system drives their feelings about themselves and their behavior. Children who think they are bad act badly. This treatment approach attacks the mistaken beliefs (also called internal working model). Parents intuitively know their child's deepest needs and emotions. With this approach, they create a story with a protagonist or hero with whom the child can best identify. Through the process of telling the child the story that identifies the child's key struggles, the parent's empathy provides a pathway of attunement to their child. This is a critical factor in strengthening attachment.

Eye movement, desensitization, and reprocessing (EMDR) is a powerful approach, highly effective at helping people resolve trauma, anxiety, disturbing memories, fears, and other emotional problems. The work is based on adaptive information processing whereby "stuck" traumatic or negative memories are linked up with positive beliefs. This leads to resolution of the negative images and beliefs to the point where they are no longer troubling to the individual. This approach is used cautiously with severely traumatized children, as mental exposure to the troubling images that haunt a child is necessary and can be very difficult for the child.

Summary of Treatment

Treatment should be trauma focused and directive. Treatments that are open-ended and just supportive have been shown to be less effective. The treatment should contain at least some of the elements described above and that have been shown to be most helpful. Because reactions to trauma reminders can pose big problems in children's lives, any effective approach will be systematic, helping the child cope with trauma reminders. In order to identify cognitive distortions, such as the child's blaming himself or herself for the abuse, the clinician should address the relationship between thoughts, feelings, and behaviors. We have found that the work that goes on in creating a trauma narrative—talking about and making some sense out of the traumatic event itself (see Chapter 10)—is very important. Therapies that do not talk about the traumatic events have been shown to be less effective. A treatment, however, needs to prepare the child for the trauma narrative by giving him or her tools and techniques for mastering fear and other negative emotions likely to come up.

Some treatments are not only ineffective but dangerous, such as "holding therapy" or "rebirthing therapy." If something sounds gimmicky, or too good to be true, trust your instincts. Avoid any therapist who is too quick to attribute any sort of symptom of unhappiness or anxiety as being "proof" of sexual abuse. Avoid a therapist who holds himself or herself up as a "guru" or asserts powers beyond those of other therapists. Hypnosis, sodium pentothal, or other treatments that a therapist claims will bring back repressed memories are dangerous and unreliable and should be avoided.

<table>
<tr>
<td>6</td>
<td>Intimate Partner Violence:
Overview, Stages of Change,
Crisis Intervention, and
Time-Limited Treatment</td>
</tr>
</table>

This chapter begins with a discussion of the experiences and dilemmas battered women encounter; the scope of this prevalent social and public health problem; the barriers to seeking help; the myths and realities about battering; medical, criminal justice, and human costs; and the 23 warning signs of a batterer. Then the key findings are provided of a study of 501 battered women, which led to a continuum of the five levels of woman battering. The concluding portions of this chapter focus on practice implications and applying each stage of Roberts's Seven-Stage Crisis Intervention Model (R-SSCIM).

Every 9 seconds a woman is battered by her current or former intimate partner somewhere in the United States. Each year, it is estimated that 8.7 million women are physically abused by a male partner, and about 2 million of these women are victims of severe violence (Roberts & Roberts, 2005). Social workers, nurses, and counselors must make assessments and treatment plans to help women to leave the battering relationship permanently. The overriding goal of all domestic

The material in this chapter originally appeared as "Overview and New Directions for Intervening on Behalf of Battered Women" in *Battered Women and Their Families*, Third Edition, edited by Albert R. Roberts (Springer Publishing Company, 2007).

violence advocates and clinicians is to reduce and stop the pain and suffering and the severe and permanent injuries, as well as domestic violence–related homicides. Green and Macaluso (in press, a) state that the victims' recovery is a process, both for the victims and for the service providers. Previous research indicates that providers find it a difficult task to understand and comprehend the impact and experience of victims. The literature indicates that victims of crime suffer further as they encounter the complexity of the existing judicial system, financial resources, mental health programs, victims' compensation, and other institutions.

Domestic violence is a global public health and criminal justice problem that has enormous consequences for the health and well-being of millions of women and children throughout the world. On November 24, 2005, the World Health Organization (WHO) in Geneva, Switzerland, published the key findings of the largest international study of domestic violence ever completed. The study findings are based on interviews with over 24,000 women residing in urban and rural areas in 10 countries, including Brazil, Ethiopia, Japan, Peru, Samoa, Serbia, and Thailand. The study indicated that women are at much greater risk from violence in their homes than on the street. One-quarter to one-half of all female victims of physical assault by their husbands and partners stated that they had sustained physical injuries as a result of the battering. More than 20% of the women who reported physical violence in this study said they had never told anyone about the abuse prior to the interview. Despite serious medical consequences of domestic violence, only a very small percentage ever sought help from health care providers or the police. Instead, those who sought help reached out only to neighbors and extended family members. Also significant was the finding that in most countries studied 4% to 12% of the pregnant women interviewed in the random sample said that they were beaten by the unborn child's father during pregnancy. One half of them reported they had been punched or kicked in the abdomen. The conclusions of this landmark study are that domestic violence by husbands and other intimate partners is still largely hidden around the world, that it is critically important for policy makers and public health officials to address the health and human costs and for each country to develop national plans, policies, and programs for the elimination and prevention of violence against women and children.

CASE SCENARIOS

Case 1: Cathy

Cathy was a 24-year-old college graduate whose childhood and adolescence had been quite normal. She grew up in a two-parent home, the oldest of three children. Upon entering high school, she had feelings of inadequacy, which are not uncommon for adolescent girls. During her junior and senior years in high school, she had a couple of boyfriends, but the relationships were not serious. During her freshman year in college, when she was living in the dormitory, she met Bryan, a college junior, at a fraternity party, and there was an immediate mutual attraction. Bryan was one of the most popular guys in the fraternity, and Cathy initially felt lucky that he was attracted to her. In the spring, when they had been dating for several months, Cathy told Bryan she wanted to work for the summer at a beach resort that was located approximately 85 miles away from the college. Bryan needed to take summer school classes and continue his part-time job near the campus, and he did not want Cathy to be so far away. Their disagreement over this issue turned into a raging argument that ended when Bryan grabbed Cathy's shoulders, shook her very hard, and punched her in the face. Cathy then called the police. When they arrived, they took Bryan to another room to calm him down, and they called the paramedics because Cathy's nose was bleeding. The paramedics took her to the hospital where she was treated for a broken nose. When the police asked Cathy if she wanted to press charges, she said no, because she didn't want Bryan to get into trouble (Roberts & Roberts, 2005).

Case 2: Julia

Julia was married to Steve, and she put her career on hold to raise their two daughters. Julia and Steve had been married for almost 2 years when he first began abusing her. They always fought about their financial difficulties, and at times Steve would get so mad that he would punch and kick her. Occasionally, the fights were so severe that Julia would call the police. When they arrived at the scene, they took Steve into a separate room to interview him, while the paramedics treated Julia, who usually had minor cuts and bruises.

The police department received calls from Julia once or twice a month, and sometimes they would arrest Steve, but Julia never pressed any charges or sought a restraining order.

One day, after a check bounced, Julia came home to find Steve furious after receiving a letter from the bank. Steve pushed her down the stairs and beat her with a baseball bat. Julia suffered a broken leg, broken ribs, and a concussion. After a long and painful recovery, Julia filed for a divorce.

Case 3: Cynthia

Cynthia was married to Anthony the summer after they both graduated from a small college in Arizona. They were both 22 years of age. Cynthia was a third-grade teacher, and her husband worked as a mechanic. After she graduated, she immediately got a job as a teacher with a starting salary of $40,000 a year. This was much more than her husband earned as a mechanic. Anthony first began hitting Cynthia a few months after they were married, when he went out with his buddies and got drunk. When Anthony lost his job 2 years after their marriage, he became even more violent, due to his increased drinking and difficulty accepting Cynthia as the "breadwinner." After 2½ years of marriage, Cynthia filed for divorce. Anthony began stalking Cynthia in order to get her back, and he ignored the restraining order that Cynthia filed. When Anthony realized he was losing Cynthia to another man, his anger reached a new extreme. After leaving school one afternoon as Cynthia approached her car, Anthony pulled out a shotgun and murdered her. He then used the same gun to kill himself.

BARRIERS TO SEEKING HELP

Many women are ashamed of being abused and are not comfortable with the idea of others knowing about their abuse. Although some may seek emergency medical treatment after an abusive incident, because of embarrassment or fears of retaliation by their abusive partners, women may lie or avoid questioning from doctors and nurses who treat them. Many of these women may want to escape from their dangerous battering environments as soon as they feel it is safe to do so, and by not talking about it they seem to remove themselves from the situation for the moment even if it means reliving it at a later time. The following four cases from the author's research files describe what typically happens in emergency rooms through the voices of battered women.

Case 1

One night the battered woman in this case was accused of cheating on her spouse. He then started pushing her around; this led to her being pushed down the stairs after some verbal abuse. Her fall resulted in a broken leg and fractured nose. When she was brought to the hospital emergency room, to avoid questioning, she lied and said she fell down the stairs. In reflecting on the incident she told an interviewer:

> Well, when my time came around to be seen by the doctor they called me into the room and asked me what happened. I told them that I fell. The nurse made a face like "yeah right" and they fixed my nose and leg and gave me crutches and aspirin and sent my ass home.

Case 2

In the evening when this woman's husband came home, he found that no dinner was prepared. This made him angry and he started verbally abusing his wife. He then picked up a frying pan and hit her face with it. She sustained a broken nose and cheekbone, and fractured jawbone from this incident of abuse. At the hospital where the woman required reconstructive surgery, the nurses and doctors kept asking questions, but she told them to just "fix me and send me home," and after that they did just that.

> All these stupid doctors and nurses came and asked me the same questions over and over again that really annoyed me. . . .

Case 3

In this case, the victim was confronted with a death threat by her husband, who was wielding a knife. The woman ran out of their house across the main street in their town, and her husband chased her down, threw her to the ground where he choked her, and subsequently slammed her head into the concrete. She had suffered a concussion and went to the emergency room (ER), where she was medically examined. She didn't want to talk about her abuse because she didn't like getting advice from strangers, so they sent her home without calling the police.

> The doctors and nurses examined me and gave me medication and they sent me home. I didn't really want to talk about [my abuse] so we didn't. They didn't give me any phone numbers or anything. I don't like strangers giving me advice—who are they to tell me how to run my life—I'd rather talk to my friends about it.

Case 4

During this victim's pregnancy, the husband kicked and punched her in the stomach; it seemed like he was trying to kill the baby she was carrying. He was convinced the baby was not his. This woman almost suffered a miscarriage and went to the hospital to get it checked out. She felt the nurses were sweet but could not understand the situation she was in.

> When I was pregnant I thought that I was going to lose my daughter, but they were able to save her. A nurse told me that I shouldn't be with a man who would cause me and my baby such harm. She was sweet, but she didn't understand I had nowhere else to go.

Women from the author's chronically abused group are oftentimes sent to the hospital for different injuries ranging from bruises to broken bones. Many of these women choose not to report the battering to ER staff, consequently neglecting themselves of services. In their minds, they are avoiding retaliation and future abuse from their battering partner. To avoid being questioned on the topic of abuse, women may forget the sequence of events prior to the abuse, blame themselves, or outright lie to the health care provider. In some cases they shut down when confronted with the topic, and in other cases they altogether push the health care provider away from giving advice on abusive relationships.

Abused women may change their stories to keep professionals at a distance. In Case 1, the victim lied about her abuse. She claimed that she sustained the injury merely by falling down a flight of stairs because of her clumsiness. This type of lying pushes the doctor away. If the doctor still suspects abuse despite the woman's story, he or she may hesitate to help the victim because they perceive her as not receptive to advice about intimate abuse.

Many of these women feel that the nurses and doctors who confront them with the advice may not understand or do not really care about their situation. The victim in Case 4 did not feel as though the nurses and doctors could help her. She said that they could not relate and really understand her situation. This prevented her from getting advice on how to break the chain of violence that plagued her.

In some cases, especially when abuse is not as obvious, health care providers may be the ones who choose not to bring up the subject of abuse. Another woman in the study claimed that when she went to the hospital, nurses and doctors treated her injuries but asked no questions and sent her on her way. She felt the health care providers may have fixed her injuries but did very little to heal her.

Many women also experience shame at being abused and want to avoid the negative stigma that accompanies victims of intimate abuse. In these cases, victims are likely going to try to do whatever it takes to avoid situations that make them vulnerable to others knowing their pain. Some of these women may not even go to the hospital to avoid this situation. This was especially true for one woman who was a nurse and was adamant about treating her own injuries to avoid going to the emergency room. Regardless of the severity of the injury, many women are hesitant to let health care providers or outsiders see their vulnerable abused side. Unfortunately, their inability to let others into this horrifying secret world often leads them to be quietly trapped in their abusive environments with no readily available means of escape.

MYTHS AND FACTS

1. **Myth:** Woman battering is a problem only in the lower socioeconomic class. **Fact:** Women battering takes place in all social classes, religions, races, and ethnic groups. There is a large hidden group of battered women living in highly affluent suburbs throughout the United States. Neighbors rarely hear the violence, because some of the battered women are living on 1-, 2-, and 3-acre estates. Although woman battering occurs in all socioeconomic classes, it is reported to be more visible and prevalent in the lowest socioeconomic groups.

2. **Myth:** Woman battering is not a significant problem because most incidents are in the form of a slap or a push that does not cause serious medical injuries. **Fact:** Woman battering is a very serious problem that places victims at risk of medical injuries as well as homicide. Many cases

of domestic violence result in life-threatening injuries and/or lethal consequences. The most frequent site of domestic violence injuries is the head, neck, or face of the battered women (Roberts & Kim, 2005).

3. **Myth:** The police never arrest the batterer because they view domestic violence calls as a private matter. **Fact:** As of 2001, all states have implemented "warrantless" arrest policies, and mandated domestic violence police training, specialized police domestic violence units, collaborative community police and prosecutor response teams, enhanced technology, and collaboration between victim advocates and police to enhance victim safety and offender accountability. The landmark federal court case of the mid-1980s—*Thurman v. City of Torrington, Connecticut*—served notice to police departments nationwide to respond as rapidly to domestic violence calls as in any other crime in which the victim and perpetrator did not know each other. It was a catalyst for the development of mandatory arrest laws.

4. **Myth:** It is extremely rare for a battered woman to be homeless. **Fact:** Domestic violence is one of the primary causes of homelessness among women.

5. **Myth:** Temporary restraining orders and protective orders rarely are effective in stopping the battering. **Fact:** In recent years, family, criminal, and specialized domestic violence courts have instituted major institutional reforms including technology enhancement, automated case-tracking systems, and more victim protection of confidentiality rights. It has been documented that many thousands of women are being helped and having their legal rights protected by court orders. Newest innovations are around-the-clock-methods of issuing temporary restraining orders and providing a pro bono attorney 24 hours a day, 7 days a week (Keilitz, 2002; Lutz, 2002).

6. **Myth:** All batterers are psychotic, and no treatment can change their violent habits. **Fact:** The majority of men who assault women can be helped. The main types of intervention are arrest, psychoeducational groups, and court-mandated group counseling. Research on over 1,200 batterers documented that mandatory arrest had a deterrent effect among abusers who were employed, white, and married. In Milwaukee, arrests for men who were minorities and unemployed, on the other hand led to an increase in battering (Roberts & Roberts, 2005).

7. **Myth:** Elder abuse is neither prevalent nor dangerous. **Fact:** More than 1.5 million older persons may be victims of abuse by their aging spouses as well as by their adult children. We can expect a sharp increase in elder abuse as baby-boom children reach retirement age and retire within the next 5 years.

8. **Myth:** Children who have witnessed repeated acts of violence by their father against their mother do not need to participate in a specialized counseling program. **Fact:** Several studies have demonstrated that the long-lasting harm and trauma to children results from exposure to violence between their parents. These child witnesses to their mothers being battered exhibit a range of adjustment and anxiety disorders. Boys who witness their mothers being assaulted have a greater likelihood of becoming abusers.

9. **Myth:** Although many battered women suffer severe beatings for years, only a handful experience symptoms of posttraumatic stress disorder (PTSD). **Fact:** Clinical studies of battered women revealed an association between extent and intensity of battering experiences and severity of PTSD (Robertiello, 2006).

10. **Myth:** Battered women who remain in a violent relationship do so because they are masochistic. **Fact:** Most battered women who stay in abusive relationships do so because of economic need, intermittent reinforcement and traumatic bonding, learned helplessness, the fear that the abuser will hunt them down and kill them if they leave, fear that leaving and moving will be a disruption for the children, and fear that they may lose custody permanently.

11. **Myth:** There are no marginalized and throwaway battered women or no women with serious mental health disorders, AIDS, PTSD, polydrug abuse, and/or developmental disabilities. **Fact:** Many thousands of battered women suffer from all of these. Recently, several model programs have been developed to provide them with legal advocacy and legal representation, medical or mental health treatment, and many community support systems.

12. **Myth:** Alcohol abuse and/or alcoholism causes men to assault their partners. **Fact:** The majority of batterers are not alcoholics, and the overwhelming majority of men classified as high-level or binge drinkers do not abuse their partners. Alcohol is used as an excuse, not a cause, for battering. Removing the alcohol does not cure the abusive personality.

The previously cited myths permeate the public's view of battered women. The false beliefs can be particularly detrimental when endorsed by women in abusive relationships whose belief in these myths may create excuses for the abuse or prevent them from taking steps to get out of abusive situations. Social workers and medical professionals should be cognizant that these myths are widely believed in our culture and should work to educate women and men on the actual facts.

23 WARNING SIGNS OF A POTENTIALLY ABUSIVE PARTNER

For professionals who are likely to come in contact with battered women and for women entering new relationships, it is helpful to be aware of common indicators of potentially abusive relationship dynamics. The next section identifies 23 warning signs or red flags (Roberts & Roberts, 2005) useful for all women and practitioners.

1. Abuser is extremely jealous and overly possessive of his date and has intense fear of being cheated on.
2. Abuser intimidates and instills fear in his date by raising a fist or kicking or mutilating a pet.
3. Abuser exhibits poor impulse control or explosive anger.
4. Most of abuser's desires need immediate response.
5. Abuser repeatedly violates his girlfriend's personal boundaries.
6. Abuser tries to dominate her by telling her what to wear.
7. Abuser uses extreme control tactics, such as monitoring the mileage on her car.
8. Abuser attacks the self-confidence of the partner (name-calling).
9. Abuser is emotionally dependent (wants her to spend her time just with him).
10. Abuser becomes hostile after binge drinking.
11. Abuser never takes responsibility for the role he played in the problem.
12. He cannot control his anger.
13. Abuser has poor communication skills.
14. Abuser has a history of having abused a previous girlfriend.
15. Abuser was on a college or high school sports team where violence was emphasized.
16. In a fit of anger sparked by jealousy or disagreement with his date, he threatens to hit, slap, or punch her.
17. He has a generational history of interpersonal violence among father or other familial male role models in which he was beaten as a child or he observed his father/stepfather beating his mother.
18. He is demanding, overly aggressive, frequently rough, and/or sometimes sadistic during sexual activity.
19. He escalates intimidating and potentially assaultive behavioral patterns when his partner is pregnant.

20. He exerts coercive control by threatening and then attempting homicide or suicide when the woman attempts to leave the relationship.
21. He exhibits a narcissistic personality disorder.
22. He exhibits an avoidant depressive personality disorder.
23. He exhibits a borderline personality disorder and is highly impulsive, self-punitive, sexually abusive, moody, resentful, and tense.

PREVALENCE AND COSTS

Each year, approximately 8.7 million women are victims of intimate partner violence (Roberts, 2002; Roberts & Roberts, 2005). Every 9 seconds somewhere in the United States a woman is battered by her current or former intimate partner. Violence among current and former intimate partners has been found to be highly prevalent in American society. Two national studies have provided methodologically rigorous national estimates of the prevalence of woman battering. The Tjaden and Thoennes (2000) National Violence Against Women survey was based on a national representative sample of 8,000 women and 8,000 men 18 years of age and older. The report from the National Violence Against Women (NVAW) survey indicated that almost 25% of the women surveyed and 7.6% of the men surveyed stated in the telephone interviews that they were raped and/or physically battered by a spouse, cohabiting partner, or date during their lifetime, and 1.5% of the women surveyed indicated that they were physically abused or raped by an intimate partner during the previous 12-month period. These estimates are probably low because of the problem of underreporting. Many battered women do not make criminal complaints and/or minimize the abuse or are in denial. Each year, for the past 20 years, approximately 1.5 to 2 million women have needed emergency medical attention as a result of domestic violence (Roberts, 1998; Straus, 1986). Annual estimates indicate that approximately 2,000 battered women are killed by their abusive partners, and the majority of these homicides take place after the victim has tried to leave, separate from, or divorce their batterer. In addition, 1,250 chronically battered women have killed their mates each year as a result of explicit terroristic or death threats, PTSD, and/or recurring nightmares or intrusive thoughts of their own death at the hands of the batterer (Browne, 1987; Cascardi, O'Leary, and Lawrence, 1993; Federal Bureau of Investigation [FBI], 2003; Roberts, 2002; Walker, 1984).

The aftermath of domestic violence assaults has a destructive impact on the battered woman and her children. Carlson (1996) estimated that each year more than 10 million children witness woman battering in the privacy of their own homes. The impact of growing up in a violent home often results in an intergenerational cycle of violence. See Shlonsky and Friend (2007) for detailed descriptions of treatment plans to help traumatized children of battered women.

Stark and Flitcraft (1988) have indicated that the impact of the battered woman syndrome results in subsequent high rates of medical problems, mental disorders, miscarriages, abortions, alcohol and drug abuse, increased risks of rape, and suicide attempts. More recently, Hamberger and Phelan (2004) reviewed 14 studies to determine the prevalence of spousal abuse among patients presenting at family medicine and internal medicine clinics; they found that incidence of health-related problems from physical abuse ranged from 13% to 46% of patients.

It has been estimated that approximately $4.1 billion has been spent annually for medical care and mental health treatment, and almost $1.8 billion on lost productivity related to morbidity and premature mortality of battered women (Centers for Disease Control and Prevention, 2003). This does not take into account the fact that hospital and physician fees are rising considerably every year. Any estimate of the costs of intimate partner violence should also include the intangible costs of pain and suffering to the battered women themselves and PTSD and other serious disorders of the children of chronically battered women. Any realistic estimate of overall domestic violence costs should also include advocacy and direct service costs of $3.3 billion that was allocated through the Violence Against Women Act—II for the years 2000 to 2005 as well as county and city criminal justice processing–related costs including law enforcement, prosecution, and court costs. Therefore, an annual cost estimate of $10 billion for intimate partner violence in the United States may well be a very low estimate.

Because domestic violence frequently results in serious medical injuries, in addition to calculating criminal justice costs, it is important to include estimates of average and total hospital costs. Domestic violence is the number one cause of emergency room visits by women (Roberts and Roberts, 2005, p. 4). Estimating average hospital costs for a battered woman can be quite challenging and complex. Injuries can range from broken bones and bruises to mental illnesses. According to a national economic study conducted within the health sector, Max et. al. (2004) estimated the prevalence and medical costs of domestic violence in terms of ER visits, outpatient visits, inpatient hospitalizations, physician visits, dental visits, ambulance/paramedic costs, and physical therapy visit costs. This economic analysis found that for intimate partner assault victims, the average cost per woman for medical care was $4,247.10 (Max et. al., 2004).

Case 3, Cynthia, is an exception to the other two cases because it is a case of domestic violence that resulted in homicide. Therefore, not only should the total hospital costs be calculated, but also the largest cost estimates, those due to a lifetime of absenteeism and lost wages, should be computed. There is an assumption that most people work until the age of 66. If a batterer kills his 23-year-old wife or ex-wife, her salary must be multiplied by the number of years to age 66.

Cathy's short-term case is the least serious of the three. Her incident involved only one hospital visit, and no overnight admission was necessary. She suffered a broken nose, and the only fee charged was the standard emergency room fee of $760. An additional $195 was added to her total for cost of stitches. Her total hospital cost was approximately $955.

Julia's case involves more medical attention. Julia suffered a broken leg, a concussion, and broken ribs when her husband threw her down the stairs. She was admitted to the hospital for a total of 2 days and charged $760 for the emergency room fee, $2320 for skull x-rays and an MRI necessitated by possible head and traumatic brain injuries, $150 for the chest film and broken ribs, and $125 for sutures. She was also charged $500 per day for admission costs. Her total equaled $4,355.

Cynthia's case is the most complex and involves the estimation of additional costs not estimated for Cathy or Julia. Within a 2-year period, Cynthia visited the emergency room a total of eight times. Each visit required an overnight stay and admission into the hospital. The initial emergency room fee for her eight visits totaled $4,880 for a 2-year period. Costs for x-rays, chest films, and sutures totaled $2,430. Admission costs totaled $5,100. Cynthia's total hospital costs for a 2-year period were estimated to be $12,410.

We also must compute Cynthia's costs due to lost wages. Cynthia died at the age of 23. At that time she was earning an annual salary of $40,000. Individuals typically work until the age of 66, so Cynthia lost 43 years of wages. Forty-three years multiplied by her salary of $40,000, totals $1,720,000 ($1.72 million) in lost wages. If we factor in 32% in fringe benefits each year and a cost of living increase in annual salary each year of approximately 4.5%, then the lost productivity total is estimated at $4.25 million.

In addition, it is necessary to also calculate lost wages due to a lengthy recovery period. On average, if there are only 4 million domestic violence cases per year, and each case costs the victim on average about $6,000, the average number of sick days directly resulting from domestic violence is 28 days per year (4 million cases × $6,000 per case = $24 billion) per year in lost wages.

CONTINUUM OF THE DURATION AND SEVERITY OF WOMAN BATTERING BASED ON 501 CASES

The next section of this chapter summarizes the findings of a 7-year study of domestic violence that included over 500 in-depth interviews with battered women survivors. The author presents a qualitative analysis that compares chronically battered women with women who ended the battering relationship relatively quickly. A model for effective crisis intervention is proposed. It involves implications for police-based domestic violence units, 24-hour crisis hotlines, crisis intervention units at local mental health centers, and court-mandated batterers group treatment programs.

The continuum the author developed focuses on circumstances, situations, and the nature and extent of battering relationships. Interview points include checking onset, duration, and severity of injuries. Particular attention was paid to critical incidents and turning points at which either the victim tried to leave the batterer or there was a lethal outcome; in the sample 105 women killed their partners. From the data collected, the author developed a classification schema based on duration and chronicity. It is based on the common themes extracted in a content analysis of the interviews.

The total sample of 501 women who participated in the study comprised four subsamples. These came from a state women's prison, two shelters for battered women, three suburban police departments, and a modified snowball sample. A 39-page standardized interview schedule was developed and pretested. The findings indicated a significant correlation among a low level of education, a chronic pattern of battering, PTSD, explicit death threats, and battered women who kill in self-defense.

The literature explaining the reluctance of women to leave their abusive husbands is inconclusive. There is no single characteristic that determines a woman's potential for leaving the batterer (Astin,

Lawrence, & Foy, 1993; Roberts, 1996, 2002). Rather, it is a group or cluster of personal and situational characteristics taken together that can provide significant indicators of the battered woman staying in the relationship.

Methodology

The study sample came from four sources:

1. A large state women's prison in the northeastern part of the United States ($N = 105$, battered women who have killed their partners).
2. Three police departments ($N = 105$).
3. Three shelters for battered women ($N = 105$).
4. A convenience subsample of 186 formerly abused women, drawn by inviting 30 graduate students in two sections of the author's MSW Family Violence course, and 15 criminal justice honor students, each to locate and interview one to three friends, neighbors, or relatives who had been battered during the past 4 years; this type of convenience subsample is also known as a modified snowball sample (Roberts, 2002).

The final sample of 501 battered women consisting of the four waves of subsamples comes very close to the author's plan of sampling battered women from different educational, income levels, and racial backgrounds. The results of this exploratory and qualitative study indicate that the duration and severity of battering varies at different levels of chronicity.

Limitations. The four subsamples of battered women all came from New Jersey. Thus, the findings are not general to all battered women. Although the study sample was carefully selected, there is always some small amount of sampling error.

All of the interviewers were college seniors or graduate students. Each interviewer received 30 hours of training on interviewing skills and qualitative research on woman battering. The training included role-playing and practice interviews. The woman battering questionnaire was prepared, pretested, and modified. It consisted of a 39-page standardized interview schedule to guide the interviews.

Findings

The 501 battered women had three experiences in common: (1) They had experienced one or more incidents of physical battering by their partners; (2) they had experienced jealous rages, insults, and emotional abuse by their partners; and (3) over one-fifth of the victims received terrorist or death threats from their abusive partners. Some of the women were hit a few times and got out of the abusive relationship quickly. These were primarily high school or college students who were not living with the abusive boyfriend. Others were assaulted intermittently over a period of several months to 2 years before leaving the batterer and filing for divorce. The largest group of the women endured chronic abuse for many years before permanently ending the relationship. The extent and degree of chronicity of battering is plotted on a five-level continuum (Table 6.1).

Duration and Severity Level of Woman-Battering Continuum

As an outgrowth of the author's study, five categories of woman battering were identified based on the duration and severity of the abuse and demographic and psychosocial variables (see Table 6.1).

Level 1+, Short-Term Victims. The level and duration of abuse experienced by short-term abused women was determined from interviews with 94 battered women who reported experiencing one to three misdemeanor abusive incidents by their boyfriend or partner. Most of the victims were high school or college students in a steady dating relationship. The overwhelming majority of the women were not living with the abuser. The abusive acts could usually be classified in the mild to moderate range of severity, for example, pushing, slapping, and punching, with no broken bones or permanent injuries. Most of these women were between 16 and 25 years of age and ended the relationship with the help of a parent or older brother. Short-term victims generally seek help from their parents and sometimes call the police to obtain a temporary protective order. Most of the women in this level were middle class (Roberts & Roberts, 2005).

Level 2+, Intermediate. The level and duration of battering of women in this category ranged from 3 to 15 incidents over a period of several months to 2 years. The 104 battered women in this category were usually living

Table 6.1

CONTINUUM OF TYPES OF WOMAN-BATTERING SITUATIONS

	SHORT-TERM (N = 94)	INTERMEDIATE (N = 104)	INTERMITTENT (N = 38)	CHRONIC AND PREDICTABLE (N = 160)	LETHAL (N = 105)
Duration	Less than 1 year	Several months to 2 years	5–40 years	5–35 years	8+ years
Type of Relationship	Dating	Cohabiting or married	Married with children	Married with children	Cohabiting or married
Severity	Mild to moderate, e.g., push, shove, sometimes severe beating	Moderate to severe, e.g., punch, kick, chokehold, or severe beating	Severe and intense violent episode without warning; long periods without violence, then another violent episode	Severe repetitive incidents; frequent, predictable pattern; violence often precipitated by alcohol or polydrug abuse	Cohabiting or married Violence escalates to homicide, precipitated by explicit death threats and life-threatening injuries
Number of Incidents	1–3 incidents	3–15 incidents	4–30 incidents	Usually several hundred violent acts per woman	Numerous violent and severe acts per woman
Socioeconomic	Usually middle class and steady dating relationship	Usually middle-class and recently married or living together	Usually upper-middle or upper class, staying together for children or status/prestige of wealthy husband	Usually lower socioeconomic or middle class, often devout Catholic with school-age children at home; husband is blue-collar, or semi-skilled	Usually lower socioeconomic class; high long-term unemployment; limited education (majority of battered women usually suffers from PTSD and BWS)

(continued)

Table 6.1

CONTINUUM OF TYPES OF WOMAN-BATTERING SITUATIONS (CONTINUED)

SHORT-TERM (N = 94)	INTERMEDIATE (N = 104)	INTERMITTENT (N = 38)	CHRONIC AND PREDICTABLE (N = 160)	LETHAL (N = 105)
Woman leaves after first or second physically abusive act	Woman leaves due to bruises or injury	Woman stays until children grow up and leave home	Abuse continues until husband is arrested, is hospitalized or dies	
Caring support system, e.g., parents or police	Caring support system, e.g. new boyfriend or parents	No alternative support system		

Source: Roberts, A. R. (2002). Duration and severity of woman battering: A conceptual model/continuum. In A. R. Roberts (Ed.), *Handbook of domestic violence intervention strategies* (pp. 64–79). New York: Oxford University Press.

with the abuser in either a cohabiting or a marital relationship. None of the women in this level had children. The women ended the relationship with the help of the police, a family member, or a friend after a severe battering incident. Many of the women had sustained severe injuries such as a broken jaw, broken ribs, a cut that required stitches, or a concussion. These women often obtained a restraining order and moved out to a safer residence. Most of the women in this level were middle class (Roberts, 2002).

Level 3+, Intermittent/Long Term. The intensity of each incident was usually severe, and the duration of battering was 5 to 40 years. Most women in this category were economically and socially dependent on their husbands. In addition, they were often religious and would not divorce for that reason. They were nurturing and caring mothers and wanted to keep the family together for the sake of the children. There might be no physical violence for several months, and then the husband vented his anger and frustration at pressures (e.g., at his job) at his wife by beating her. Most of these 38 women were middle or upper class and rarely went to the hospital. When they went to their family physician for treatment, they had an excuse for the causation of the injury (e.g., they claimed to be accident-prone).

Level 4+, Chronic and Severe With a Regular Pattern. The duration of battering was 5 to 35 years, with the intensity of the violence increasing over the years. The 160 battered women comprised in this category all reported a discernible pattern of abuse during the recent past (e.g., every weekend, every other weekend, and/or every Friday night). Many of the batterers (68%) had serious drinking problems including binge drinking, drunkenness, and blackouts. However, about three-fourths battered their partners when they were sober. After many years, especially when the children are grown and out of the house, the battering became more extreme and more predictable and included the use of weapons, forced anal and genital sex, and generalized death threats. The injuries for these victims were extensive and included sprains, fractures, numerous stitches, head injuries, and other injuries that required treatment in the hospital emergency room (Roberts & Kim, 2005; Roberts & Roberts, 2005).

Level 4.5, Subset of Chronic With a Discernible Pattern—Mutual Combat. Twenty-four (24) of the 160 Level 4 cases fit the mutual combat category.

This mutual combat and chronic category sometimes led to dual arrests; at other times the police arrested the partner who appeared to have the lesser injuries. The level of violence was usually severe, and the duration of woman battering in this category lasted from 1 to 25 years. The study identified two types of mutual combat. In the first type, the man was the primary aggressor and initiated a violent act such as punching the woman, and she retaliated (e.g., slapping or punching him back). He then retaliated more violently by beating her severely. In the second type of mutual combat, the woman used a weapon (typically a knife) to attack the man, usually in retaliation for physical or emotional abuse. The 10 battered women in this category had either a chronic alcohol problem or a drug problem, or a history of violent aggressive acts in adolescence (e.g., cutting another girl, boy, or adult with a knife). In 14 of the 24 cases, both the abusive male and the female had a drug problem. Generally, there were severe injuries to one or both parties. Most of the women in this level were lower class. Many of these couples separated after a few years.

Level 5+, Homicidal. The duration of the battering relationship in this category was generally 8 years or longer, although the range was 2 years to 35 years. The majority of these women are usually in a common-law relationship (cohabiting for 7 years or longer), in a marital relationship, or recently divorced. The overwhelming majority (59.2%) of these women lacked a high school education and the skills to earn a decent income on their own (Roberts, 2002). Almost half (47.6%) of the homicidal battered women had been on public assistance for many years during the battering episodes (Roberts, 2002).

The 105 women in this category began at Level 2, and usually escalated to either Level 4 or Level 5 for several years, after which the death threats became more explicit and lethal. Also in a number of cases, the victim had finally left the abuser and obtained a restraining order, which he violated. Many of the women in this category suffered from PTSD, nightmares, and insomnia; and some had attempted suicide. A smaller group of the homicidal women indicated that at the time they killed their batterer, they were delusional or hallucinating from heavy use of LSD, methamphetamines, cocaine, or other drugs. The most significant finding related to the homicidal battered woman is that *the overwhelming majority (65.7%) of the women received specific lethal death threats in which the batterer specified the method, time, and/or location of their demise.*

PRACTICE IMPLICATIONS

Interventions and treatment plans should be geared to the type of abuse pattern detected. The short-term and intermediate patterns of abuse may be more amenable to crisis intervention, brief psychotherapy, support groups, and restraining orders. Crisis intervention can bolster the survivor's self-confidence, as well as suggest new coping and safety skills that can facilitate a permanent end to the battering relationship. The prognosis for the chronic/long-term category, whether it be intermittent or a weekly pattern of battering, is much more guarded. The chronic recidivist cases are frequently put into a life-threatening situation. However, when there are specific death threats and a loaded handgun in the house, even the short-term and intermediate battering cases can also escalate to a *code blue—life and death situation.*

In chronic cases, the human suffering, degradation, and emotional and physical pain sometimes end in permanent injuries to the victim or in the death of the batterer or the battered woman. At other times, the chronically battered woman temporarily escapes to a shelter, a relative's home, or the police precinct. In many of the chronic cases the victim returns to the batterer or is dragged back to the violent home. Finally, a small but growing number of chronically battered women leave the batterer and stay free of violence because they are empowered through a support group and counseling, legal advocacy, an out-of-state relative or friend who provides temporary housing, or the death of the batterer by drug overdose, cirrhosis of the liver, or other terminal illnesses. The final section of this chapter applies a structured and sequential crisis intervention model developed by the author.

ROBERTS'S SEVEN-STAGE CRISIS INTERVENTION MODEL

The Seven-Stage Crisis Intervention Model (Figure 1.2; Roberts, 2000, 2005; Roberts & Roberts, 2005) includes the following stages. It is important to note that Stages 1 and 2 need to take place simultaneously, immediately on making contact with the battered woman.

Stage 1. Assessing Lethality: Assess whether caller is in any current danger and consider future safety concerns in treatment planning and referral. Maintain active communication with the client. Evaluating issues: severity of crisis, client's current emotional state, immediate psychosocial needs, and level of the client's current coping skills.

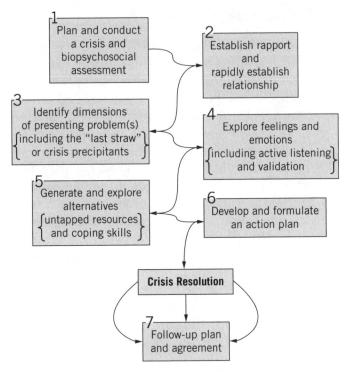

Figure 6.1 Roberts' Seven-Stage C.I. Model (R-SSCIM)

Stage 2. Establishing Rapport and Communication: Active listening and empathic communication skills are essential in establishing rapport and engagement of the client.

Stage 3. Identifying the Major Problems: Crisis worker should help the client prioritize the most important problems or impacts by identifying these problems in terms of how they affect the survivor's current status. First priority of this stage is meeting the basic needs of emotional and physical health and safety.

Stage 4. Dealing With Feelings and Providing Support: It is critical for crisis worker to show empathy and understanding, validating and assurance.

Stage 5. Exploring Possible Alternatives: Crisis workers help clients recognize and explore a variety of alternatives such as situational supports, coping skills, and positive and rational thinking patterns.

Stage 6. Formulating an Action Plan: Crisis worker must help the client look at both the short-term and long-range impacts in planning intervention. Main goals are to help the client achieve an appropriate level of functioning and maintain adaptive coping skills and resources.

Stage 7. Follow-Up Measures: Help determine whether these results from the last stage have been maintained or whether more work needs to be done. At this stage, four tasks of crisis resolution should have been addressed: physical safety and survival, venting and expressing feelings, cognitive mastery, and interpersonal adjustments.

The crisis intervention model will now be specifically applied to domestic violence.

Stage 1: Assessing Lethality: Assessment in this model is ongoing and critical to effective intervention at all stages, beginning with an assessment of the lethality and safety issues for the battered woman. With victims of family violence, it is important to assess whether the caller is in any current danger and to consider future safety concerns in treatment planning and referral. In addition to determining lethality and the need for emergency intervention, it is crucial to maintain active communication with the client, either by phone or in person, while emergency procedures are being initiated.

To plan and conduct a comprehensive assessment, the crisis counselor needs to evaluate the following issues: (a) the severity of the crisis, (b) the client's current emotional state, (c) client's immediate psychosocial and safety needs, and (d) level of client's current coping skills and resources. In the initial contact, assessment of the client's past or precrisis level of functioning and coping skills is useful, however, past history should not be a focus of intake or crisis assessment, unless related directly to the immediate victimization or trauma. The goals of this stage are assessing and identifying critical areas of intervention, while also recognizing the duration and severity of violence and acknowledging what has happened.

Stage 2: Establishing Rapport and Communication: Survivors of acute crisis episodes and trauma may question their own safety and vulnerability, and trust may be difficult for them to establish at this time. Therefore, active listening and empathic communication skills are essential to establishing rapport and engagement of the client. Even though the need for rapid engagement is essential, the crisis worker should try to let the client set the pace of intervention. Many crisis victims feel out of control or powerless and should not be coerced or confronted into action until they have stabilized and dealt with the initial crisis and trauma reactions (Roberts, 2005).

Stage 3: Identifying the Major Problems: The crisis counselor should focus on helping the battered women to prioritize the most important problems or impacts by identifying these problems in terms of how they affect the survivor's current status. Encouraging the client to ventilate about the precipitating event can lead to problem identification, and some clients have an overwhelming need to talk about the specifics of the battering situation. This process enables the client to figure out the sequence and context of the event(s), which can facilitate emotional ventilation, while providing information to assess and identify major problems to be worked on.

Stage 4: Dealing With Feelings and Providing Support: It is important for the crisis counselor to demonstrate empathy and an anchored understanding of the victim's experience, so that her symptoms and reactions are normalized and can be viewed as functional strategies for survival. Self-blame is a common reaction, and many victims blame themselves, so it is important to help the client accept that being a victim is not her fault. Validation and reassurance are especially useful in this stage because survivors may be experiencing confusing and conflicting feelings. Catharsis and ventilation are critical to healthy coping, and throughout this process, the crisis worker must recognize and support the client's courage in facing and dealing with these emotional reactions and issues (Roberts & Roberts, 2005).

Stage 5: Exploring Possible Alternatives: In this stage, effective crisis counselors help the client to recognize and explore a variety of alternatives, such as (1) situational supports, which are people or social work agencies that can be helpful to the client in meeting needs and resolving crisis related problems; (2) coping skills, which are behaviors or strategies that promote adaptive responses and help the client reach a precrisis level of functioning; and (3) positive and rational thinking patterns, which can lessen the client's levels of anxiety, stress, and crisis.

The crisis counselor can facilitate healthy coping skills by identifying client strengths and resources. Many crisis survivors feel they do not have a lot of choices, and the crisis worker needs to be familiar with both formal and informal community services to provide referrals. For example, working with a battered woman often requires relocation to a safe place for her and the children. The client may not have the personal resources or financial ability to move out of the home, and the crisis worker needs to be informed about the possible alternatives, which could include an emergency shelter program, a host home or safe home, a protective order, traveler's aid, or other emergency housing services (Roberts, 2005).

Stage 6: Formulating an Action Plan: In this stage, an active role must also be taken by the crisis worker; however, the success of any intervention plan depends on the client's level of involvement, participation, and commitment. The crisis worker must help the client look at both the short-term and the long-range impacts in planning intervention. The main goals are to help the client achieve an appropriate level of functioning and maintain adaptive coping skills and resources. It is useful to have a manageable treatment plan with short attainable goals, so that the client can follow through and be successful. Do not overwhelm the client with too many tasks or strategies, which can set her up for failure. Clients must also feel a sense of ownership in the action plan, so that they can both increase the level of control and autonomy in their lives and ensure that they not become dependent on other support persons or resources. Termination begins when the client has achieved the goals of the action plan or has been referred. It is important to realize that many survivors may need longer term therapeutic help, and referrals for individual, family, or group therapy should be considered at this stage. For further discussion of termination see Burman (2007) and Roberts and Burman (2007).

Stage 7: Follow-Up Measures: The sixth stage should result in significant changes and resolution for the client in regard to her postcrisis level of functioning and coping. This last stage should help determine whether these results have been attained or whether further work remains to be done. Typically, follow-up contacts should be done within 2 to 8 weeks after termination. At this stage, the four tasks of crisis resolution should have been addressed, which are (1) physical safety and survival, (2) venti-lation and expression of feelings, (3) cognitive mastery, and (4) interpersonal adjustments and adapting to a new environment.

CONCLUSION

The hospital costs, judicial costs, and law enforcement costs that result from domestic violence cases are enormous. Although the vast majority of cases coming into the criminal justice system from intimate partner vio-lence never go to trial and are partially remedied by family court judges or through plea bargaining, the costs still remain high. The amount of money paid in overtime to law enforcement officers for working extra hours on many cases alone constitute significant costs. As Roberts and Roberts (2005) suggest, the police and courts can be used effectively to stop battering. The role of the police and the courts is to protect victims of domestic violence better. If state and county criminal justice agen-cies begin to have the same commitment with general revenue funds as the federal government has had through the federal Violence Against Women Act (VAWA II) and the $3.3 billion allocated for 2000 to 2005 for criminal justice and other domestic violence services, then the future holds much promise. With the passage of VAWA III on October 30, 2005, the 5-year allocation was increased to $3.9 billion for fiscal years 2005 to 2010. This is very promising in terms of the delivery of much needed social services and criminal justice services to underserved groups of battered women throughout the nation.

The rapid assessment of the duration, intensity, and lethality of woman battering are among the most critical issues in forensic mental health and social work. This chapter provides a new evidence-based continuum for evaluating battered women and improving risk assessments of danger. It should be used to determine the number and length of treatment ses-sions by behavioral health clinicians, family counselors, as well as other mental health clinicians. It can also facilitate court decisions on whether battered women are at low, moderate, or high risk of continued battering, life-threatening injuries, and/or homicide (Roberts & Roberts, 2005).

Biopsychosocial and lethality assessments should begin with an evalu-ation of the psychological harm and physical injury to the victim, duration and chronicity of abusive incidents, and the likelihood of the victim escaping and ending the battering cycle. The continuum presented in this chapter provides a classificatory schema by which forensic specialists and clinicians can make reasonably clear predictions of lethality and a likely repeat of the violence. It is important for all counseling, social work, public health, and criminal justice practitioners to document the duration and intensity of battering histories among clients in order to provide customized safety planning, risk assessments, crisis intervention, and effective services.

When working with the strengths and empowerment models to assist people to gain or maintain independence after being a victim of domestic violence, key objectives are to provide them with education, information, and resources to maintain or gain their independence from an abuser and maintain a safe, healthy lifestyle (Green & Macaluso, in press, b).

7 Sexual Assault

The U.S. Department of Justice (2005) defines sexual assault as any type of sexual contact or behavior that occurs without the explicit consent of the recipient of the unwanted sexual activity (e.g., forced sexual intercourse, sodomy, child molestation, incest, fondling, and attempted rape). One result of sexual assault is a loss of trust and the loss of feeling safe. One's assumptive world is shattered at the very core.

The annual National Crime Victimization Survey includes statistics on reported and unreported crimes in America, with sexual assault being one of the most underreported crimes. The Rape, Abuse & Incest National Network (2007) reports the following from the National Crime Victimization Survey:

- Every 2½ minutes, somewhere in America, someone is sexually assaulted.
- One in six American women, and 1 in 33 American men, is a victim of sexual assault.
- In 2004–2005, there were an average annual 200,780 victims of rape, attempted rape, or sexual assault.
- About 44% of rape victims are under age 18, and 80% are under age 30 at the time of the rape.
- Since 1993, the incidents of rape/sexual assault have fallen by over 69%.

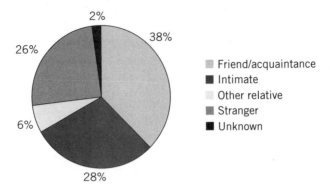

2%

38%

26%

6%

28%

- Friend/acquaintance
- Intimate
- Other relative
- Stranger
- Unknown

Figure 7.1 Perpetrator's Relationship to Victim

According to the 2005 National Crime Victimization Survey, there were 191,670 victims of rape, attempted rape, or sexual assaults in 2005. Of the average annual 200,780 victims in 2004–2005, about 64,080 were victims of completed rape, 51,500 were victims of attempted rape, and 85,210 were victims of sexual assault. Figure 7.1 depicts the relationship of the perpetrator to the victim, indicating that 72% of sexual assaults were perpetrated by a nonstranger: 38% of perpetrators were friends or acquaintances of the victim, 28% were intimates, and 6% were other relatives. Almost two-thirds of the rapes/sexual assaults occurred at night between 6 p.m. and 6 a.m. A staggering statistic is that between 1976 and 2002, approximately 11% of murder victims were determined to have been killed by an intimate partner (National Crime Victimization Survey, 2005).

The National Crime Victimization Survey (2005) includes statistics on reported and unreported crimes in America. Sexual assault is one of the most underreported crimes, with more than half still going unreported. Using services such as the National Sexual Assault Hotline can help encourage victims to get help and report what has happened to them so that more perpetrators can be brought to justice. Males are the least likely to report a sexual assault, although it is estimated they make up 10% of all victims. Young females are four times more likely than any other group to be a victim of sexual assault (Rape, Abuse & Incest National Network, 2007). Additionally, rape victims are 8.7 times more likely to attempt suicide than are nonvictims in the general population. Teens who are 16 to 19 years old are 3.5 times more likely to be raped than the general population. Table 7.1 addresses rape myths and realities (Standing Together Against Rape, 2007).

Table 7.1

RAPE MYTHS AND REALITIES

MYTH	REALITY
Rape is a sex crime, a "crime of passion."	Rape is an act of power, control, domination, anger, and hostility. Sex is used to express these feelings. Rapists do not consider the victim's needs or feelings. Rapists think only about themselves.
Rapists are insane, perverse, sexually deprived, or "over-sexed."	Rapists tend to look and act "normal." However, they may have a greater than average tendency toward violent behavior.
Rape is an impulsive, uncontrollable act of sexual gratification. Most rapes are spontaneous.	Many rapists are already in consenting sexual relationships when they perpetrate an assault. Rapes are often planned in advance.
Most rapists are strangers to the victim.	The majority of rapes—80%—are committed by persons known and trusted by the victim.
Most rapes are interracial.	Nationally, 90% of rapes involve a rapist and victim of the same race. In Anchorage, Alaska, however, there is a high incident of white men assaulting Native women.
Rapes usually happen in secluded places like dark alleys and empty parking lots.	Rapes can and do occur anywhere and at anytime. The most common places for a rape to occur are in the victim's home, in the perpetrator's home, or in a vehicle.
Only young, attractive women are raped.	Anyone can be raped. The rapist seeks someone who is vulnerable. Children, the elderly, and the disabled are at especially high risk.
Women frequently "cry rape" when they regret their choice of having had sex.	Studies show that only 2 percent of sexual assault reports are false, no more than the incidence of false reports for other felonies. More commonly, a victim will not report a sexual assault because of feeling of shame, fear and humiliation.
Rape victims "ask for it."	Victims are not responsible for the actions of the rapist. Nothing a person says or does justifies rape.
Rape does not have much effect on a person.	Survivors of rape have experienced a violent and dangerous attack that deeply affects their lives.

Summarized from Standing Together Against Rape (2007).

ASSESSMENT

Special Issues in Sexual Assault Cases

Because of the personal nature of sex crimes, psychological effects often follow. Studies over the past two decades have consistently demonstrated that sexual assault victims often experience significant symptoms of anxiety, depression, and posttraumatic stress (Green, Streeter, & Pomeroy, 2005; Kilpatrick, Resnick, Saunders, & Best, 1998; Kilpatrick, Resick, & Veronen, 1981). Studies have indicated that social support may be instrumental in the overall well-being of sexual assault victims (Green & Pomeroy, 2007). Assessing successful coping strategies can also assist in the recovery of victims.

The immediate symptoms of rape trauma include posttraumatic stress disorder (PTSD), obsessive-compulsive disorder, dissociative identity disorder, self-injury, self-blame, panic attacks, flashbacks, body memories, and sleeping disorders. These effects can often be lifelong if the victim does not receive immediate support and care. Rape trauma syndrome (RTS) is a common human reaction to an unnatural or extreme event such as a rape or sexual assault. RTS was recognized and named by Ann Burgess and Lytle Holmstrom (1974). This syndrome of behavioral, somatic, and psychological reactions is an acute stress reaction to a life-threatening situation and consists of the following two phases:

Acute Phase: Disorganization

Impact reactions: within hours victims may present in a variety of ways, including

- expressed style: feelings shown in behavior such as crying, sobbing, smiling, restlessness, tenseness, joking
- controlled style: feelings are masked or hidden behind a calm, composed, or subdued effect

Immediate effects: in the first weeks, some of the somatic manifestations may be

- physical trauma
- skeletal muscle tension
- gastrointestinal irritability

- genitourinary disturbance
- sexual dysfunction

Emotional reactions that may be present are shock, numbness, embarrassment, guilt, powerlessness, loss of trust, fear, anxiety, anger, disbelief, shame, depression, denial, retriggering, and disorientation.

Reorganization Phase

Short-term effects—up to 3–4 months—may include

- generalized anxiety and fear
- disturbances in eating, sleeping, thoughts, relationship
- life disruptions (for example, changing phone number to create safety)
- impaired social functioning
- difficulty in maintaining/establishing relationships
- guilt for not preventing assault (often)
- sudden, unpredictable changes of residences and disappearances
- negative impact of legal processes

Intermediate effects—up to 1 year—may include

- disruption and change in lifestyle (e.g., move, change job)
- increased dependence on family or others
- sleep disturbance, often with nightmares
- fear and phobias (e.g., fears about going out or being alone; exaggerated cleanliness)
- disturbance of sexuality (e.g., body image issues, flashbacks, loss of enjoyment)
- thoughts of past rape/incest—brings up past abuse
- sense of being "damaged" goods—thinks others can tell

Long-term reactions—up to 4 years—may include

- anger toward offender, legal system, family/friends
- diminished capacity to enjoy life
- hypervigilance to danger (e.g., fearful of new or risky situations)
- continued sexual dysfunction—may engage in regular sex as before, but with decreased desire and arousal, and many experience flashbacks (Rape, Abuse & Incest National Network, 2007)

Victims often feel that the healing was more painful than the rape. Smith and Kelly (2001) found several themes in recovering rape victims:

- Reaching out: talking to others. This might include women, family members, friends, church members, therapists, and other supportive individuals.
- Reframing the rape: attempting to make sense of what happened by possibly finding a reason for the rape. Many often found that this gave them a stronger appreciation for life, perhaps bringing them closer to their spiritual being.
- Redefining self: redefining to reclaim what was lost and allowing for personal growth. This often includes forgiveness of self and of the perpetrator.

Victim Assessment

As with all victims of crime, a thorough assessment must be conducted prior to beginning treatment. Components of this assessment should include creating a trauma history with numbers and types of trauma experienced, and the violent nature of those traumas (Falsetti & Bernat, 2000). Social support, self-esteem, coping strategies, distress levels, and appraisal should also be evaluated.

Forensic nursing provides a medical assessment of the victim that is often used in court. This assessment consists of injury assessment, health history, information about the crime, screenings for sexually transmitted diseases (STDs), helping the victim, and collecting and preserving evidence for law enforcement. The National Center for Justice Reference Service (2004) has developed a protocol for those working with sexual assault victims. In it, they identified a dual purpose for assessment. One purpose is to address the needs of individuals disclosing sexual assault. This is accomplished (with the individual's permission) by

- evaluating and treating injuries
- conducting prompt examinations
- providing support, crisis intervention, and advocacy
- providing prophylaxis against STDs
- assessing female patients for pregnancy risk and discussing treatment options, including reproductive health services
- providing follow-up care for medical and emotional needs

The other purpose is to address justice system needs. This is accomplished by

- obtaining a history of the assault
- documenting exam findings
- properly collecting, handling, and preserving evidence
- interpreting and analyzing findings (postexam)
- subsequently presenting findings, and providing factual and expert opinions related to the exam and evidence collection.

Sexual Assault Response Teams (SARTs) are being created all over the country in response to the protocol. These teams use an interdisciplinary approach, and coordination is strongly recommended in order to simultaneously address the needs of victims and the justice system. Ensuring that victims' needs are met can increase their level of comfort and involvement with the legal system.

Key responder roles can be described in these ways:

- Advocates may be involved in initial victim contact (via 24-hour hotline or face-to-face meetings). They may offer victims advocacy, support, crisis intervention, information, and referrals before, during, and after the exam process; they may also help ensure that victims have transportation to and from the exam site. They often provide follow-up services designed to aid victims in addressing related legal and nonlegal needs.
- Forensic scientists analyze forensic evidence and provide results of the analysis to investigators and/or prosecutors.
- Health care providers assess patients for acute medical needs and provide stabilization, treatment, and/or consultation. Ideally, sexual assault forensic examiners perform the medical forensic exam, gather information for the medical forensic history, and collect and document forensic evidence from patients. They offer information, treatment, and referrals for STIs and other nonacute medical concerns; assess pregnancy risk and discuss treatment options with the patient, including reproductive health services; and testify in court if needed. They typically coordinate with advocates to ensure that patients are offered crisis intervention, support, and advocacy during and after the exam process, and encourage use of other victim services. They may follow up with patients for medical and forensic purposes. Other health

care personnel that may be involved include, but are not limited to, emergency medical technicians, staff at hospital emergency departments, gynecologists, surgeons, private physicians, and/or local, tribal, campus, or military health services personnel.

■ Law enforcement representatives (e.g., 911 dispatchers, patrol officers, officers who process crime scene evidence, and investigators) respond to initial complaints, work to enhance victims' safety, arrange for victims' transportation to and from the exam site as needed, interview victims, coordinate collection and delivery of evidence to designated labs or law enforcement property facilities, and investigate cases.

■ Prosecutors determine whether there is sufficient evidence for prosecution and, if so, prosecute the case. They should be available to consult with first responders as needed. A few jurisdictions involve prosecutors more actively, paging them after initial contact and having them respond to the exam site so that they can become familiar with the case and help guide the investigation. Prosecutors may want to consider whether participation in a SART would be beneficial. (National Center for Justice Reference Center, 2004, p. 23)

Use of Standardized Measures

The Coping Inventory for Stressful Situations (CISS) (Endler & Parker, 1994) can be used to assess appraisal and coping strategies. "Coping strategies concern cognitive assessment and behavior while trying to manage an emotional encounter; and appraisal is an evaluation of what might be thought or done in that encounter" (Lazarus, 1991, p. 113). The CISS is a 48-item self-report instrument measuring problem-focused coping, emotion-focused coping, and avoidance-oriented coping. Scores for all items on each factor are summed for scale scores. The higher score indicates a greater use of that coping strategy. Alpha reliability coefficients range from .76 to .90. Test-retest reliability correlations have been reported ranging from .51 to .73. There are a variety of instruments assessing coping strategies, but the CISS has been demonstrated to come closest to measuring the emotion-focused, problem-focused, and avoidance-oriented factors of coping strategies for stressful situations.

Social support may influence the coping strategies and level of stress experienced by victims of crime. Social support has been shown to play an important role in victim recovery from crime-related psychological trauma (Hanson, Kilpatrick, Falsetti, Resnick, & Weaver, 1996). Most studies find that support from friends, family, and the community assists in recovery (Kaniasty & Norris, 1994). Received social support can be assessed using a 12-item scale developed by Kaniasty (1988) for use with victims of crime. The development of this scale was based on the Inventory of Socially Supportive Behaviors (Barrera, Sandler, & Ramsay, 1981). This is a 40-item scale that assesses the frequency with which individuals actually receive specific supportive behaviors from people around them. A short form of the scale (12 items), created for crime victims, was accomplished by identifying the items with the highest factor loadings (Kaniasty, 1988). The scale evaluates emotional, tangible, and informational help.

Perceived social support can be measured with a 12-item scale developed by Kaniasty (1988) for victims of crime. This scale was created using principal-components analysis of 12 items from the Social Support Appraisal Scale (Vaux, 1986). These items were chosen to parallel the tangible, emotional, and informational subscales of the received social support measurement. The Social Support Appraisal Scale assesses perceived availability of social support from family and friends. The psychometric properties have been established with internal consistency coefficients ranging from .76 to .83 and an alpha of .90 (Cohen & Hoberman, 1983; Cohen & Willis, 1985).

The PTSD Symptom Scales Self-Report (Falsetti, Resnick, Resick, & Kilpatrick, 1993) is a 17-item self-report measure that assesses symptoms of PTSD. This scale is a modification of the PTSD Symptom Scale (Foa, Riggs, Dancu, & Rothbaum, 1993), which was a precursor of the Posttraumatic Stress Diagnostic Scale. The major modifications are that the items are not keyed to any particular traumatic event and that the MPSS-SR includes severity ratings in addition to the original measure's frequency ratings for each item. Thus, items are rated on 4-point frequency (ranging from 0 = "not at all" to 3 = "5 or more times per week") and intensity scales (ranging from A = "not at all upsetting" to D = "extremely upsetting"). In addition, for each item, respondents are asked to identify, if they can, an event to which each symptom is linked. Respondents are asked how they have been feeling for the past 2 weeks. The MPSS-SR can be used to make a preliminary determination of the diagnosis of PTSD. It can be scored as a continuous measure of PTSD symptom severity.

Rosenberg's (1989) Self-Esteem Scale is a 10-item self-report measure of global self-esteem, or an individual's sense of personal value or worth. It consists of 10 statements related to overall feelings of self-worth or self-acceptance. It has demonstrated good reliability and validity across a large number of different sample groups. The scale has been validated for use with both male and female adolescent, adult, and elderly populations.

The World Assumptions Scale was developed by Janoff-Bulman (1989). It is a 32-item scale measuring basic assumptions with two subscales. The two subscales include general statements about people and the world and measure the core assumption of benevolence of the world. There are three additional subscales that assess more specific assumptions of justice, control, and randomness relating to the core assumption of meaningfulness of the world. The last three subscales measure one's perceived self-controllability, sense of personal luck, and self-worth, therefore assessing the core assumption of self-worth. Cronbach's Alpha values have been .82 for benevolence of the world, .60 for benevolence of people, .73 for randomness, .86 for justice, .75 for controllability, .80 for self-worth, .75 for self-controllability, and .71 for luck. The scale has demonstrated reliability and validity.

The Trauma Symptom Inventory (TSI) is a measurement containing 100 items claiming to measure the evaluation of acute and chronic posttraumatic symptomatology, including the effects of rape, spouse abuse, physical assault, combat experiences, major accidents, and natural disasters, as well as the lasting sequelae of childhood abuse and other early traumatic events. The various scales of the TSI assess a wide range of psychological impacts. These include not only symptoms typically associated with PTSD or acute stress disorder (ASD), but also those intra- and interpersonal difficulties often associated with more chronic psychological trauma.

The clinical scales are

- *Anxious Arousal* (AA) (symptoms of anxiety, including those associated with posttraumatic hyperarousal)
- *Depression* (D) (depressive symptomatology, both in terms of mood state and depressive cognitive distortions)
- *Anger/Irritability* (AI) (angry or irritable affect, as well as associated angry cognitions and behavior)
- *Intrusive Experiences* (IE) (intrusive symptoms associated with post-traumatic stress, such as flashbacks, nightmares, and intrusive thoughts)
- *Defensive Avoidance* (DA) (posttraumatic avoidance, both cognitive and behavioral)

- *Dissociation* (DIS) (dissociative symptomatology, such as depersonalization, out-of-body experiences, and psychic numbing)
- *Sexual Concerns* (SC) (sexual distress, such as sexual dissatisfaction, sexual dysfunction, and unwanted sexual thoughts or feelings)
- *Dysfunctional Sexual Behavior* (DSB) (sexual behavior that is in some way dysfunctional, either because of its indiscriminate quality, its potential for self-harm, or its inappropriate use to accomplish nonsexual goals)
- *Impaired Self-reference* (ISR) (problems in the "self" domain, such as identity confusion, self-other disturbance, and a relative lack of self-support)
- *Tension Reduction Behavior* (TRB) (the respondent's tendency to turn to external methods of reducing internal tension or distress, such as self-mutilation, angry outbursts, and suicide threats). (Briere, 2007).

Treatment Planning

With the use of pretest/posttest assessments, subjective degrees of pain and sorrow can be identified and fully explored. The following are recommendations for care providers and other responders to facilitate victim-centered care:

- Give sexual assault patients priority as emergency cases.
- Provide the necessary means to ensure patient privacy.
- Adapt the exam process as needed to address the unique needs and circumstances of each patient.
- Be aware of issues commonly faced by victims in specific populations.
- Understand the importance of victim services within the exam process. Involve victim service providers/advocates in the exam process (including the actual exam) to offer support, crisis intervention, and advocacy to victims, their families, and friends.
- Respect patients' requests to have a relative, friend, or other personal support person present during the exam, unless considered harmful by responders.
- Accommodate victims' requests for responders of a specific gender as much as possible.
- Prior to starting the exam and conducting each procedure, describe what is entailed and its purpose to patients. After

providing this information, seek patients' permission to proceed and respect their right to decline any part of the exam.

■ However, follow exam facility and jurisdictional policy regarding minors and adults who are incompetent to give consent.

■ Assess and respect patients' priorities.

■ Integrate exam procedures where possible.

■ Address patients' safety concerns during the exam. Sexual assault patients have legitimate reasons to fear further assaults from their attackers. Local law enforcement may be able to assist facilities in addressing patients' safety needs.

■ Provide information that is easy for patients to understand and that can be reviewed at their convenience.

■ After the exam is finished, provide patients with the opportunity to wash, brush their teeth, change clothes, get food or drink, and make needed phone calls. Assist them in arranging transportation home or to another location if needed. (The National Center for Justice Reference Service, 2004, p. 41)

Summary of Assessment

Falsetti and Bernat (2000) state the following: Before effective treatment can be implemented with rape victims, a thorough assessment must be conducted. The assessment should entail a detailed trauma history, including information about the lifetime number and types of trauma experienced by the victim, as well as an evaluation of trauma characteristics, such as whether the person experienced a threat to life or injury during the rape—factors that are associated with increased PTSD. It is important that trauma-screening questions are direct and behaviorally specific. For example, questions that use legal terms (e.g., "Have you ever been raped?") yield lower endorsement rates than questions that use behaviorally specific terms (e.g., "Has a man or boy ever made you have sex by using force or threatening to harm you or someone close to you?") (Koss, Gidycz, & Wisniewski, 1987). It is also essential that clinicians assess for disorders that co-occur with PTSD, such as major depression, panic disorder, and substance abuse. Finally, it is important to assess factors that may influence adjustment, such as social support, coping skills, and available resources. For a more detailed description of assessment of trauma and PTSD instruments, please refer to Research Tools and Resources, Screening Measures for Violence.

TREATMENT: ISSUES AND INTERVENTIONS

Overview: General Principles of Treatment

The following are the practice guidelines for rape and sexual assault developed by Falsetti and Bernat (2000). Treatments that are effective in reducing PTSD symptoms associated with rape and sexual assault are behavioral and cognitive behavioral. This is not to say that other treatments are ineffective. A sample of treatments that have been studied for use with sexual assault victims include stress inoculation training, prolonged exposure, cognitive processing therapy, multiple channel exposure therapy, and eye movement desensitization and reprocessing.

Stress Inoculation Training

Stress inoculation training (SIT) is a behavioral treatment developed by Meichenbaum (1974) and adapted by Kilpatrick, Veronen, and Resick (1982) to treat the fear and anxiety symptoms often experienced by rape victims. SIT consists of three phases: education, training in coping skills, and application/exposure to real or simulated situations for the victim to practice using the coping skills learned.

During the education phase, individuals learn how fear develops as a learned response to trauma; they learn to identify cues in the environment that trigger fear (e.g., dark places that resemble the location of the sexual assault; being alone), and they learn relaxation exercises such as progressive muscle relaxation (PMR).

In the skill-building phase, clients learn to control their fear reactions through exercises designed to reduce physiological sensations (e.g., diaphragmatic breathing, PMR) and fearful thoughts (e.g., thought stopping, mental rehearsal, guided self-talk, and role playing) (Falsetti, 1997).

In the application phase, clients apply the skills they have learned to engage in fear-producing behavior, control self-criticism, and manage avoidance behavior. Clients are taught to reward themselves for their progress. SIT usually takes between 10 and 14 sessions. Several studies have shown SIT to be beneficial for female rape victims. SIT was found to be the most effective treatment for short-term improvement of symptoms (Foa, Dancu, Hembree, Jaycox, Meadows, & Street, 1999). Long-term improvement was seen with both SIT and Prolonged Exposure (see below). SIT has been shown to be effective in reducing PTSD symptoms in rape victims compared to a wait-list control condition (Foa et al., 1999).

Prolonged Exposure Therapy

Prolonged Exposure (PE) Therapy is a cognitive-behavioral treatment program for individuals suffering from PTSD. PE is also known as flooding, and is a form of exposure therapy that is based on learning and information processing theories. One of the primary goals of PE is to have individuals repeatedly confront fearful images and memories of their traumatic event so that fear and anxiety decrease (Falsetti, 1997; Foa & Rothbaum, 1998).

During PE, the therapist helps the individual recount the trauma memory in an objectively safe environment (therapist's office). Clients are encouraged to describe their rape experience in detail. The oral narrative is repeated several times during each session to reduce fear associated with the memory. Clients also are asked to tape-record sessions and listen to the tapes to facilitate exposure. In general, the technique is similar to watching a frightening movie repeatedly. Although at first the movie may be very scary, eventually, after repeated viewing (perhaps as often as 20 times), it is not as scary.

As part of exposure, clients are also asked to confront situations that are not dangerous but that have been associated with danger at the time of the trauma (e.g., dating, going out with friends, dark places). This is called *in-vivo* exposure, as it generally involves exposure to objects or situations in real life, whereas recounting the thoughts, memories, or images of the rape is called *imaginal* exposure (Falsetti, 1997).

PE has been shown to be an effective treatment for rape victims with PTSD for over 20 years. PE has been shown to be superior to no treatment, traditional counseling, and SIT in reducing PTSD symptoms in a group of rape victims (Foa, Rothbaum, Riggs, & Murdock, 1991). Foa, Hearst-Ikeda, and Perry (1995) also found that brief PE (in combination with relaxation training and cognitive techniques) applied shortly following sexual assault decreased PTSD symptoms in recently assaulted rape victims. More recently, Foa, Dancu, Hembree, Jaycox, Meadows, and Street (1999) compared PE, SIT, and their combination in a group of women who had experienced sexual or physical assault and who met criteria for PTSD. Results showed that at follow-up, PE was superior to SIT and PE-SIT on measures of PTSD, depression, anxiety, and adjustment. It should be noted, however, that the exposure component of SIT was left out in this study (so as not to confound the individual treatments), which may have reduced the effectiveness of SIT.

Cognitive Processing Therapy

Cognitive processing therapy (CPT) is a multicomponent treatment package developed by Resick and Schnicke (1993) for treatment of rape victims suffering from PTSD and depression. CPT is based on an information-processing model and combines elements of exposure therapy and cognitive restructuring. The goal of CPT is to help integrate the rape by processing emotions and by confronting cognitive distortions and maladaptive beliefs concerning the rape. Exposure involves writing narratives of the rape in detail and reading the narratives aloud in sessions and for homework. Clients write about the meaning of the rape, and themes of safety, trust, power, esteem, and intimacy are addressed in sessions. Clients are provided basic education about feelings, given information about how self-statements affect emotions, and are encouraged to identify "stuck points" (i.e., inadequately processed emotions about the trauma) in their narratives. Specific cognitive strategies are used to challenge maladaptive beliefs about the rape (e.g., self-blame), helping the victim accommodate the experience in a healthy manner while maintaining a balanced and realistic perception of the world.

CPT can be conducted in individual or group format and completed in 12 weekly sessions. In an uncontrolled trial of CPT, Resick and Schnicke (1992) reported significant improvements on measures of PTSD and depression in female sexual assault victims compared to a wait-list control condition. For the CPT condition, rates of PTSD went from a pretreatment rate of 90% to a posttreatment rate of 0%. Rates of major depression also decreased from 62% to 42%. A large, controlled study is currently underway to further test this treatment.

Multiple Channel Exposure Therapy

Multiple channel exposure therapy (MCET) is a treatment adapted from CPT (Resick & Schnicke, 1992), SIT (Kilpatrick, Veronen, & Resick, 1982), and Mastery of Your Anxiety and Panic (Barlow & Craske, 1988). MCET is used to treat both panic attacks and PTSD, conditions that often co-occur in rape victims. MCET was originally developed for the treatment of civilian trauma in general (e.g., domestic violence, physical assault, rape), and may be adapted for rape victims specifically.

Because exposure therapy may cause initial high levels of physiological arousal (i.e., panic symptoms), individuals who experience panic attacks may not be able to tolerate this treatment at first. Thus, MCET focuses on panic-symptom reduction before trauma-exposure work begins. Clients are provided education about panic and trauma, are taught diaphragmatic breathing exercises to reduce panic, and learn methods to counteract negative and distorted thinking. Individuals are then instructed to bring about panic symptoms through structured exposure exercises, such as tensing their muscles, holding their breath, spinning in a chair, hyperventilating, or shaking their head from side to side. Clients gradually learn that the sensations they fear (i.e., panic symptoms) are not actually harmful or dangerous; rather, it is the interpretations of these symptoms that are problematic. Following successful panic reduction, individuals begin writing about their rape following the procedures outlined in CPT. Cognitive strategies are also adapted from CPT to facilitate emotional processing of the trauma. Finally, in-vivo exposure to environmental cues associated with the rape (e.g., sights, sounds, smells, locations) is conducted after the rape has been processed emotionally.

MCET lasts 12 weeks and can be conducted in individual or group format. Although data await publication, preliminary evidence shows that MCET is effective in reducing both PTSD and panic symptoms in female civilian trauma victims compared to a minimal-attention control group (Falsetti & Resnick, 1998). Among women who received MCET in a group format, rates of PTSD went from a pretreatment rate of 100% to a posttreatment rate of 8.3%. Rates of panic attacks also decreased from a pretreatment rate of 100% to 50% at 1 month posttreatment. Treatment studies with sexual assault and rape victims specifically are needed.

SUMMARY

It has been documented for decades that significant numbers of people experience sexual assault. Sexual assault is one of the most underreported violent crimes in the United States. Rape is almost always a life-changing experience. One's core assumptions about the world are shattered, resulting in emotional, behavioral, and often somatic manifestations. Recovery from such an experience presents a myriad of challenges. Burgess and Holstrom (1974) assert that recovery is when "she or he can honestly say that the memory is not as frequent, the physical distress not as great, and the intensity of the memory has decreased. The victim will then have psychologically let go of the pain, fear, and memory, and will feel a degree of calm that enables him or her to go about the business of living again" (p. 982). Professionals need to provide a supportive, empathic, and nonjudgmental environment that allows the victim to feel safe so that recovery may begin.

8   Homicide Victims

Homicide is of particular interest not only because of its severity but also because it is a fairly reliable barometer of all violent crime. At a national level, no other crime is measured as accurately and precisely. Homicide is the killing of one human being by another. Included among homicides are murder and manslaughter, but not all homicides are considered crimes, particularly when there is a lack of criminal intent. Noncriminal homicides include incidents such as killing in self-defense, hunting accidents, automobile accidents not involving a violation of law, and legal government executions. Generally, murder is committed by a person with a criminal state of mind (i.e., intentionally, with premeditation, knowingly, recklessly, or with criminal negligence). The U.S. Department of Justice Bureau of Statistics indicates that homicide rates recently declined to levels last seen in the late 1960s.

- The homicide rate nearly doubled from the mid 1960s to the late 1970s.
- In 1980, the homicide rate peaked at 10.2 per 100,000 in the population and subsequently fell off to 7.9 per 100,000 in 1984.
- The homicide rate rose again in the late 1980s and early 1990s to another peak in 1991 of 9.8 per 100,000.
- From 1992 (23,438) to 2000 (15,586), the rate declined sharply. Since then, the rate has been stable.

153

After falling rapidly in the mid to late 1990s, the number of homicides began increasing in 2001 but remains at levels below those experienced in the early 1970s. The demographic characteristics of homicide victims and offenders in the period 1976–2005 differed from the general population as can be seen in Table 8.1.

- Blacks were disproportionately represented as both homicide victims and offenders. The victimization rates for blacks were 6 times higher than those for whites. The offending rates for blacks were more than 7 times higher than the rates for whites.
- Males represented 77% of homicide victims and nearly 90% of offenders. The victimization rates for males were 3 times higher

Table 8.1

VICTIMS AND OFFENDERS BY DEMOGRAPHIC GROUP, 1976–2005

	Percent of			Rate per 100,000 population	
	VICTIMS	OFFENDERS	POPULATION	VICTIMS	OFFENDERS
Total	100.0%	100.0%	100.0%	7.8	8.7
Age					
Under 14	4.8%	.5%	20.5%	1.8	.2
14–17	5.0%	10.4%	6.1%	6.4	14.9
18–24	23.9%	36.6%	10.8%	17.0	29.3
25–34	28.8%	28.4%	15.7%	14.2	15.8
35–49	22.8%	17.3%	20.5%	8.6	7.3
50–64	9.3%	5.1%	14.2%	5.1	3.1
65+	5.3%	1.7%	12.3%	3.4	1.2
Gender					
Male	76.5%	88.8%	48.8%	12.3	15.8
Female	23.5%	11.2%	51.2%	3.6	1.9
Race					
White	50.9%	45.8%	83.7%	4.7	4.8
Black	46.9%	52.2%	12.3%	29.6	36.9
Other	2.1%	2.0%	4.0%	4.1	4.4

Source: Federal Bureau of Investigation (2007).

than the rates for females. The offending rates for males were 8 times higher than the rates for females.

■ Approximately one third of murder victims and almost half of offenders were under the age of 25. For both victims and offenders, the rate per 100,000 in the population peaked in the 18-to 24-year-old age group.

Family homicides most often involve spouses or ex-spouses, although such crimes have declined recently. After spousal killing, parents killing their children is the most frequent type of family homicide. Siblings are murder victims less often than other family members. Fathers are more likely than mothers to be killed by their children. Teenage sons are most often the perpetrators in parental killings. Brothers are more likely than sisters to kill a sibling. Older teen and young adult males are most often the perpetrators in killings of brothers. Males who kill their sisters tend to be younger than males who kill their brothers. Sisters rarely kill their siblings (United States Department of Justice, 2005).

The mix of circumstances surrounding homicides has changed over the last two decades. As can be seen in Figure 8.1, the number of homicides

■ in which the circumstances were unknown was greater than any category of known circumstances
■ resulting from arguments had declined in recent years but remains the most frequently cited circumstance of the known circumstances

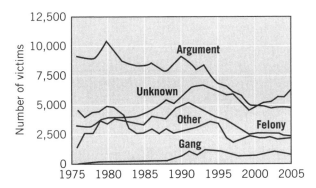

Figure 8.1 Homicide by Circumstance, 1976–2005

- that occurred during the commission of another felony such as a robbery or burglary had declined since 1991 but had stabilized in recent years
- involving adult or juvenile gang violence had increased almost eightfold between 1976 and 2005

Changes in homicide trends have been driven by changes in the number of homicides in large American cities. Between 1976 and 2005,

- Over half of the homicides occurred in cities with a population of 100,000 or more.
- Almost one quarter of the homicides occurred in cities with a population of over 1 million (United States Department of Justice, 2005).

"Violent crimes, like homicide, rape and physical assault touch the lives of millions of Americans each year and produce persistent emotional effects which can last for years" (Kilpatrick, Saunders, Veronen, Best, & Von,.1987, p. 3). Thompson, Norris, and Ruback (1996) conducted a study exploring the experiences of homicide survivors (family members of the murdered), including experiences with the criminal justice system and activities therein. The authors found that fragmented services provided by the criminal justice system increased levels of distress, which could lead to long-term emotional difficulties. They found that fragmented services often led to the victims feeling a loss of control, lack of social support, and fear, resulting in increased levels of low self-esteem, depression, and complicated grief. Therefore, services provided within the criminal justice system can impact the recovery of a victim (Amick-McMullan, Kilpatrick, & Veronen, 1989).

After experiencing a great loss, as when one loses a loved one to homicide, there are many reactions a person may have. In the beginning some people go numb and "shut down." Others cry uncontrollably, feel angry, or both. All of these reactions are normal. There are three different types of reactions a person may have to loss—emotional, behavioral, and physical—and a person may experience one, some, or all of these.

Emotional reactions to loss are the feelings one experiences. Apart from the most obvious feeling of pain and sadness, there are other normal reactions a person can experience during grieving. These include anxiety, or a feeling of extreme worry and panic; anger; irritability; guilt; or abandonment. It is common for a person to feel numb and empty immediately following the loss, which helps protect the person from the extremely difficult emotions that can seem overwhelming in the early stages of grief. As time goes by, the loss becomes more real, and a person begins to realize fully that his or her loved one will not come back to life. When this occurs, the feelings of pain, loss, and grief may become worse, especially if support from others in the person's life has decreased. Everyone experiences grief differently. It is important to remember that experiencing and showing these painful feelings and reactions is not "weak" or shameful; rather, experiencing and showing these feelings are normal parts of healing.

When dealing with grief, a person may also experience some behavioral reactions, or changes in the way he or she acts. It may suddenly seem impossible to make decisions or to keep track of things. Someone who is normally very active may feel uninterested in doing any usual activities or projects. Additionally, because of the extreme emotions associated with grief and the serious adjustments that must be made in one's life after losing a loved one to homicide, a survivor may feel disoriented and may behave in a confused or "lost" manner. A person may become short-tempered or snap at others, even if the person had not been like that before the loss. A variety of behavior changes may occur following loss, and it is normal to experience them.

Losing a loved one can hit a person with an almost physical force, so it is normal to experience physical difficulties as well as emotional ones. These reactions can include nausea, a feeling of tiredness, stomach ache, or a general feeling of being unwell. Many people experience a change in sleep patterns or appetite, and some become clumsy and more prone to accidents. Very often, survivors are so busy taking care of various arrangements and consoling other people who have shared their loss that they forget to take care of themselves (Rheingold, Grier, & Whitworth, 2005, p. 1–3)

ASSESSMENT

Special Issues in Homicide Cases

Homicide survivors (family and loved ones of the homicide victim) have been shown to have depression manifested by shock, disbelief, numbness, changes in appetite, sleeping difficulties, heightened anxiety, and phobic reactions (Redmond, 1989). Tasks of grieving should be a focus of intervention in an attempt to alleviate depressive symptomatology. Homicide survivors must deal with a myriad of issues at once: the finality of the death, the loss of relationships and roles with the victim, and ultimately a questioning of their philosophies of life and life assumptions. The nature of grief that is experienced following the death of a loved one is a difficult dynamic to understand. The ensuing shattered assumptions and search for meaning form a continuous process that may last for years following the loss.

Victim Assessment

Usually, psychotherapy treatment involves an initial clinical assessment that focuses on determining how best to help a survivor cope with the aftermath of homicide. The process of bereavement and mourning are influenced by the nature of the death. The sudden and unexpected nature of homicide complicates the assessment of the victim, and as such, the assessment must be an ongoing process. The time that has passed from the homicide to the assessment must also be taken into consideration. Understanding how an individual has coped with stressors in the past may facilitate the recovery process. Victims also experience a tremendous amount of anger at the situation as well as the criminal justice system, and often have homicide-related intrusions and avoidance behaviors indicative of posttraumatic stress disorder (PTSD).

Use of Standardized Measures

Folkman and Lazarus (1988) developed the Ways of Coping Questionnaire, which measures coping using the following eight subscales:

1. Confrontive Coping (6 items)
2. Distancing (6 items)
3. Self-controlling (7 items)
4. Seeking Social Support (6 items)
5. Accepting Responsibility (4 items)
6. Escape-avoidance (8 items)
7. Planful Problem Solving (6 items)
8. Positive Reappraisal (7 items)

Folkman and Lazarus state that

> the Ways of Coping Questionnaire is designed to identify the thoughts and actions an individual has used to cope with a specific stressful encounter. It measures coping processes, not coping dispositions or styles. To assess

coping styles with the instrument, the investigator would need to assess an individual's coping processes in a range of stressful encounters, then evaluate consistencies in those processes across encounters. The Ways of Coping Questionnaire can be used as a stimulus for discussion in clinical, training, and workshop settings. Fruitful areas for discussion include identification of what was at stake in the stressful encounter as well as identification of the possible options for coping and the strategies that were actually used. Another utility is to use the Questionnaire as a research tool in clinical settings, for example, in relation to types and degree of pathology, or in measuring the effects of interventions. (p. 1)

Bard and Sangrey (1980) found that appropriate social support is important in the recovery process of victims. Gottfredson, Reiser, and Tsegaye-Spates (1987) state that "the conduct of family and friends of victims, bystanders, investigating police officers, medical and paramedical personnel, judges, prosecutors, and court staff may either alleviate or exacerbate the difficulties that victims face" (p. 318). Most studies find that support from friends, family, and the community assist in the recovery process (Kaniasty & Norris, 1994). Cutrona and Russell (1990) classified emotional support as most beneficial to victims since it fosters feelings of acceptance and comfort. Material or tangible support and informational support were also identified as assisting the victim in the recovery process (Cutrona & Russell, 1990). Social support is considered an asset in providing resources that the victimization experience depletes (Hobfall, Freedy, Geller, & Lane, 1990).

Assault-related injuries often need immediate medical services and crisis intervention for accompanying emotional crises. Steps need to be taken at this point to possibly alleviate long-term physical injuries and emotional distress. Medical treatment and psychological counseling for injuries associated with types of crime are frequently justified for short-term concerns. However, the mediating and moderating role of perceived and received support may have implications for long-term health and mental health as well.

The Inventory of Socially Supportive Behaviors (ISSB) can be used to assess social support (Barrera, Sandler, & Ramsay, 1981). This is a 40-item, Likert-scaled survey that measures the nature of supports received from natural helpers, such as family members and friends. It has demonstrated internal consistency with Cronbach's Alpha = 0.926 to 0.94 (different administrations) (Barrera et al., 1981). Cognitive/informational support and appraisal/emotional support have been found to be the most robust dimensions of the ISSB.

The Social Support Appraisals Scale is a subjective measure of social support with good reliability and appropriate subscale intercorrelation. Evidence of construct validity has included significant associations with another social support appraisal measure, measures of other social support dimensions, and family-reported data.

Many victims of crime express anger at the crime event, the criminal justice system, and themselves. The assessment of anger can be accomplished through the use of the State-Trait Anger Expression Inventory (STAXI) (Spielberger, 1979). STAXI-2 is a 57-item inventory that measures the intensity of anger as an emotional state (State Anger) and the disposition to experience angry feelings as a personality trait (Trait Anger). The instrument consists of six scales: Trait Anger, Anger Expression-Out, Anger Expression-In, Anger Control-Out, Anger Control-In, and State Anger. The STAXI-2 also includes 5 subscales and an Anger Expression Index. This scale defines state anger as "an emotional state or condition that consists of subjective feelings of tension, annoyance, irritation, fury and rage, with concomitant activation or arousal of the autonomic nervous system" (Spielberger, 1996, p. 10). The S-Anger scale consists of a 20-item, 4-point Likert scale. Respondents report the intensity of their feelings, with 1 being "not at all" and 4 being "very much." Alpha coefficients have been reported at .93. The STAXI has strong convergent and construct validity, as evidenced by reported correlations of this scale ranging from .39 to .45 with other anger and personality scales (Spielberger et al., 1985).

Posthomicide stress and postcrime stress have been shown to result from certain coping responses. Research has suggested that emotion-focused coping strategies are most effective in moderating adaptation to crimes that typically result in PTSD symptomatology. The Impact of Events Scale (IES) (Zilberg, Weiss, & Horowitz, 1982) can be used to operationalize posttraumatic stress. This scale is a 15-item, self-report scale that measures emotional reactions, specifically avoidance and intrusion following a traumatic event such as a crime. Split-half reliability for the scale has been reported at $r = .86$. Internal consistency of the subscales has been reported for the avoidance component (.82) and for the intrusion component (.78). An Alpha of .93 has been reported for the total Impact of Events Scale. While the intrusion and avoidance subscales have been shown to be correlated ($r = .42$), they have also been shown to measure different concepts. The IES has been found reliable and to have concurrent validity with respect to the Trauma Symptom Checklist and the Los Angeles Symptom Checklist.

Treatment Planning

It is important to recognize all the potential problems survivors may experience. Identifying and addressing these issues are paramount for effective treatment planning. The following list of potential problems, barriers, feelings, and issues that a homicide survivor may encounter and/or experience is provided by the National Organization of Parents of Murdered Children (2007).

1. isolation and helplessness in a world that is seen as hostile and uncaring and that frequently blames the victim
2. feelings of guilt for not having protected the victim
3. memory of a mutilated body at the morgue: "How much did my loved one suffer?"
4. getting back the personal belongings of a murder victim
5. sensational and/or inaccurate media coverage
6. lack of information
7. endless grief
8. loss of ability to function on the job, at home, or in school
9. strain on marriages (frequently resulting in divorce) and the strain on family relationships
10. effects on health, faith and values
11. effects on other family members, children, friends, and coworkers, among others
12. indifference of the community, including professionals, to the plight of survivors
13. society's attitude regarding murder as a form of entertainment
14. financial burden of medical and funeral expenses
15. medical expenses for stress-related illnesses and professional counseling for surviving family members
16. financial burden of hiring private investigators or similar others
17. public sympathy for murderers
18. feeling that the murderer, if found, gets all the help but survivors of homicide victims have few rights
19. outrage about the leniency of the murderer's sentence
20. disparities in the judicial system (frequently, punishments for property crimes are as great or greater than punishments for the crime of taking a human life)
21. anger over a plea-bargain arrangement/agreement
22. frustration at not being allowed inside the courtroom at the time of trial

23. unanswered questions about the crime, such as "What really happened?"
24. unanswered questions about postponements and continuous delays throughout the trial
25. bitterness and loss of faith in the American criminal justice system
26. after conviction, living with a long appeals process
27. constantly reliving your story through the dreaded parole process

Summary of Assessment

When a person loses a loved one to homicide, there are many possible reactions. In the beginning some people go numb and "shut down." Others cry uncontrollably, feel angry, or both. All of these reactions are normal. The three different types of reactions a person may have to loss are emotional, behavioral, and physical. A person may experience one, some, or all of these. The unexpected and violent nature of homicide is a traumatic life event. Much research has found that the loss of a loved one through homicide results in anxiety states, panic, and often depression. It is important to assess survivors adequately so that services can be provided to alleviate the unrelenting grief that they may feel for years. Each survivor experiences the loss as well as the interaction with the criminal justice system in a way that is uniquely his or her own.

TREATMENT: ISSUES AND INTERVENTIONS

Overview: General Principles of Treatment

Treatment for mental health issues arising from experiencing a traumatic event has been shown to be effective (Harvey, Bryant, & Tarrier, 2003). Coping with the aftermath of murder is a difficult and long-lasting process. Recovery is often prolonged as a result of complex interactions between the homicide survivor and the criminal justice system, and the ensuing multiple losses felt by the survivor. Interventions should focus on every aspect of these losses. Individuals who have lost a loved one from homicide experience overwhelming eruptions of emotions for years. The individual may have been able to recover initially, but once the trial begins, the wounds may be opened and deepened again. Involvement with the criminal justice system can be devastating and can result in complicated grief. Survivors may have feelings of ambivalence about attending and participating in the trial; they may experience rage, despair, and guilt as they relive aspects of the murder. A combination of therapeutic approaches (e.g., crisis intervention; individual, family, and group therapy; peer support groups; pharmacological intervention) may assist the survivor in working through the trauma and grief of such a violent loss. A combination of approaches (e.g., trauma-focused counseling, pharmacological approaches) is more effective than use of any single approach.

Revictimization Issues

Rheingold, Grier, and Whitworth (2005) found that perhaps one of the most frustrating factors that can complicate grief reactions is the difficulty a survivor may encounter when dealing with law enforcement. When a person is murdered, there are many things a survivor has to handle that he or she would not normally encounter. Autopsies, investigations, legal meetings, hearings, and trials can make the difficult situation of losing a loved one even more challenging. Because the judicial system takes a very long time to complete its processes, a survivor may have to wait months or even years before dealings with law enforcement end, thereby delaying a person's opportunity to put some of the trauma to rest. Despite these difficulties, it is important for the survivor to cooperate with law enforcement officials in order to help ensure that justice is served. Most police departments have victim advocates, who are available to help survivors navigate the complexities of the legal system and help make this added stressor a little more manageable.

Victims are also often revictimized by the media, the hospital and emergency room, victim service providers, and victim compensation and social service workers. The sudden loss creates a sense of chaos for survivor, who is trying to balance the devastating news of the loss with the unrelenting needs of the criminal justice system. This period of chaos hinders survivors' ability to grasp the full extent of their reality and can last for weeks, months, and years as their lives continually intersect with various criminal justice and health management systems. It is a critical time for involvement of practitioners in assisting with the grief process.

Grief Therapy and Meaning Reconstruction

Upon hearing the news that a loved one has been murdered, survivors have a difficult time comprehending the difference between the unconscious wish for a normal life with the loved one and the sudden, unresolved reality that they have a life without him or her now. The struggle for comprehension of the gap between their lifelong desires and expectations and a new, previously unperceived reality grips them emotionally and mentally.

A grief resolution approach uses a variety of methods that can include guided imagery, visualization, art therapy, journaling, or reflection techniques, to name a few. Initially, the goal is to use reflective practice to validate the expressions of grief, acknowledge the real losses present, and recognize changes in the person's life as a result of this loss. It is necessary to explore with the survivor ways of coping with the loss and managing the stress that is created by the event and the criminal justice system.

Since all individuals process grief and loss differently, it is important to identify a variety of ways to help survivors grieve. Narrative therapy is often helpful in the grieving process, although not during the initial aftermath of the homicide. The central idea of narrative therapy is that the person is never the problem—the person *has* a problem. The person does not have to change who he or she is, but has to attempt to fight the influence of the problem in his or her life. Complicated grief arises when a survivor essentially gets "stuck" in the story. Through narrative therapy, the survivor rediscovers his or her past and who he or she was prior to the homicide. The new story brings the person into liberation with a clearer insight (Epston & White, 1992). Grief therapy becomes an opportunity for narrative repair and reinforces resilience. Some of the goals and objectives of narrative therapy are to

- use narrative methods to reveal turning points in the survivor's history associated with the loss
- diagnose complicated grief based on the identification of signs and symptoms of traumatic disruption
- recognize the role of narrative gaps and identify areas of reconstruction
- recognize the silent questions that the survivor must reveal in order to find a new orientation for their loss
- listen beneath the story that the survivor tells himself or herself about the loss, thus enabling the survivor to grasp and transform the event's personal significance
- Use metaphoric listening and externalizing grief to find the personal meaning of the loss
- create a biopsychosocial-spiritual framework to support survivor resilience
- link current research on grief to specific clinical interventions

Chapter 8 Homicide Victims **165**

Crisis Intervention

The immediate aftermath of a murder of a loved one probably will be the biggest crisis a person will have to face. It is scary and frightening beyond imagination. However, in many cases, the experience of this type of crisis can be lessened when those left behind allow themselves to ask for help. The goals of crisis intervention are to resolve the immediate crisis and teach the individual effective coping strategies for dealing with future difficulties. Aquilera (1990) described three factors that affect the way individuals deal with crisis: prior coping abilities, presence of social support, and the individual's perception of the event. The increased sense of vulnerability that individuals experience often motivates those in crisis to seek assistance in addressing the problem. It may be possible to correct distorted perceptions and improve the client's ability to cope with the crisis in the very early stages following a murder. Crisis intervention refers to the methods used to offer immediate, short-term help to individuals who experience an event that produces emotional, mental, physical, and behavioral distress or problems. Crisis intervention may include elements from one or more of these models:

- Equilibrium model: The goal of this model is to help the client recover to a state of precrisis equilibrium, whereby coping mechanisms and problem-solving methods are used to meet the survivor's needs.
- Cognitive model: The goal of this model is to help the client become aware of and change his or her views and beliefs about the crisis. Survivors can gain control of the crisis by changing their thinking and focusing on rational and self-enhancing elements.
- Psychosocial transition model: The goal of this model is to help the client choose workable alternatives to current behavior, attitudes, and use of environmental resources.

The crisis intervention process involves (1), identifying and clarifying the elements of the crisis, (2) developing problem-solving strategies, and (3) mobilizing the person to act on these strategies (Shulman, 2000). Allowing the survivor to vent feelings of loss and grief may lead to lessening the feeling of loss of control and disorganized thinking. The ultimate task is to help the survivor discover solutions and access support networks, resources, and concrete services.

The crisis intervention approach should also contain a focus on the terrorist grief and recovery process model, which is based on the premise that part of the grieving and recovery process is relinquishing an attachment to previously held beliefs and values about self, human nature, the world, and spirituality (Jordan, 2005). See Chapter 4 for more detailed discussion of crisis intervention.

Stress Reduction Group

Homicides produce a great amount of stress and anxiety, both immediately and over the weeks and months that follow. In *Coping with Disasters: A Guide to Psychosocial Intervention*, Ehrenreicht and McQuaide (2001) provide a variety of techniques that may be useful in reducing stress and anxiety.

Rest and Recreation

Brief periods of rest in the course of the day's activities and adequate sleep are important for both relief workers and survivors. Understandably, the emergency created by a disaster may interfere with rest and sleep in the first hours or days after the disaster. As soon as the most urgent, life-and-death rescue needs are met, however, encourage relief workers to permit themselves to take a break or a short nap, and ensure that adequate facilities are available. Encourage those supervising relief efforts to schedule relief workers' shifts so as to ensure that workers get adequate sleep. Recreational activities, ranging from card games to watching television to participating in games, may be helpful, both for adults (relief workers and primary disaster victims) and for children and adolescents. In part, these activities serve as diversions, preventing "ruminating" about the disaster. They also help restore a sense of normalcy and control over one's life.

Ventilation

Allowing relief workers and survivors to talk about their experiences and feelings in both informal and formal settings relieves stress. Repetitive restatements or rumination, however, do not relieve stress and may promote depression; for these reasons, they should be discouraged. Divert the discussion to other topics, provide diversions, or use other approaches to promote relaxation.

Exercise

Physical activity helps dissipate stress. Provide opportunities for relief
workers and primary disaster victims (e.g., those in a shelter) to get exercise: taking a walk, jogging, engaging in a group exercise "class," engaging in an athletic event, or dancing.

Relaxation Exercises

Several types of relaxation exercises can be adapted easily for use in
disaster settings to help clients reduce anxiety and stress. These include
breathing exercises, visualization exercises, muscle relaxation exercises,
and combinations.

- *Breathing exercises:* The client is taught to breathe in a controlled way, while attending closely to his or her own breathing.
- *Visualization exercises:* The client is asked to provide an account of a setting or situation he or she finds very relaxing
  (e.g., walking in the woods), and is then asked to visualize this
  scene in a very detailed way. The particular scene to be visu-
  alized should be worked out in discussion with the intended
  user of the exercise.
- *Muscle relaxation exercises:* The client is asked to practice first
  contracting, then relaxing different muscle groups until the
  entire musculature is relaxed, while concentrating on the feelings of relaxation in the muscle.

First, the counselor leads an individual or a small group of individuals through these exercises. If the victims have tape cassette play-
ers available, it may be helpful to record a relaxation exercise for each
client to listen to and engage in on his or her own. Individuals can
also be taught how to use the procedures on their own without a tape
recording.

Relaxation procedures can be used on an "as needed" basis (i.e.,
at a time when the relief worker or survivor is feeling "stressed out"),
either on his or her own, or with the help of the counselor. A regularly
scheduled relaxation event, whether consisting of relaxation exercises,
prayer, stretching exercises, or other techniques, may be offered at a
consistent time once or twice a day. Many people also find that following
the relaxation procedure on their own several times a day, on a routine

basis, increases their ability to deal with stress throughout the day. After learning a full relaxation exercise, a shortened form can be developed. Such brief forms are especially useful "as needed."

For a person to be willing to allow himself or herself to relax by following the directions of another person (the disaster counselor) requires some trust. Teaching relaxation exercises should be delayed until the counselor and the client have created a trusting relationship. This is especially true of disaster survivors who have developed PTSD. People who are very anxious or very depressed may find relaxation exercises problematic. Relaxation exercises should be approached with caution with such clients. *If the client begins to become agitated, stop the exercise.*

Contraindications to the Use of Relaxation Exercises

Relaxation exercises are not for everyone. They should be used with extreme caution or not at all in the following circumstances:

- presence of marked dissociative symptoms
- anger as the primary response to trauma
- state of acute grief
- state of extreme anxiety or panic
- history of severe psychopathology prior to the trauma
- current substance abuse
- severe depression and/or suicidal ideation
- presence of marked ongoing stressors

CONCLUSION

With interventions that have a reasonable likelihood of being beneficial for a survivor, the important issues for the practitioner become understanding the nature of the risks in order to minimize them to the extent possible, fully informing the survivor as to the nature of the risks within the context of the possible benefits, and ultimately allowing the survivor to make an informed decision regarding treatment options. The most basic information needed is the status of the case, the opportunity to make a victim impact statement, information about the release of the offender, the right to compensation and restitution, and the role of the victim in the criminal justice process. State-level victims' bills of rights cannot help if victims are not aware of what they can ask for and expect.

Social workers can actively influence changes in social policy that would ensure the same rights and services for victims as those that offenders receive. Professionals can combat the lack of rights provided to victims through the types of programs offered and the ways these programs are developed. Social workers need to actively involve victims in identifying what programs are needed and in designing, implementing, and managing the programs.

Previous research indicates the need for mandates to be in place for the evaluation of existing services for victims. Sheriffs' offices and police departments should evaluate the extent to which crime victims use their professional help through victim service departments. How crime victims rate the quality of professional services and the effects of those professional services on the victims' recovery processes should be addressed. Victims' compensation funds continue to pour money into services that may or may not be effective in reducing psychological distress of victims. Evaluations answering questions regarding effectiveness would better inform legislators about cost-effective expenditures for victim assistance.

The serious nature and increasing number of criminal acts and their aftermath demand that future studies be conducted concerning the experience of crime victims and their needs. Research will assist in promoting legislative and policy changes necessary to improve the treatment of victims. Legislative bodies would be able to provide technical assistance to victim advocates, such as how to propose legislation on victim rights and services, and how to design and implement strategies to ensure proper enactment (National Organization for Victim Assistance, 1998). Other implications for policy include the development of certification and standards for victim assistance programs and service providers.

Social service agencies should be encouraged to become active in local, state, and national efforts that address ways to support the rights of victims and simplify the ways in which victims employ those rights. By becoming active advocates, social workers can improve the awareness of lawmakers regarding the needs and issues of victims, and can take the lead in the development of social justice for victims of crime. Shachter and Seinfeld (1994) embrace this approach with the following statement: "Social workers have a vital stake in influencing change in the politics and values that shape the culture of violence" (p. 347). The following principles promote victim success in the recovery process:

- All people should be treated with respect and dignity.
- The results of our actions should lead to "just consequences."
- Worker actions should lead to increased freedom for the survivor.
- Worker actions should be state-of-the-art.
- Criminal justice workers, social workers, support staff, and others should be treated with the same respect and dignity as survivors (Schachter & Seinfeld, 1994, p. 349).

Elder Abuse

Currently, there are an estimated 35 million people age 65 or older in the United States. Older adults are now the fastest growing segment of the U.S. population. In 2011, the first group of baby boomers will turn 65, and by 2030, nearly 20% of the population is expected to be 65 or older. According to the National Committee for the Prevention of Elder Abuse (2007):

- Approximately 450,000 Americans have been victims of elder abuse.
- As many as 1.2 million seniors have been abused at some point in their lives.
- Those most at risk of being abused are people who suffer from dementia.
- Dementia is an effect of Parkinson's disease.

Elder abuse is a relatively new field that raises many complex ethical, legal, and clinical questions. It has challenged our understanding of such fundamental concepts as personal freedom, the role of culture in defining family responsibility, and society's obligations to its members. Older people today are more visible, more active, and more independent than ever before. They are living longer and remain in better health longer. But as the population of older Americans grows, so does the hidden problem of elder abuse, exploitation, and neglect. Every year, an estimated 2.1

million older Americans are victims of physical, psychological, or other forms of abuse and neglect. Those statistics may not tell the whole story. For every case of elder abuse and neglect that is reported to authorities, experts estimate that there may be as many as five cases that have not been reported (National Committee for the Prevention of Elder Abuse, 2007). Recent research suggests that elders who have been abused tend to die earlier than those who are not abused, even in the absence of chronic conditions or life-threatening diseases. Elder abuse is doing something or failing to do something that results in harm to an elderly person or puts a helpless older person at risk of harm. This includes

■ physical, sexual, and emotional abuse
■ neglecting or deserting an older person for whom you are responsible
■ taking or misusing an elderly person's money or property

Elder abuse can happen within the family. It can also happen in settings such as hospitals, nursing homes, or in the community. Elder abuse is a serious problem in this country. All 50 states have laws against elder abuse. The laws differ, but all states have systems for reporting suspected abuse. The National Committee for the Prevention of Elder Abuse distinguishes among seven different types of elder abuse. These include physical abuse, sexual abuse, emotional abuse, financial/material exploitation, neglect, abandonment, and self-neglect.

■ *physical abuse*: use of physical force that may result in bodily injury, physical pain, or impairment
■ *sexual abuse*: nonconsensual sexual contact of any kind with an elderly person
■ *emotional abuse*: infliction of anguish, pain, or distress through verbal or nonverbal acts
■ *financial/material exploitation*: illegal or improper use of an elder's funds, property, or assets
■ *neglect*: refusal, or failure, to fulfill any part of a person's obligations or duties to an elderly person
■ *abandonment*: desertion of an elderly person by an individual who has physical custody of the elder, or by a person who has assumed responsibility for providing care to the elder
■ *self-neglect*: behaviors of an elderly person that threaten the elder's health or safety

Currently, there are no official national statistics relating to the prevalence of this dilemma. However, recent research estimates that approximately 1 to 2 million Americans age 65 or older have been abused or neglected by the very people they entrust with their care and protection. The majority of elder abuse victims are female, whereas the majority of the perpetrators are male. Overall, adult children are most often the perpetrators of elder abuse, followed by other family members and spouses. Unfortunately, institutional abuse of the elderly (e.g., in hospitals, convalescent homes, and board-and-care homes) is also becoming a major concern, particularly since more families are unable to provide appropriate care for the elderly at home (National Committee for the Prevention of Elder Abuse, 2005).

Just as in other forms of abuse, elder abuse is a complex problem, and it is easy for people to have misconceptions about it. Many people who hear "elder abuse and neglect" think about older people living in nursing homes or about elderly relatives who live all alone and never have visitors. But elder abuse is not just a problem of older people living on the margins of our everyday life. It is right in our midst.

- Most incidents of elder abuse don't happen in a nursing home. Occasionally, there are shocking reports of nursing home residents who are mistreated by the staff. Such abuse does occur, but it is not the most common type of elder abuse. At any one time, only about 4% of older adults live in nursing homes, and the vast majority of nursing home residents have their physical needs met without experiencing abuse or neglect.

- Most elder abuse and neglect takes place at home. The great majority of older people live on their own or with their spouses, children, siblings, or other relatives—not in institutional settings. When elder abuse happens, family, other household members, and paid caregivers usually are the abusers. Although there are extreme cases of elder abuse, often the abuse is subtle, and the distinction between normal interpersonal stress and abuse is not always easy to discern.

- There is no single pattern of elder abuse in the home. Sometimes the abuse is a continuation of long-standing patterns of physical or emotional abuse within the family. Perhaps, more commonly, the abuse is related to changes in living situations and relationships brought about by the older person's growing frailty and dependence on others for companionship and for meeting basic needs.

■ It is not just infirm or mentally impaired elderly people who are vulnerable to abuse. Elders who are ill, frail, disabled, mentally impaired, or depressed are at greater risk of abuse, but even those who do not have these obvious risk factors can find themselves in abusive situations and relationships (National Committee for the Prevention of Elder Abuse, 2005).

ASSESSMENT

Special Issues and Assessment in Elder Abuse Cases

Physical Abuse

Physical abuse is physical force or violence that results in bodily injury, pain, or impairment. It includes assault, battery, and inappropriate restraint. Perpetrators may be acquaintances, sons, daughters, grand-children, or others. Perpetrators are likely to be unmarried, to live with their victims, and to be unemployed. Some perpetrators have alcohol or substance abuse problems. Some are caregivers for those they abuse. As a group, victims of physical abuse do not differ significantly from seniors who are not abused. Physical indicators may include injuries or bruises, while behavioral indicators are ways victims and abusers act or interact with each other. Many of the indicators listed below can be explained by other causes (e.g., a bruise may be the result of an accidental fall), and no single indicator can be taken as conclusive proof. Rather, one should look for patterns or clusters of indicators that suggest a problem.

Physical Indicators

■ sprains, dislocations, fractures, or broken bones
■ burns from cigarettes, appliances, or hot water
■ abrasions on arms, legs, or torso that resemble rope or strap marks
■ internal injuries evidenced by pain, difficulty with normal functioning of organs, and bleeding from body orifices
■ bruises—especially the following types, which are rarely accidental:
  ■ bilateral bruising to the arms (may indicate that the person has been shaken, grabbed, or restrained)

- bilateral bruising of the inner thighs (may indicate sexual abuse)
- "wraparound" bruises that encircle an older person's arms, legs, or torso (may indicate that the person has been physically restrained)
- multicolored bruises (indicating the bruising was sustained over time)
- injuries healing through "secondary intention" (indicating the injuries did not receive appropriate care)
- signs of traumatic hair and tooth loss

Behavioral Indicators

- unexplained injuries or implausible explanations (do not "fit" with the injuries observed)
- differing explanations from family members of how injuries were sustained
- history of similar injuries or numerous or suspicious hospitalizations
- victims brought to different medical facilities for treatment (perhaps to prevent medical practitioners from observing a pattern of abuse)
- delay between onset of injury and seeking medical care (National Committee for the Prevention of Elder Abuse, 2005)

Sexual Abuse

Sexual abuse is any form of nonconsensual physical contact. It includes rape, molestation, or any sexual conduct with a person who lacks the mental capacity to exercise consent. Perpetrators of sexual abuse include attendants, employees of care facilities, family members (including spouses), and others. Those who are at risk of sexual abuse include

- women
- persons with physical or cognitive disabilities
- persons who lack social support and are isolated

Physical indicators may include injuries or bruises, while behavioral indicators are the ways victims and abusers act or interact with each other. Some of the indicators listed below can be explained by other causes (e.g., inappropriate or unusual behavior may signal dementia or drug interactions), and no single indicator can be taken as conclusive proof. Rather, one should look for patterns or clusters of indicators that suggest a problem.

Physical Indicators

■ genital or anal pain, irritation, or bleeding
■ bruises on external genitalia or inner thighs
■ difficulty walking or sitting
■ torn, stained, or bloody underclothing
■ sexually transmitted diseases

Behavioral Indicators

■ inappropriate sex-role relationship between victim and suspect
■ inappropriate, unusual, or aggressive sexual behavior (National Committee for the Prevention of Elder Abuse, 2007)

Domestic Violence

Domestic violence is an escalating pattern of violence or intimidation by an intimate partner, which is used to gain power and control. Several categories of domestic violence against the elderly have been identified: "Domestic violence grown old" is when domestic violence had started earlier in life and has persisted into old age. "Late onset domestic violence" begins in old age. There may have been a strained relationship or emotional abuse earlier that got worse as the partners aged. When abuse begins or is exacerbated in old age, it is likely to be linked to

■ retirement
■ disability
■ changing roles of family members
■ sexual changes

Some older people enter into abusive relationships late in life. Perpetrators are spouses or intimate partners. The majority are men, and some perpetrators abuse drugs or alcohol. Indicators of domestic violence are similar to those associated with physical abuse and sexual abuse (see physical abuse and sexual abuse). The following additional patterns are also characteristic:

- The frequency and severity of injuries are likely to increase over time.
- Victims often experience intense confusion and disassociation.
- Violent incidents are often preceded by periods of intensifying tension and followed by periods of apparent contrition on the part of perpetrators (National Committee for the Prevention of Elder Abuse, 2007).

Psychological Abuse

Psychological abuse is the willful infliction of mental or emotional anguish by threat, humiliation, or other verbal or nonverbal conduct. Cultural values and expectations play a significant role in how psychological abuse is manifested and how it affects its victims. Perpetrators may be family members, caregivers, or acquaintances. Persons who are isolated and who lack social or emotional support are particularly vulnerable.

Physical indicators may include somatic changes or decline, while behavioral indicators are ways victims and abusers act or interact. Some of the indicators listed below can be explained by other causes, and no single indicator can be taken as conclusive proof. Rather, one should look for patterns or clusters of indicators that suggest a problem.

Physical Indicators

- significant weight loss or gain that is not attributed to other causes
- stress-related conditions, including elevated blood pressure

Behavioral Indicators

The perpetrator

- isolates the elder emotionally by not speaking to, touching, or comforting him or her

The elder

- has problems sleeping
- exhibits depression and confusion
- cowers in the presence of abuser
- is emotionally upset, agitated, withdrawn, and nonresponsive

- exhibits unusual behavior usually attributed to dementia (e.g., sucking, biting, rocking) (National Committee for the Prevention of Elder Abuse, 2007)

Financial Abuse

Elder financial abuse spans a broad spectrum of conduct, including

- taking money or property
- forging an older person's signature
- getting an older person to sign a deed, will, or power of attorney through deception, coercion, or undue influence
- using the older person's property or possessions without permission
- promising lifelong care in exchange for money or property, and not following through on the promise
- using confidence crimes ("cons") or deception to gain victim's confidence
- using scams or other fraudulent or deceptive acts
- engaging in fraud: the use of deception, trickery, false pretense, or dishonest acts or statements for financial gain
- engaging in telemarketing scams: calling victims and using deception, scare tactics, or exaggerated claims to get them to send money; making charges against victims' credit cards without authorization

Perpetrators may be family members, including sons, daughters, grandchildren, or spouses. One or more family members may

- have substance abuse, gambling, or financial problems
- stand to inherit and feel justified in taking what they believe is "almost" or "rightfully" theirs
- fear that their older family member will get sick and use up their savings, depriving the abuser of an inheritance
- have had a negative relationship with the older person and feel a sense of "entitlement"
- have negative feelings toward siblings or other family members whom they want to prevent from acquiring or inheriting the older person's assets

Predatory individuals seek out vulnerable seniors with the intent of exploiting them. They may

- profess to love the older person ("sweetheart scams")
- seek employment as personal care attendants, counselors, or similar roles to gain access
- identify vulnerable persons by driving through neighborhoods (to find persons who are alone and isolated) or contact recently widowed persons they identify through newspaper death announcements
- move from community to community to avoid being apprehended (transient criminals)

Unscrupulous professionals or businesspersons, or persons posing as such may

- overcharge for services or products
- use deceptive or unfair business practices
- use their positions of trust or respect to gain compliance

The following conditions or factors increase an older person's risk of being victimized:

- isolation
- loneliness
- recent losses
- physical or mental disabilities
- lack of familiarity with financial matters
- having family members who are unemployed and/or have substance abuse problems

Why are the elderly attractive targets?

- Persons over the age of 50 control over 70% of the nation's wealth.
- Many seniors do not realize the value of their assets (particularly homes that have appreciated markedly).
- The elderly are likely to have disabilities that make them dependent on others for help. These "helpers" may have access to

homes and assets, and may exercise significant influence over the older person.

- They may have predictable patterns (e.g., because older people are likely to receive monthly checks, abusers can predict when an older people will have money on hand or need to go to the bank).
- Severely impaired individuals are also less likely to take action against their abusers as a result of illness or embarrassment.
- Abusers may assume that frail victims will not survive long enough to follow through on legal interventions, or that they will not make convincing witnesses.
- Some older people are unsophisticated about financial matters.
- Advances in technology have made managing finances more complicated.

Indicators

- unpaid bills, eviction notices, or notices to discontinue utilities
- withdrawals from bank accounts or transfers between accounts that the older person cannot explain
- bank statements and canceled checks no longer coming to the elder's home
- new "best friends"
- legal documents, such as powers of attorney, which the older person did not understand at the time he or she signed them
- unusual activity in the older person's bank accounts, including large, unexplained withdrawals, frequent transfers between accounts, or ATM withdrawals
- care not commensurate with the size of elder's estate
- excessive interest by caregiver in the amount of money being spent on the older person
- missing belongings or property
- suspicious signatures on checks or other documents
- absence of documentation about financial arrangements
- implausible explanations about the elderly person's finances by the elder or the caregiver
- elder's lack of awareness or understanding of financial arrangements that have been made for him or her (National Committee for the Prevention of Elder Abuse, 2007)

Neglect

Neglect is the failure of caregivers to fulfill their responsibilities to provide needed care. "Active" neglect consists of behavior that is willful: the caregiver intentionally withholds care or necessities. The neglect may be motivated by financial gain (e.g., the caregiver stands to inherit) or reflect interpersonal conflicts. "Passive" neglect comprises situations in which the caregiver is unable to fulfill his or her caregiving responsibilities as a result of illness, disability, stress, ignorance, lack of maturity, or lack of resources. Self-neglect consists of situations in which there is no perpetrator, and neglect is the result of the older person refusing care. Perpetrators may be paid attendants, family members, employees of long-term care facilities, or others. Caregivers who perpetrate may lack adequate skills, training, time, or energy. Additionally, caregivers who perpetrate may be mentally ill, or have alcohol, substance abuse, or other mental health problems. In self-neglect cases, there are no perpetrators.

Persons with physical or mental disabilities as well as persons with high care needs who depend on others for care are at risk. The literature on caregiving suggests that certain conditions are particularly stressful for caregivers. These include fluctuations in the older person's need for care, disturbed sleep, incontinence, and lack of support from other family members. Self-neglect is often associated with mental health problems, including substance abuse, dementia, and depression.

Indicators of neglect include the condition of the older person's home (environmental indicators), physical signs of poor care, and behavioral characteristics of the caregiver, the older person, or both. Some of the indicators listed below may not signal neglect but rather reflect lifestyle choices, lack of resources, or mental health problems. One should look for patterns or clusters of indicators that suggest a problem.

Signs of Neglect Observed in the Home

- absence of necessities including food, water, heat
- inadequate living environment evidenced by lack of utilities, sufficient space, and ventilation
- animal or insect infestations
- signs of medication mismanagement, including empty or unmarked bottles or outdated prescriptions
- Housing that is unsafe as a result of disrepair, faulty wiring, inadequate sanitation, substandard cleanliness, or architectural barriers

Physical Indicators

- poor personal hygiene including soiled clothing, dirty nails and skin, matted or lice-infested hair, odors, and the presence of feces or urine
- Lack of clothing or lack of proper clothing for weather
- decubiti (bedsores)
- skin rashes
- dehydration, evidenced by low urinary output; dry, fragile skin; dry, sore mouth; apathy; lack of energy; and mental confusion
- untreated medical or mental conditions including infections, soiled bandages, and unattended fractures
- absence of needed dentures, eyeglasses, hearing aids, walkers, wheelchairs, braces, or commodes
- exacerbation of chronic diseases despite a care plan
- worsening dementia

Behavioral Indicators

The caregiver/abuser

- expresses anger, frustration, or exhaustion
- isolates the elder from the outside world, friends, or relatives
- obviously lacks caregiving skills
- is unreasonably critical and/or dissatisfied with social and health care providers, and changes providers frequently
- refuses to apply for economic aid or services for the elder, and resists outside help

The victim

- exhibits emotional distress such as crying, depression, or despair
- has nightmares or difficulty sleeping
- has had a sudden loss of appetite that is unrelated to a medical condition
- is confused and disoriented (this may be the result of malnutrition)
- is emotionally numb, withdrawn, or detached
- exhibits regressive behavior
- exhibits self-destructive behavior
- exhibits fear toward the caregiver

■ expresses unrealistic expectations about his or her care (e.g., claims that care is adequate when it is not, or insists the situation will improve) (National Committee for the Prevention of Elder Abuse, 2007)

Summary of Assessment

Caregiver personal problems that can lead to abusing a frail, older person include caregiver stress, mental or emotional illness, addiction to alcohol or other drugs, job loss or other personal crises, financial dependency on the older person, and a tendency to use violence to solve problems. Sometimes the person being cared for may be physically abusive to the caregiver, especially when the older person has Alzheimer's or another form of dementia. Caregiver stress is a significant risk factor for abuse and neglect. When caregivers are thrust into the demands of daily care for an elder without appropriate training and without information about how to balance the needs of the older person with their own needs, they frequently experience intense frustration and anger that can lead to a range of abusive behaviors. The risk of elder abuse becomes even greater when the caregiver is responsible for an older person who is sick or who is physically or mentally impaired. Caregivers in such stressful situations often feel trapped and hopeless and are unaware of available resources and assistance. If they have no skills for managing difficult behaviors, caregivers can find themselves using physical force. Particularly with a lack of resources, neglectful situations can arise. Sometimes the caregiver's own self-image as a "dutiful child" may compound the problem by causing him or her to feel that the older person deserves and wants total care from the caregiver alone and that considering respite or residential care is a betrayal of the older person's trust.

Dependency is a contributing factor in elder abuse. When the caregiver is dependent financially on an impaired older person, there may be financial exploitation or abuse. When the reverse is true, and the impaired older person is completely dependent on the caregiver, the caregiver may experience resentment that leads to abusive behavior.

TREATMENT: ISSUES AND INTERVENTIONS

Overview: General Principles of Treatment

In a longitudinal study by Dura, Stukenberg, and Kiecolt-Galser (1991), caregivers listed fewer people in their support networks, and reported less frequent contact, less closeness, and less emotional and tangible support than others in a comparable population. The lack of support is significant because this has been shown to be a contributing factor in the stress experienced by the caregiver. Gormley (2000) asserts that caregiver interventions assist by directly providing tangible and emotional support to the caregiver and by providing the resources to facilitate the caregiving task, thus reducing the incidence of abuse. The forms of intervention include providing education, teaching coping skills and problem-solving techniques, and involving the caregiver with support groups, respite care, family therapy, and/or individual counseling. The educational intervention can focus on medical, psychosocial, and legal aspects of their current situation. The intervention can also include teaching caregiving skills such as behavior modification, communication, and basic skills of daily living.

Prevention/Treatment

A variety of health and social services are available to address the underlying causes of abuse, stop it, and reduce the likelihood that it will occur again. Still other services treat the emotional, physical, and financial effects. Some of these services are federally funded and available in every community, while others are specific to certain communities. Below are descriptions of services that are frequently needed by victims.

Mental health assessments are often needed to determine whether an older person is capable of meeting his or her own basic needs, making decisions about services, offering testimony, and protecting himself or herself against abuse. Assessments of an alleged abuser's mental status are sometimes needed to determine whether the person poses a danger to others and is in need of treatment.

Counseling for victims or vulnerable adults can help them assess their options, plan for their safety, resolve conflicts, and overcome trauma. Group or individual counseling may be available from private therapists, health maintenance organizations, or mental health clinics. In abuse cases, counseling typically focuses on the following issues:

- educating victims about resources and options
- breaking through denial and shame
- planning what to do if abuse occurs (safety planning)
- building support networks
- addressing codependency

- identifying and addressing traumatic or posttraumatic stress
- providing family counseling to resolve or mediate conflicts, and to address tensions or stresses that give rise to abuse or neglect

Legal assistance is needed in many abuse cases. Legal services are provided by private attorneys, programs operated by local or state bar associations, or subsidized legal aid programs. The Older Americans Act established a network of free legal services for persons over the age of 60. These programs are becoming increasingly adept at handling elder abuse cases. The following interventions may be needed in abuse cases:

- lawsuits to recover assets or property
- annulments of bogus marriages
- restraining orders to restrict contact between perpetrators and victims
- guardianship (called conservatorship in some states): a process by which courts assign responsible persons or agencies to act on behalf of people who are unable to protect themselves or their interests as a result of physical or cognitive impairments. Guardians may be family members or professionals from public or private guardians or in private practice. Some communities have programs that use volunteers to serve as, or monitor, guardians
- prosecution of offenders
- assistance with obtaining restitution

Support Services

When abuse or neglect is related to the stresses associated with caregiving, risk can be reduced by providing services that reduce the older person's dependency and isolation, and also provide relief to caregivers. Specific support services include the following:

- Daily money management services address financial abuse that may occur when an older person has lost the ability to manage his or her finances. Arranging for trustworthy people to help can reduce this risk. The help may be informal, where the money manager simply helps the elder with simple tasks like paying bills, or it may involve formal transfers of authority, including representative payeeship, power of attorney, or guardianship.

■ Home delivered meal programs deliver nutritious meals to seniors in their homes.

■ Attendants assist vulnerable people with their daily activities, including bathing, shopping, and preparing meals.

■ Adult day health centers provide an array of services, including nursing care; physical, occupational, and speech therapy; and socialization for frail seniors.

■ Friendly visitors make home visits to isolated seniors.

■ Telephone reassurance programs can make routine, "check in" calls to isolated seniors or provide telephone counseling to seniors who are in emotional distress.

■ Support groups for caregivers address the emotional demands and stresses of providing care. They also provide instruction and guidance in meeting the older person's needs and handling difficult behaviors. They may relieve the tensions, resentments, and stresses that give rise to abuse and neglect.

■ Respite programs give caregivers a break. Respite care comes in many forms. Attendants, professionals, or volunteers may come to the older person's home to provide a few hours of relief to the caregiver, or the older person may come to an agency. Some communities offer extended respite care of several days or longer.

Case management is an approach to providing services to individuals who have multiple and changing care needs. Case managers, who may work for public or private agencies or be in private practice, provide the following services:

■ conducting comprehensive assessments of the older person's general health, mental capacity, and ability to manage in the home and community

■ developing "care plans," often in consultation with other professionals from several disciplines, for meeting clients' service needs

■ arranging for needed services

■ responding to problems or emergencies

■ conducting routine reassessments to detect changes in the older person's health or ability to manage, and anticipate problems before they occur

Victim witness assistance programs, which are usually located within prosecutors' offices, help victims whose cases are in the criminal justice system. They provide

- information to victims about the court process and the status of their cases
- advocacy on behalf of victims: victim advocates inform courts about victims' special needs for protection or assistance, their preferences and concerns regarding what happens to perpetrators, and other similar information
- information about and assistance with compensation, restitution, and community services

Domestic violence programs provide an array of services for battered women. Some offer special services for older women or can accommodate older women's special needs. Domestic violence services include

- shelters
- counseling for victims and abusers
- crisis lines
- support groups

Services for Abusers

Some situations can be remedied by providing services to abusers. Abusers who are dependent on their victims for money or a place to live may benefit from job training or placement, financial assistance, counseling in independent living, or mental health or substance abuse treatment. While it is difficult to convince some abusers to accept treatment voluntarily—particularly mental health, domestic violence, or substance abuse treatment—these services are often mandated by courts or are offered as conditions of probation or as alternatives to prosecution.

Determining what interventions are appropriate in neglect cases depends on many factors, including the caregivers' willingness to improve care, the families' resources, and the willingness of the elder to accept help. Caregivers who are willing and able to improve the care they provide can be assisted by support services. A caregiver whose motive for providing care is self-interest may need to be replaced by a responsible person. Mental health services may also be needed, particularly in self-neglect cases.

Caregiver stress is a complex phenomenon. Several studies have revealed that caregivers find certain behaviors of care receivers to be particularly stressful, which can lead to abuse. Therefore, one primary prevention strategy is to intervene with caregivers prior to that point. Assuming that caregiver abuse is related to caregiver stress, several researchers have attempted to discern whether or not the predictors of stress also predict abuse. This line of reasoning has yielded some promising results. Depression, which is highly predictive of caregiver stress, has also been found to be a strong predictor of elder abuse, particularly when caregivers' level of depression reaches near-clinical levels. The likelihood that caregivers will abuse also appears to be strongly linked to how they perceive their situations. Abusive caregivers are more likely than nonabusive caregivers to feel that they are not receiving adequate help from their families, social networks, or public entities. Abusive caregivers report that certain behaviors are particularly stressful to them. These include verbal aggression, refusal to eat or take medications, calling the police, invading the caregiver's privacy, noisiness, "vulgar habits," disruptive behavior, embarrassing public displays, and physical aggression.

As the population ages and caregiving becomes a fact of life for many families, a myriad of new services have been developed to meet caregivers' need for support and assistance. These programs and services have been designed to help caregivers and their families reduce their stress and isolation, handle difficult behaviors, improve their coping skills, and delay or prevent nursing home placement. Services for caregivers are typically funded by states through general revenue funds or as part of multipurpose, publicly funded home and community-based care program that serves both care recipients and their family caregivers. Fifteen states now have comprehensive, state-funded caregiver support programs, which typically offer respite care and four or more other services, including specialized information and referral, family consultation or care planning, support groups, care management, and education and training (Coleman, 2000). These states vary considerably in how they deliver and fund these services, and how they define eligibility. Other states have developed smaller, innovative programs.

According to Whittier, Coon, and Aaker (2001), the use of multiple interventions has the best outcome when working with caregivers. These interventions include educating the caregiver about caregiving and providing individual and family therapy, support groups, and/or respite care. Mittelman, Ferris, Shulman, Streinberg, and Levine (1996) conducted a longitudinal intervention that focused on increasing family involvement in care and offered family therapy. The intervention reduced primary caregiver depression by increasing social support and enhancing caregiver problem-solving skills. Moreover, increased social support has proven to affect caregiver well-being in a positive way. Having a strong support system in place results in decreased caregiver burden and depression, greater life satisfaction, and a reduction in health problems (Dunkin & Anderson-Hanley, 1998).

It is often necessary to intervene with the caregiver and assist him or her, therefore potentially preventing elder abuse. Mittelman, Roth, Coon, and Haley (2004) also indicate that a combination of strategies is most effective in treating caregivers with depression. The first component of the intervention they described consisted of two individual sessions with the caregiver and four family sessions. These sessions did not include the care receiver. The content of these sessions was based on the individual needs of each caregiver. This included things such as learning how to address difficult behaviors of the care receiver appropriately as well as how to foster communication among family members. Additionally, individuals were educated about the aging process and the community resources available to them. The next component of the intervention entailed joining a support group. The final component consisted of ad hoc counseling.

Beauchamp, Irvine, Seeley, and Johnson (2005) have ascertained that caregivers can also access information on the Internet, join Web-based media learning, participate in online discussion and support groups, and communicate with family members via the Internet. As part of the REACH initiative (Resources for Enhancing Alzheimer's Caregiver Health), one study enabled family therapy through the use of a computer-telephone system (Eisdorfer, Czaja, & Lowenstein, 2003). Outcomes indicated that caregivers found it helpful to be able to communicate regularly with their families and with their therapists. They found online discussion groups and the online resource guide to be instrumental (Czaja & Rubert, 2002).

10   Terrorism/Mass Violence

The Federal Bureau of Investigation (FBI) (2007) recorded five terrorist incidents and five terrorism preventions in 2004. Domestic extremists were responsible for each incident. Three of the incidents involved possible associates of the Earth Liberation Front environmental extremist movement, who used incendiary devices against car dealerships, construction sites, and housing developments. In a fourth incident, associates of the Animal Liberation Front conducted two attacks against an animal science facility on the campus of Brigham Young University, which resulted in more than $75,000 in damages. Another incident involved a white supremacist affiliated with Aryan Nations, who firebombed a synagogue in Oklahoma City, Oklahoma.

In 2005, the FBI recorded five terrorist incidents and three terrorism preventions. All of the incidents involved arson or attempted arson. Domestic terrorists associated with the Earth Liberation Front were responsible for three of the incidents, which targeted commercial and residential construction sites. The other two incidents targeted the residences of persons involved with animal research. Responsibility for one of these incidents was claimed by the Animal Liberation Front, and the other was possibly attributable to animal rights extremists as well.

Many people throughout the United States reported mental distress symptoms following the September 11, 2001, attack, the Oklahoma City bombing, and all of the school shootings (Schuster, Stein, & Jaycox, 2001).

The psychological sequelae for terrorism or mass violence victims include a wide variety of factors, and survivors of such traumatic events respond in myriad ways. Some survivors recover successfully from the trauma, while other survivors have great difficulty recovering. The recovery may be more complicated for those who have experienced trauma previously, those who feel constant stress, and those with limited social support systems. Following the terrorist attacks, individuals reported high levels of mental distress that were related to the event. Whether the individual was directly or indirectly affected by the attack is not indicative of the severity of symptoms. The literature on epidemiology indicates that mental disorders are common outcomes of terrorism.

There are typically three classifications for disasters. One classification is for natural disasters (e.g., hurricanes, tornadoes). A second class includes technological disasters (e.g., chemical spills). The third class includes mass violence (e.g., terrorism or riots). Those mass violence disasters that reportedly have numerous injuries are typically associated with a higher risk of psychological effects that are persistent and acute (Herman, Felton, & Susser, 2002). The Code of Federal Regulations defines terrorism as "the unlawful use of force or violence against persons or property to intimidate or coerce a government, the civilian population, or any other segment thereof, in furtherance of political or social objectives" (28 C.F.R. Section 0.85). The United States Department of Justice defines domestic terrorism (groups or individuals entirely based within the United States) and international terrorism (violent acts that violate criminal laws of any foreign government or state). Under the USA PATRIOT Act, the definition of "domestic terrorism" is limited to conduct that (1) violates federal or state criminal law and (2) is dangerous to human life.

The Homeland Security Act of 2002 (HR 5005-2) and the Public Health Security and Bioterrorism Preparedness and Response Act of 2002 (Public Law 107–188) indicated that bioterrorism is a continuing threat for the United States. Recent threats of anthrax are clear evidence that the United States is vulnerable to the pervasive threat of bioterrorism (Jernigan, Raghunathan, Bell, Brechner, Bresnitz, & Butler, 2002). Bioterrorism uses biological weapons (bacteria, viruses, toxins) that can kill or injure people. The Centers for Disease Control (CDC) (2001) identifies the following four categories of bioweapons:

1. bacteria (plague, anthrax, and so forth)
2. viruses (smallpox and viral hemorrhagic fevers, among others)

3. rickettsias (Q fever)
4. toxins (botulinum, ricin, and mycotoxins)

The CDC has further identified the highest risk to include smallpox, anthrax, plague, tularemia, botulism, and viral hemorrhagic fevers. The greatest impact of bioterrorism has been shown to be the psychological impact, which can be from panic to acute stress disorder, posttraumatic stress disorder (PTSD), phobias, sleep disorders, and substance abuse (DiGiovanni, 1999). Public panic has been seen following anthrax attacks: only 22 cases were identified as being exposed, and 40,000 individuals took the antibiotic (Shilne, 2003).

PTSD is a common consequence of terrorist attacks or mass violence. According to the *Diagnostic and Statistical Manual of Mental Disorders* (4th ed., text revision; *DSM-IV-TR*; American Psychiatric Association, 2000), a person with PTSD must have been exposed to some event during which he or she felt fear, helplessness, or horror. The person continues to reexperience the event through memories, reenactments, nightmares, or flashbacks. Cues that remind the person of the event are avoided, and emotional responsiveness is numbed. Often, such individuals are chronically overaroused, easily startled, and quick to anger. The *DSM-IV-TR* (2000) subdivides PTSD into acute and chronic types.

1. Acute PTSD may be diagnosed 1–3 months after the traumatic event, whereas chronic PTSD is diagnosed after 3 months. PTSD cannot be diagnosed sooner than 1 month posttrauma.
2. Chronic PTSD is associated with more long-term avoidance and greater comorbidity than acute PTSD.
3. If a person does not show any symptoms until long after the traumatic event, then a diagnosis of delayed onset PTSD is warranted.

Acute stress disorder is a new disorder in the *Diagnostic and Statistical Manual of Mental Disorders* (4th ed., *DSM-IV*; American Psychiatric Association, 1994) and refers to PTSD occurring within the first month after a trauma. The different name emphasizes the very severe reaction that some people have immediately following a traumatic event. In this case, PTSD symptoms are accompanied by severe dissociative symptoms.

North, Nixon, and Shariat (1999) found PTSD had developed in over 34% of the victims of the Oklahoma City bombing at a 6-month assessment. Seventy-five percent of those individuals reported that their symptoms began the day of the bombing, and 94% had symptoms 1 week following the bombing. Additionally, individuals who resided in Oklahoma City and were indirectly exposed reported PTSD symptoms (7.8%). This suggests that one's physical proximity to the event and the magnitude of the event largely influence the emotional distress experienced. North, McCutcheon, Spitznagel, and Smith (2002) conducted a 3-year follow-up of survivors of a mass shooting episode. They found that PTSD and major depression were most prevalent shortly after the disaster and tended to drop off over time. Conversely, individuals with other psychopathologies did not recover until 3 years had passed. They concluded that previous psychopathology and gender were predictor variables for the development of PTSD; however, these variables did not predict individual recovery.

Terror victims and their families will often suffer emotional and psychological distress following the event. Acute stress disorder, PTSD, depression, and severe grief (see Chapter 3) may affect the ability to function in everyday life in both the short and long term.

ASSESSMENT

Special Issues in Mass Violence Cases

Traumatic events shatter one's basic assumptive world (see Chapter 2). Almost everyone exposed to a terrorist or mass violence attack experiences a range of emotional and psychological symptoms. For some individuals, this is short-term, but for others, it results in long-term, often debilitating emotional outcomes.

Terrorism involves accepting horrific facts that may include the idea that human life is cheap and that murder, misery, and torture can be used in cold, calculating ways for symbolic or political purposes. Most victims of terror attacks/mass violence have a psychiatric/emotional reaction that challenges their meaning of life—their assumptive world that impacts them on several levels. There are many kinds of trauma associated with the impact and aftermath of a terrorist incident. The literature examining the mental aftermath of a terrorist or act of mass violence indicates that large numbers of victims report symptoms indicative of PTSD, anxiety disorders, and depression. With few exceptions, all those associated with terrorism will experience certain "hidden injuries" that inevitably result from the attempt to face reality while at the same time attempting to deny any responsibility or role in it. Marin (1995) has called this "moral pain": those who are closest to the terrorist act or mass violence act have to "numb" themselves emotionally in some way, and those who consider themselves lucky enough to have "survived" are challenged by guilt processes. A terrorist act or mass violence act can be considered a crisis event, which Parad and Caplan (1960, p. 11–12) defined as having five elements:

1. The stressful event poses a problem which is, by definition, insoluble in the immediate future.
2. The problem overtaxes the psychological resources of the family, since it is beyond their traditional problem-solving methods.
3. The situation is perceived as a threat or danger to the life goals of the family members.
4. The crisis period is characterized by tension that mounts to a peak, then falls.
5. The crisis situation awakens unresolved key problems from both the near and distant past.

In these conditions, crisis assessment should be an ongoing evaluation of the level of intervention needed and a monitoring of victims' reactions.

Victim Assessment

A thorough assessment of a terrorism/mass violence victim can be complicated by the difficulty that the victim has in answering specific questions about the traumatic event. Clinicians should be aware of potential mood states that may arise from the discussion of difficult situations. It is not uncommon for these victims to present with PTSD, acute stress disorder, anxiety disorders, major depressive disorder, sleep disorders, adjustment disorders, and substance-related disorders. PTSD is not, by any means, the most typical reaction to trauma, since PTSD depends in large part on whether a person has any preexisting traumas, personality disorders, or other chronic conditions in their life history (Hendin, 1983; Goodwin, 1988). If the victim becomes overly distressed during the course of the assessment, a self-report measure may be the most appropriate option. Myers (2001) identified five assessment approaches:

1. diagnostic assessment (also called the medical model)
2. standardized testing assessment
3. symptom assessment

4. psychological history assessment
5. crisis assessment

Assessment of victims of terrorism or mass violence should begin with triage assessment/crisis assessment as described in Roberts's Seven-Stage Crisis Intervention Model (see Chapter 4). The ACT model (Assessment, Crisis Intervention, and Trauma Treatment) is a set of assessments and intervention strategies integrating various assessment and triage protocols with the seven-stage crisis intervention model and the 10-step acute traumatic stress management protocol. It is a three-stage framework and intervention model that should be useful in helping mental health professionals provide acute crisis and trauma treatment services. Roberts's (2002a) ACT model is outlined below:

A: **1.** assessment/appraisal of immediate medical needs, threats to public safety and property damage undertaken

2. triage assessment, crisis assessment, trauma assessment, and the biopsychosocial and cultural assessment protocols implemented

C: **1.** connections to support groups, disaster relief and social services, and critical incident stress debriefing (Mitchell and Everly's CISD model [1996]) provided

2. crisis intervention (Roberts's seven-stage model) implemented; strengths perspective and coping attempts bolstered

T: **1.** traumatic stress reactions, sequelae, and PTSD

2. ten-step acute trauma and stress management protocol (Lerner & Shelton, 1991), trauma treatment plans, and recovery strategies implemented

Use of Standardized Measures

The Impact of Event Scale (IES) (Zilberg, Weiss, & Horowitz, 1982) can be used to operationalize posttraumatic stress. This is a 15-item, self-report scale that measures emotional reactions, specifically avoidance and intrusion following a traumatic event such as a crime. Split-half reliability for the scale has been reported at $r = .86$. Internal consistency of the subscales has been reported for the avoidance component (.82) and for the intrusion component (.78). An alpha of .93 has been reported for the total scale. Although the intrusion and avoidance subscales have been shown to be correlated ($r = .42$), they have also been shown to be measuring different concepts. The IES has been found to be reliable and to have concurrent validity with respect to the Trauma Symptom Checklist and the Los Angeles Symptom Checklist.

The PTSD Symptom Scale (PDS) is a 49-item, paper and pencil or online, self-report instrument that is designed to assist with the diagnosis of PTSD. The PDS is based on the *DSM-IV* (1994) diagnostic criteria for PTSD. The PDS takes 10–15 minutes to complete and 5 minutes to hand score (Axford, 1999). Convergent validity has been established with the Beck Depression Inventory (.79), State-Trait Anxiety Inventory (.73), Impact of Event Scale intrusion index (.80), and the Impact of Event Scale avoidance index (.66). It has demonstrated high internal consistency with Cronbach's Alpha of .92 being reported by the author for the 17 items used to calculate the symptom severity score. It has also demonstrated test-retest reliability.

The Trauma Symptom Inventory (TSI) is a 100-item scale claiming to measure posttraumatic stress and other psychological sequelae of traumatic events. It was devised to be used in the assessment of "acute and chronic traumatic symptomatology," such as rape, physical assault, spouse abuse, major accidents, combat trauma, natural disasters, and the enduring effects of childhood abuse and early childhood trauma (Briere, 1995). The TSI assesses a broad range of psychological symptoms including those related to PTSD and acute stress disorder. It is self-administered and is intended for a fifth-grade and above reading level (Briere, 1995). Items are scored on a four-point scale with 0 = "never" to 3 = "often," and are rated in terms of frequency of occurrence over the previous 6 months. The TSI takes approximately 20 minutes to complete and about 15 minutes to score (Briere and Elliott, 1997). The TSI has been standardized on a random sample of men and women from the general population ($n = 828$). The TSI is appropriate for all adult sex-by-age combinations. The 10 clinical scales of the TSI are internally consistent (mean alphas of .86, .87, .84, and .84 in standardization, clinical, university, and military samples, respectively), and exhibit reasonable convergent, predictive, and incremental validity.

The Davidson Trauma Scale (DTS) is a 17-item self-report measure that assesses the 17 *DSM-IV* (1994) symptoms of PTSD. Items are rated on five-point frequency (0 = "not at all" to 4 = "every day") and severity scales (0 = "not at all distressing" to 4 = "extremely distressing"). Respondents are asked to identify the trauma that is most disturbing to them and to rate, in the past week, how much trouble they have had with each symptom. The DTS yields a frequency score (ranging from 0 to 68), severity score (ranging from 0 to 68), and total score (ranging from 0 to 136). It can be used to make a preliminary determination about whether the symptoms meet *DSM-IV* (1994) criteria for PTSD. Scores can also be calculated for each of the three PTSD symptom clusters (i.e., B, C, and D) (Davidson, Book, Colket, Tupler, Roth, David, et al., 1997).

The Clinician-Administered PTSD Scale (CAPS) is the gold standard in PTSD assessment. The CAPS is a 30-item structured interview that corresponds to the *DSM-IV* (1994) criteria for PTSD and can be used to make a current (past month) or lifetime diagnosis of PTSD, or to assess symptoms over the past week. In addition to assessing the 17 PTSD symptoms, questions target the impact of symptoms on social and occupational functioning, improvement in symptoms since a previous CAPS administration, overall response validity, overall PTSD severity, and the frequency and intensity of five associated symptoms (guilt over acts, survivor guilt, gaps in awareness, depersonalization, and derealization). The CAPS was designed to be administered by clinicians and clinical researchers with a working knowledge of PTSD, but it can also be administered by appropriately trained paraprofessionals. The full interview takes 45–60 minutes to administer, but it is not necessary to administer all parts (e.g., associated symptoms). Table 10.1 lists additional trauma measures from the United States Department of Veteran Affairs (2007).

Treatment Planning

Van der Veer (1998) concluded from studying the responses of those who witnessed the first World Trade Center attack in 1993 that there is a hierarchy of suffering that can be indicative of victims' experiences. This hierarchy refers to a belief some victims articulate that some individuals have more of a right to be traumatized by the attack than others, thus leading to the perspective that some individuals have a right to receive interventions and services more than others. This can be seen in the 1993 World Trade Center attack, when the individuals who were across the street became heroes in comparison to those who were not at work that day for various reasons. This public display of holding up those individuals as heroes led to those who were not there feeling guilty (indirect exposure effects).

Table 10.1

THE FOLLOWING IS A CHART OF ADDITIONAL TRAUMA MEASURES FROM THE UNITED STATES DEPARTMENT OF VETERAN AFFAIRS (2007)

TRAUMA EXPOSURE MEASURES	TARGET GROUP	FORMAT	# OF ITEMS	TIME TO ADMINISTER (MINUTES)	ASSESSES *DSM-IV* CRITERION A
Combat Exposure Scale (CES)	Adult	Self-Report	7	5	No
Evaluation of Lifetime Stressors (ELS)	Adult	Self-Report & Interview	56	60–360	Yes
Life Stressor Checklist-Revised (LSC-R)	Adult	Self-Report	30	15–30	Yes
National Women's Study Event History	Adult	Interview	17	15–30	A-1 only
Potential Stressful Events Interview (PSEI)	Adult	Interview	62	120	Yes
Stressful Life Events Screening Questionnaire (SLESQ)	Adult	Self-Report	13	10–15	No
Trauma Assessment for Adults (TAA)	Adult	Self-Report & Interview	17	10–15	A-1 only
Trauma History Screen (THS)	Adult	Self-Report	13	2–5	Yes
Trauma History Questionnaire (THQ)	Adult	Self-Report	24	10–15	A-1 only
Traumatic Events Questionnaire (TEQ)	Adult	Self-Report	13	5	A-1 only
Traumatic Life Events Questionnaire (TLEQ)	Adult	Self-Report	25	10–15	A-1 only
Traumatic Stress Schedule (TSS)	Adult	Interview	9	5–30	A-1 only

United States Department of Veteran Affairs. Retrieved September 9, 2007, from http://www.ncptsd. va.gov/ncmain/ncdocs/assmnts/nc_chart_trauma_exp.html

It is important to take into consideration all the factors listed in this chapter when planning an intervention or treatment for victims of terrorism or mass violence. The primary goals of treatment planning are to

1. help victims find effective coping strategies as a response to the stress
2. identify the assumptive world that has been shattered
3. identify and attend to unhealthy coping responses
4. help victims overcome trauma and emotional disorders

Evaluations made during the immediate aftermath of a crisis must have specific goals: to identify those in need of urgent services and to expedite their referrals. Until additional resources become available, longer and more in-depth evaluations should be postponed. Reactions and responses to a crisis are both immediate and long-term, and may be observed for months or even years after an event.

TREATMENT: ISSUES AND INTERVENTIONS

Overview: General Principles of Treatment

Most people experience symptoms after a traumatic stress. All victims are at risk, including the immediate victims, families, friends, and rescue workers. In 2001, the National Institute of Mental Health (NIMH) conducted a workshop with 58 experts in disaster mental health from six countries. The goal was to address the impact of early psychological interventions and identify needs. The following are the key components that were identified for assessment and early intervention (National Institute of Mental Health [NIMH], 2002, p. 13):

Basic Needs

- Provide survival, safety, and security.
- Provide food and shelter.
- Orient survivors to the availability of services/support.
- Communicate with family, friends, and community.
- Assess the environment for ongoing threats.

Psychological First Aid

- Protect survivors from further harm.
- Reduce physiological arousal.
- Mobilize support for those who are most distressed.
- Keep families together and facilitate reunions with loved ones.
- Provide information, and foster communication and education.
- Use effective risk communication techniques.

Needs Assessment

- Assess the current status of individuals, groups, and/or populations and institutions/systems. Ask how well needs are being addressed, what the recovery environment offers, and what additional interventions are needed.

Rescue and Recovery Environment Observation

- Observe and listen to the most affected.
- Monitor the environment for toxins and stressors.
- Monitor past and ongoing threats.
- Monitor services that are being provided.
- Monitor media coverage and rumors.

Outreach and Information Dissemination

- Offer information/education and "therapy by walking around."
- Use established community structures.
- Distribute flyers.
- Host Web sites.
- Conduct media interviews and programs, and distribute media releases.

Technical Assistance, Consultation, and Training

- Improve capacity of organizations and caregivers to provide what is needed to
  - reestablish community structure

- foster family recovery and resilience
- safeguard the community
- Provide assistance, consultation, and training to relevant organizations, other caregivers and responders, and leaders.

Fostering Resilience and Recovery

- Foster but do not force social interactions.
- Provide coping skills training.
- Provide risk assessment skills training.
- Provide education on stress responses, traumatic reminders, coping, normal versus abnormal functioning, risk factors, and services.
- Offer group and family interventions.
- Foster natural social supports.
- Look after the bereaved.
- Repair the organizational fabric.

Early Intervention

Early intervention is any psychological intervention that is delivered to the victim within the first 4 weeks following a terrorist or mass violence act. Brief, focused psychotherapy and some cognitive behavioral approaches are considered early intervention. The NIMH reports that mass education and media outlets may produce more unintended harm than benefit. It also reports that early intervention that is limited to reliving or creating a narrative of the event may actually lead to the later development of mental health problems. There is a dearth of literature exploring the effects of psychological interventions following a terrorist attack or mass violence (NIMH, 2002). The following offers NIMH findings from studies of other traumatic events:

- Early, brief and focused psychotherapeutic intervention can reduce distress in bereaved spouses, parents, and children.
- Selected cognitive behavioral approaches may reduce the incidence, duration, and severity of acute stress disorder, PTSD, and depression in survivors.
- Early intervention in the form of single, one-on-one recitals of events and emotions evoked by a traumatic event do not consistently reduce risks of later PTSD or related adjustment disorders.

■ There is no evidence that eye movement desensitization and reprocessing (EMDR) as an early mental health intervention following mass violence and disasters is a treatment of choice over other approaches (p. 2).

Triage

Triage is the screening of victims according to their need for treatment and the resources available, and the process of evaluating and sorting victims by immediacy of treatment needed and directing them to immediate or delayed treatment. "The goal of triage is to do the greatest good for the greatest number of victims" (NIMH, 2002, p. 27). A typical triage assessment should include but not be limited to sociodemographic information on the victim, how the victim perceives the event, and the victim's coping strategies. Additionally, information regarding any trauma previously experienced, perceived and received special support, and substance use/abuse issues should be gathered, and a suicide/homicide risk assessment should be completed. The three levels of triage as applied to an example of school violence are

1. *Primary assessment of psychological trauma* begins as soon as possible/appropriate, before individual students and/or staff are offered any school crisis intervention. It is designed to identify those who are considered at risk for becoming psychological trauma victims and to help make initial school crisis intervention treatment decisions. It typically includes assessment of crisis exposure (physical and emotional proximity) and personal vulnerabilities.
2. *Secondary assessment of psychological trauma* is designed to identify those who are actually demonstrating signs of psychological trauma and to make more informed crisis intervention treatment decisions.
3. *Tertiary assessment of psychological trauma* focuses on screening for psychiatric disturbances (e.g., PTSD) and typically begins weeks after a crisis event has ended. It is designed to identify those victims who will require mental health treatment. It typically includes the careful monitoring of crisis reactions. "Survivors of traumatic events that do not manifest symptoms after approximately two months generally do not require follow-up" (NIMH, 2002, p. 9).

Cognitive Behavioral Therapy

"The basic assumption . . . is that people contribute to their own psychological problems, as well as specific symptoms, by the way in which they interpret events and situations in their life. To a large degree, cognitive-behavioral therapy is based on the assumption that a reorganization of one's self-statements will result in a corresponding reorganization of one's behavior" (Corey, 1996).

Cognitive behavioral therapy (CBT) is based on the idea that critical or negative automatic thoughts and unpleasant physical or emotional symptoms combine to form maladaptive cycles that maintain and exaggerate initial problems, resulting in emotional disorders. The goal of CBT is to identify and modify the negative, self-defeating cognitions that are maintaining the distress. Overarching goals, according to Beck (1979), are to

1. Correct faulty information processing, modify dysfunctional beliefs and assumptions that maintain maladaptive behaviors and emotions.
2. Help victims recognize their distorted thoughts, evaluate their cognitive distortions, and then change their automatic thoughts to be more adaptive and less distorted. By focusing on the victim's automatic thoughts, therapists and clients can eventually see the faulty underlying assumptions with which the victims are operating.

There are several types of cognitive distortions/errors that potentially lead to emotional distress (Beck, 1979):

- *catastrophizing or minimizing:* expecting disaster, weighing an event as too important, or failing to weigh it enough
- *dichotomous thinking:* thinking of things as black or white/good or bad
- *emotional reasoning:* believing that what you feel must be true (e.g., if you feel you are ugly and boring, then you must be)
- *fortune-telling:* anticipating that events will turn out badly
- *labeling:* generalizing one or two qualities into a global perspective of a person (e.g., a person who forgets something one time is an idiot)
- *mental filter:* ignoring either the positive or the negative of one situation or issue; magnifying negative details and filtering positive ones

- *mind reading:* believing that what a person thinks can be known solely from his or her behaviors.
- *overgeneralization:* jumping to a general conclusion based on a single event (e.g., expecting something bad to happen over and over again)
- *personalization:* assuming everything said or done around you is directly related to you
- *"should" statements:* having a certain way you think and feel things "should" be done, and getting angry or frustrated when they are not done in that way

CBT has a realistic expectation for a minimum timeline of 1–12 months, as outlined below. This outline can, and most likely will, change to suit each individual's specific needs.

1–3 months in CBT sessions

3–6 months in follow-up, retraining, and reassessment sessions

6–12 months recovery to refine skills and learning techniques

CBT is one type of counseling that is used in individual, family, and group therapy. It appears to be the most effective type of counseling for PTSD. In cognitive therapy, the therapist helps the victim understand and change how he or she thinks about the trauma and its aftermath. The goal is for the victim to understand how certain thoughts about the trauma cause stress and make symptoms worse.

Victims learn to identify thoughts that result in feelings of fear and upset. Victims learn to replace these thoughts with less-distressing thoughts; additionally, they develop new coping strategies to deal with their emotions. Victims often blame themselves following a mass violence event. Cognitive therapy, a type of CBT, helps with understanding that the traumatic event they lived through was not their fault. In general, cognitive behavioral methods have proven very effective in producing significant reductions in PTSD symptoms.

Critical Incident Stress Management

Critical Incident Stress Management (CISM) is an intervention that was developed specifically for dealing with traumatic events. It is a formal, highly structured process for helping those involved in a critical incident.

CISM interventions range from the precrisis phase, through the acute crisis phase, and into the postcrisis phase. CISM may be applied to individuals, small functional groups, large groups, families, organizations, and even communities. Table 10.2 captures the core components of the CISM model.

1. *Precrisis preparation.* This includes stress management education, stress resistance, and crisis mitigation training for both individuals and organizations.
2. *Disaster or large-scale incident.* This includes school and community support programs such as demobilizations, informational briefings, "town meetings" and staff advisement.
3. *Defusing.* This is a three-phase, structured, small-group discussion provided within hours of a crisis for the purposes of assessment, triaging, and acute symptom mitigation.
4. *Critical Incident Stress Debriefing (CISD).* This refers to the "Mitchell model" (Mitchell & Everly, 1999), a seven-phase, structured group discussion, usually provided 1–10 days postcrisis. CISD is designed to mitigate acute symptoms, assess the need for follow-up, and if possible, provide a sense of postcrisis psychological closure.
5. *One-on-one crisis intervention/counseling or psychological support.* This is provided throughout the full range of the crisis spectrum.
6. *Family crisis intervention and organizational consultation.* These are provided as needed based on the situation.
7. *Follow-up and referral mechanisms.* These are relied on as necessary for assessment and treatment.

Psychotraumatology

Everly (2006) uses the term "psychotraumatology" as a framework for understanding posttraumatic stress. He defines it as "the study of psychological trauma, more specifically, the study of the processes and factors that lie antecedent to, concomitant with, and subsequent to psychological trauma" (Everly, 1993, p. 1). It implies there is something broken. The goal in treatment of victims of mass violence is to find what is broken and then treat the break. We all have an assumptive world (see Chapter 2), and trauma destroys our cognitive schemas regarding safety and self-efficacy. Trauma represents an insult or injury to the structure and

Table 10.2

THE SEVEN CORE COMPONENTS

INTERVENTION	TIMING	ACTIVATION	GOALS	FORMAT
1. Precrisis preparation	Precrisis phase	Anticipation of crisis	Set expectations. Improve coping Encourage stress management	Group organization
2. Demobilization & staff consult (rescuers); group info. briefing for civilians, schools, businesses	Postcrisis, or shift disengagement	Event driven	Inform, consult Allow psychological decompression Encourage stress management	Large group organization
3. Defusing	Postcrisis (within 12 hrs)	Usually symptom driven	Symptom mitigation Possible closure Triage	Small group
4. Critical Incident Stress Debriefing (CISD)	Postcrisis (1–7 days)	Usually symptom driven; can be event driven	Facilitate psychological closure Mitigation Triage	Small group
5. Individual crisis intervention (1:1)	Any time, anywhere	Symptom driven	Symptom mitigation Return to function, if possible Referral if needed	Individual
6. Family CISM; org. consultation	Any time	Either symptom driven or event driven	Foster support, communications Symptom mitigation Closure if possible Referral if needed	Organizations
7. Follow-up; referral	Any time	Usually symptom driven	Assess mental status Access higher level of care	Individual, family

(Adapted from Everly and Mitchell, 1997)

function of one's personality. Human beings require an assumptive world for normal development; therefore, they create assumptions about

- themselves
- others
- the world in general

These beliefs may be thought of as "assumptive worldviews." There are several core worldviews:

- the belief in a just and fair world
- the assumption that some people can be trusted
- the belief in the self as a "good," self-efficacious person
- the need for "safety"
- the belief in some order to life (e.g., through spirituality, science, religion)

Psychological trauma results from a violation of one or more of these core assumptive worldviews. These violations include

- injustice, lack of fairness
- betrayal, treachery
- guilt, lack of control
- lack of safety
- unpredictability, lack of meaning, events that one cannot understand

    Understanding psychotraumatology can assist in the recovery process for victims of mass violence. The focus should be on the symptoms more than the event itself, as horrific as the event may have been. The goal is to find what is "broken" in the survivor, and then work on that area to assist in recovery.

    The needs and stresses confronting victims of mass violence and terrorism are complex and often overwhelming. Social, cultural, and economic conditions have significant and measurable effects on violence in the United States. One result is a growing awareness of the demands of services needed by mass trauma victims.

School Violence: Crisis Intervention Protocols and Prevention Strategies

INTRODUCTION

For over 30 years, children, youth, and staff at public and private schools have been traumatized, injured, and/or murdered in school violence acts. One of the earliest documented violent crimes against school children took place on July 15, 1976, when a school bus with 19 girls and 7 boys, ages 5–14, was hijacked in Chowchilla, CA. The children and bus driver were forced to a remote location and transferred to an 8-foot by 16-foot moving van trailer, which was then buried in a secluded rock quarry ravine. This horrendous kidnapping and captivity lasted for 27 hours until they were rescued. None of the victims sustained life-threatening physical injuries. However, follow-up studies 4 years later found that many of the children were still suffering from anxiety disorders, emotional trauma, and posttraumatic stress disorder (PTSD) (Terr, 1983).

Some of the more recent crisis-inducing violent events include the following: On May 7, 2004, a drive-by shooting took place in Randallstown, MD, following a charity basketball game at the local high school. Four students were critically wounded. One of the two shooters arrested the next day was a 17-year-old student who attended the high school. According to the police report, the shootings were in retaliation for a name-calling incident involving a girl.

The Columbine High School massacre occurred on Tuesday, April 20, 1999, at Columbine High School in unincorporated Jefferson County, CO near Denver and Littleton. Two students embarked on a shooting rampage, killing 12 students and a teacher, as well as wounding 23 others, before committing suicide. It was the fourth-deadliest school killing in U.S. history, after the 1927 Bath School disaster, the 2007 Virginia Tech massacre, and the 1966 University of Texas sniper massacre.

On September 3, 2004, a school was taken over in Beslan, Russia. School children, staff, parents, and relatives were celebrating a national holiday at this neighborhood school when armed terrorists took hundreds of these children and adults hostage in the school. Shooting broke out between the terrorists and Russian security, and 344 children and adults were killed. In addition, several hundred survivors were wounded.

On October 2, 2006, in an Amish school in Nickel Mines, PA, 10 girls were taken hostage. After several hours, the 32-year-old perpetrator shot all 10 of the youths, and then fatally shot himself.

The Jonesboro school massacre occurred on Tuesday, March 24, 1998, in Craighead County, AK, near northwestern Jonesboro. Four female students and a teacher were killed, and nine other students and a teacher were wounded, all by two armed middle school boys.

Aggressive and violent behavior by students in our schools has serious consequences for the individuals involved. Each year, many thousands of student victims experience physical injuries, psychological trauma, mental health disorders, and death. No school is immune to multiple acts of simple assault, aggravated assault, terroristic threats, bullying, date abuse, and school stabbings and shootings. Today, crisis intervenors and victim advocates emphasize the importance of early crisis assessment and crisis intervention in the aftermath of school violence, focusing on immediate emotional reactions and needs, and facilitating recovery. All schools should have effective crisis intervention plans, school-based crisis teams, regional multidisciplinary crisis teams, school security/suppression plans, school–police liaison programs, behavior management programs for aggressive and acting-out youths, and alternative education programs.

Terr (1990) focuses on two types of crises: Type I, which focuses on an acute single event (e.g., the mass shootings at Columbine High School) that precipitates a crisis; and Type II crises, which are responses to chronic and prolonged events (e.g., chronic and repeated episodes of child abuse or intimate partner violence). Most discussions of response to school violence, including ours, focus on Type I crises, the type which Roberts (2005) has referred to as an "acute situational crisis." A sudden, hazardous, and unpredictable event is encountered. The individual then perceives the event as an imminent threat to his or her life, psychological well-being, or social functioning. The individual tries to cope, escape the dangerous situation, gain necessary support from a significant other or close family member or friend, and/or adapt by changing lifestyle or environment. Coping attempts fail, and the person's severe emotional state of imbalance escalates into a full-blown crisis (Roberts, 2005, p. 12–13).

This chapter will identify and discuss immediate, short-term crisis intervention and crisis team protocols for dealing with acute situational crises.

Historically, schools have had emergency response plans for natural disasters (e.g., fire drills, tornado drills). The need for crisis prevention/intervention protocols and teams in school settings has become more evident with increases in school violence, terrorist threats/acts, and other traumatic situations. In the past, crisis preparedness may have seemed more important to schools at high risk for natural disasters, but it is clear that being prepared for potential crisis situations and their aftermaths is today's reality for all schools. Much has been learned from research and intervention with those who have experienced tragic school shootings and other violent incidents, and that knowledge and experience have contributed to more comprehensive planning and development to meet the needs of the local community and school community.

This chapter provides an overview of the research studies and literature on how to develop school crisis prevention/intervention protocols and teams, and a discussion of the empirical evidence that supports best practices with victims and survivors of school violence. A crisis intervention model is presented as a guideline for planning at the regional, district, and school levels. Specific steps for crisis intervention services and debriefing in the aftermath of a school crisis are also provided, as well as resources and Web sites that can aid school personnel in crisis preparedness, training, and response. Although this chapter identifies some of the typical issues and impacts of school violence, each situation is unique, and even the most comprehensive plans cannot anticipate all possible scenarios and effects. However, crisis planning and preparedness can help address the traumatic impacts and provide short-term treatment for those affected.

REVIEW OF THE LITERATURE

Crisis Impacts and Treatment Issues for Children and Adolescents Experiencing School Violence and Community Disasters

The empirical research on children and adolescents experiencing community disasters and school violence examines a variety of impact and treatment issues, including specific issues associated with certain types of catastrophic events: mass school shootings, terrorist attacks, hurricanes, tornados, earthquakes, and floods (Asarnow et al., 1999; Feinberg, 1999; Newgass & Schonfeld, 2005; Shaw, Applegate, & Shorr, 1996; Zenere, 2001). For example, the warning time or advance notice associated with hurricanes can give people time to gather belongings and seek refuge, but it also allows more time for fear and anxiety to increase. In contrast, the sudden mass carnage during a school shooting spree leave people little time to prepare and may result in more confusion and panic responses (Roberts, 2005).

Literature addressing other impact issues such as PTSD symptoms; effects of relocation; parental reactions; coping styles; and developmental, cultural, and ethnic considerations contributes to the knowledge base for best practices in this field (Bolton, O'Ryan, Udwin, Boyle, & Yule, 2000; Goenjian, Molina, Steinberg, & Fairbanks, 2001; Jones, Fray, Cunningham, & Kaiser, 2001; La Greca, Silverman, Vernberg, & Prinstein, 1996; Lazarus & Gillespie, 1996; Prinstein, La Greca, Vernberg, & Silverman, 1996; Raid & Norris, 1996; Wasserstein & La Greca, 1998). This literature provides insights from previous personal experiences and research studies on how school-based mental health and social work professionals can plan, prepare for, and intervene after unpredictable catastrophic events. Current research emphasizes collaboration among school, community, state, and federal organizations and programs with the goals of teaching children and adolescents effective coping strategies, fostering supportive relationships among peers and with their families, and helping survivors process their emotions and reactions (Brock, Sandoval, & Lewis, 2001; Lazarus, Jimerson, & Brock, 2002).

School-Based Crisis Intervention

Those with personal experience with school crises and tragedies have also authored the majority of the literature on school crisis intervention/

prevention. Training manuals and journal articles from the 1990s describe how school professionals responded to actual experiences involving school crises to increase awareness about the effects on those involved and stress the need for crisis preparedness (Kennedy, 1999; Kline, Schonfeld, & Lichtenstein, 1995; Lichtenstein, Schonfeld, Kline, & Speese-Linehan, 1995; Pitcher & Poland, 1992; Poland & Pitcher, 1990; Roberts, 1991; Young, 1997).

More recent models of crisis intervention have been developed, such as the Integrative ACT (Assessment, Crisis Intervention, and Trauma Treatment) Intervention Model, which is a three-stage framework and intervention model that integrates various assessment and triage protocols for a sequential set of assessment and intervention strategies (Roberts, 2002a). Other current literature focuses on practical guides and steps in developing school crisis protocols and teams (Allen, Burt, Bryan, Carter, Orsi, & Durkan, 2002; Brock, Lazarus, & Jimerson, 2002; Brock, Sandoval & Lewis, 2001; Eaves, 2001; Newgass & Schonfeld, 2005; Rock, 2000; Sandoval, 2002; Schonfeld, Lichtenstein, Pruett, & Speese-Linehan, 2002; Wanko, 2001; Watson & Watson, 2002). These manuals and handbooks are excellent resources that include strategies on how to plan and intervene in specific crisis situations, training curriculum, case vignettes, samples of forms, and ideas for supplies and crisis kits. Table 11.1 outlines the major contributors and their literature and can be used as a reference guide for the best practices in school crisis intervention.

Other resources for school crisis management can be found on the Internet through these Web sites:

- http://www.aaets.com (American Academy of Experts in Traumatic Stress)
- http://www.apa.org (American Psychological Association's Disaster Response Network)
- http://www.colorado.edu/cspv/blueprints (Blueprints for Violence Prevention)
- http://www.clemson.edu/olweus (Bullying Prevention Program)
- http://www.compassionatefriends.org (Compassionate Friends support groups for bereaved parents)
- http://www.crisisinfo.org (national standards for responding to university and school-based crises)
- http://www.fema.gov (Federal Emergency Management Agency)
- http://www.keepschoolssafe.org (National Association of Attorneys General and National School Boards Association)

Table 11.1

SCHOOL-BASED CRISIS INTERVENTION LITERATURE AND MANUALS

CONTRIBUTORS/ YEAR	TITLE/PUBLISHER	DESCRIPTION
Brock, S. E., Lazarus, P. J., & Jimerson, S.R.(Eds.). (2002).	*Best practices in school crisis prevention and intervention.* Bethesda, MD: NASP Publications.	Chapters cover crisis theory, primary prevention plans and preparing for crises, responding to crisis events, specific types of crises, long-term treatment of trauma, and special topics such as legal and ethical issues, research needs, and advocacy in this field.
Brock, S. E., Sandoval, J., & Lewis, S. (2001).	*Preparing for crises in the schools: A manual for building school crisis response teams.* NY: John Wiley & Sons.	Training manual with curriculum that includes lectures, experiential exercises, and handouts for an intensive 2-day in-service on crisis intervention and PTSD; also includes samples of forms and evaluation instruments for safe schools.
Decker, R. H. (1997).	*When a crisis hits: Will your school be ready?* Thousand Oaks, CA: Corwin Press.	Ten-step approach outlines district-wide planning components for crisis management; also provides various case scenarios and recommendations for specific steps and actions to take for a variety of types of crises.
Educational Service District 105, Yakima, Washington (1997).	*Quick response: A step-by-step guide to crisis management for principals, counselors, and teachers.* Alexandria, VA: Association for Supervision and Curriculum Development.	Training manual for developing a crisis management plan and creating teams; includes specific guidelines, checklists, and resources for prevention planning and crisis intervention, including flip charts for references to local and national resources and contact information.
Sandoval, J. (Ed.). (2002).	*Handbook of crisis counseling, intervention, and prevention in the schools* (2nd ed.). Mahwah, NJ: Lawrence Erlbaum.	Reference for mental health professionals on school-based crises, with discussion of the research that underlies best practices; chapters cover crisis preparedness and counseling, types of crises during childhood and adolescence, and developmentally appropriate intervention activities.
Schonfeld, D. J., Lichtenstein, R., Pruett, M. K., & Speese-Linehan, D. (2002).	*How to prepare for and respond to a crisis.* Alexandria, VA: Association for Supervision and Curriculum Development.	Chapters cover the crisis intervention model and how to establish crisis teams, with guidelines on how to develop a school crisis plan and samples of forms, a school crisis kit, and case vignettes for training.

- http://www.ncptsd.org (National Center for PTSD: Disaster Mental Health Services: A Guidebook for Clinicians & Administrators, and info on PTSD in children and adolescents)
- http://www.ojp.usdoj.gov/ovc/infores/crt/pdfwelc.htm (Community Crisis Response Team training manual from the U.S. Department of Justice's Office for Victims of Crime)
- http://www.schoolcrisisresponse.com (practical guide for school crisis response planning)
- http://www.tlcinstitute.org (National Institute for Trauma and Loss in Children)

School Crisis Response Model

A school crisis response model should address the levels and types of intervention, as well as the opportunities for collaboration between the school system, the local community, state resources, and federal programs. School crisis intervention models typically have three levels:

- *primary prevention* activities such as creating emergency response planning and training; providing crisis drills in schools; establishing a crisis team; and preparing for medical, security, communication, and media responses
- *secondary intervention* steps to be taken during a school shooting or other crisis event to minimize the effects and keep the situation from escalating, including evacuating students to safety, notifying family members and parents, and following immediate crisis intervention strategies to address the emotional impacts and physical safety needs of those involved
- *tertiary intervention* in the aftermath when debriefing, support groups, short-term counseling, and referral to other community-based programs and long-term services may be needed

These three levels of intervention require participation and support from key personnel at different levels or divisions of the school system—from the central administration to school principals and other campus faculty/staff—and may vary depending on the needs of the community and the size and number of school districts and campuses involved. Newgass & Schonfeld (2005) recommend a hierarchical model as follows:

- *regional resource team* composed of a multidisciplinary representatives from school administration, mental health, police, academic, and social services that meets to develop and review programs, protocols, and policies; to provide support and training to district level teams; and to act as an information clearinghouse
- *district level teams,* which provide crisis response oversight for the school system and technical assistance to the schools within the district at the time of crisis; teams should include central office administrators and mental health staff who oversee district policies and procedures, resource allocation, staff training, and supervision
- *school-based crisis teams,* which consist of the school administrator(s), school nurse, social workers, school counselors, teachers, and support/security staff, all of whom may provide direct crisis intervention services and ongoing counseling services

This type of crisis response model allows flexibility to meet the needs of different levels of crisis situations from incidents involving only one school campus, to those involving more than one school in a district, or to the entire community. A comprehensive model must incorporate all the different levels of intervention and resources to adequately plan for and respond to the variety of school crises situations that could be anticipated. Coordinating and implementing the many needs involved in a school crisis can be confusing and cause response delays if previous planning has not been established.

The following school crisis response model provides a guide for planning and developing a region-wide plan. Although this model does not include all the specific tasks and activities involved at each level, it does give a framework for how to distribute and organize the various steps and procedures that need to be implemented for a timely and coordinated response. Other pertinent issues and obstacles will need to be developed for the unique needs of each school and the surrounding community. For example, larger metropolitan areas with several school districts may have more problems with coordinating services and personnel because of student body size and geographical considerations, while smaller school districts may have limitations in resources and technical assistance.

School-Based Crisis Teams

The overriding goal of the school-based crisis response team is to delegate and implement the roles and duties that are needed before, during and after a crisis. (See table 11.2). Team size varies depending on the size of the school district and of the individual schools within the district, but it

Table 11.2

CRISIS INTERVENTION MODELS AND CRISIS TEAMS			
LEVELS OF INTERVENTION	**REGIONAL LEVEL**	**DISTRICT LEVEL**	**SCHOOL LEVEL**
Primary Prevention	Community-level crisis response plan Team policies and procedures Support and resources Networking	Emergency response policies/ procedures Safety and security issues Training and education Communication systems	Emergency and evacuation plans and drills Prevention programs Support services Crisis intervention team
Secondary Intervention	Activate community response team and plan involving school, emergency medical personnel, police, mental health and social service providers Technical assistance	Activate district level plan and procedures Coordinate school-level crisis teams Link to regional level response Communication and media Resource allocation for schools	Activate school crisis plan and teams Emergency and evacuation procedures Notification/ communication Debriefing/ demobilization Short-term crisis counseling
Tertiary Intervention	Networking with community resources Policy and procedures evaluation Ongoing planning and needs assessment for the region	Ongoing support and resources Program and response plan evaluation District team meetings to improve procedures and prevention strategies	Referral for long-term counseling or other services Memorialization needs Follow-up with school crisis team members Practice evaluation of interventions

typically ranges from four to eight members. If the team is too large, it can be unmanageable, making it difficult to schedule meetings and trainings. If the team is too small, there may not be enough members to cover critical tasks. It is recommended that teams be multidisciplinary, including school administrators, school counselors, social workers, school nurses, teachers, security officers, and support staff. There should also be alternates or members who serve in a back-up or on a rotating basis to address potential situations when members are unavailable or suffering burn out.

Schonfeld, Kline, and members of the Crisis Intervention Committee (1994) suggest that roles for the school-based crisis team members include a *team leader,* responsible for planning and presiding at team meetings, and overseeing the functioning of the team and its members, and an *assistant team leader,* who assists in these tasks and is responsible if the team leader is unavailable. Other important roles include a *media coordinator,* who serves as the contact person for all media inquiries, and a *staff notification coordinator,* who establishes and initiates a telephone tree or alternate communication system. The communication system is used to notify team members and other school staff after hours in order to communicate in an organized manner with people affected by the crisis, including students, families, and staff. The communication system can be designed in levels similar to a pyramid: at the top is the team leader, who notifies the assistant team leader, who then notifies the designated group leaders, who then call other people, and so forth.

Also needed is the *in-house communication coordinator,* who screens all incoming calls, maintains a phone log, assists the staff notification coordinator, and maintains a phone directory of regional and district level teams/staff and community resources. A *crowd management coordinator* collaborates with school security personnel, local law enforcement, and emergency departments to supervise evacuation and crowd control procedures, and to ensure the safe and organized movement of students and staff to minimize the risk of harm (Schonfeld et al., 1994).

Brock, Sandoval, and Lewis (2001) recommend assigning a team member to the role of *evaluator,* whose main responsibilities include conducting drills and readiness checks, designing questionnaires and structured interviews, and collecting data on crisis team performance and outcome. The evaluator can also be responsible for the debriefing and demobilization with the crisis team members after a crisis response.

Debriefing refers to stress-relieving activities and the processing of the incident. Typically, this occurs between 24 and 72 hours after the critical incident; it can be done individually and with the team as a group. Debriefing entails activities that encourage team members to ventilate their feelings and emotional reactions to the crisis and its impacts. Debriefing meetings should encourage team members to support each other and not be critical. The evaluator works toward the successful resolution of the trauma experienced during the crisis and the team's response. Some members of the crisis team may need referral for professional counseling, so there should be a plan for recruiting or rotating team members to minimize burnout.

Demobilization refers to evaluative information-gathering strategies for the purpose of improving responses and prevention planning. Information and feedback is gathered through written surveys or structured interviews with individuals or in a group setting after the crisis situation has been contained and resolved. Information on the school crisis intervention process and procedures, problems with the implementation of the crisis response plan, and other unforeseen circumstances or factors affecting the efforts are examples of the types of information gathered during demobilization.

It is important to have a *building plan* to provide space for medical triage, safety, shelter, communication, and other emergency needs of law enforcement and medical personnel during the immediate crisis situation. There should also be designated support rooms that are adequately staffed by qualified counseling personnel and crisis team members to provide mental health triage, referral, and brief, time-limited interventions. School crisis team members need to develop guidelines for referring students and monitoring their status, as well as procedures for obtaining parental permission for treatment, referrals for ongoing treatment or school-based support groups, and other follow-up services as needed (Schonfeld, et al., 1994).

The school crisis team may also need to deal with issues of grief and loss, such as how to convey formally the condolences of the school or class; how to handle personal belongings; appropriate displays of memorials, such as flowers, candles, or photos; attendance at funeral services; and school memorial or recognition services. The nature and timing of such memorializations need to be given careful thought and planning to ensure that they do not escalate the effects of the crisis situation or prematurely try to create closure (Newgass & Schonfeld, 2005).

Training and resources for school crisis teams require time, money, and effort that many financially burdened school districts may be reluctant or unable to fund. However, there are training curricula, manuals, and workshops available to assist in this process. School districts may want to cross train crisis team members at various levels, or provide specialized training relevant to the team members' roles and responsibilities. In-service trainers, who could conduct workshops on a regular basis as needed, would be cost-effective and would provide continuity in the training, which should be viewed as an ongoing need. School crisis team members who provide direct counseling and crisis intervention services would need more in-depth and specialized training on crisis counseling skills and types of crises. Collaboration among community professionals with experience and expertise in crisis intervention could be another resource for ongoing training.

SUMMARY

Current literature and research indicates that collaboration and planning between schools and communities is necessary to develop intervention and prevention plans for natural disasters and other types of crisis situations. Important points to address in this effort include the following:

- *School crisis intervention models* usually have three levels: primary prevention planning and preparation, secondary intervention during the crisis situation, and tertiary intervention in the aftermath.
- *School crisis response levels* are typically at the regional, district, and school levels.
- *School crisis teams* delegate and implement the roles, duties, and responsibilities that are needed during and after a crisis situation, and include a team leader; assistant team leader; coordinators for the media, staff notification, in-house communication, and crowd management; and an evaluator.
- *Debriefing* involves stress-relieving activities and the processing of the crisis by the team and other first responders within 24 to 72 hours.
- *Demobilization* refers to strategies to gather information and feedback from the crisis team members to improve responses and procedures in the future.

■ *Impact issues* such as relocation, parental reactions, coping styles, grief and loss, and a wide variety of developmental, cultural, and ethnic considerations are important to address in counseling disaster survivors.

■ *Follow-up strategies* to provide support and long-term services from local community organizations and programs should also be included.

References

Abramson, L. Y., Metalsky, G. L., & Alloy, L. B. (1989). Hopelessness and depression: A theory-based subtype of depression. *Psychological Review, 96,* 358–372.

Administration for Children and Families. (2007). Retrieved March 28, 2008, from http://www.acf.dhhs.gov/

Alexander, F., & French, T. (1984). *Studies in psychosomatic medicine: An approach to the cause and treatment of vegetative disturbances.* New York: Ronald.

Allen, M., Burt, K., Bryan, E., Carter, D., Orsi, R., & Durkan, L. (2002). School counselors' preparation for and participation in crisis intervention. *Professional School Counseling, 6*(2), 96–102.

American Psychiatric Association. (1994). *Diagnostic and statistical manual of mental disorders* (4th ed.). Washington, DC: American Psychiatric Press, Inc.

American Psychiatric Association. (2000). American Psychiatric Association *Diagnostic and statistical manual of mental disorders* (4th ed., text revision.). Washington, DC: American Psychiatric Press, Inc.

American Psychological Association Task Force on Crime Victims. (1984). *Final report of the task force on the victims of crime and violence.* Washington, DC: Henley.

Amick-McMullan, A., Kilpatrick, D. G., & Resnick, H. S. (1991). Homicide as a risk factor for PTSD among surviving family members. *Behavior Modification, 15*(4) 545–559.

Amick-McMullan, A., Kilpatrick, D., & Veronen, L. (1989). Family survivors of homicide victims: A behavioral analysis. *Behavior Therapist, 12,* 75–79.

Amick-McMullan, A., Kilpatrick, D. G., Veronen, L. J., & Smith, S. (1989). Family survivors of homicide victims: Theoretical perspectives and an exploratory study. *Journal of Traumatic Stress, 2,* 21–35

Amir, M., Weil, G., Kaplan, Z., Tocker, T., & Wirzum, E. (1998) Debriefing with group psychotherapy in a homogenous group of non-injured victims of a terrorist attack: A prospective study. *Acta Psychiatrica Scandinavica, 98,* 237–242.

Anderson, C. L. (2000). Revisiting the Parenting Profile Assessment to Screen for Child Abuse. *Journal of Nursing Scholarship, 32(1),* 53.

Antonucci, T. (1985). *Social support: Theory, research and applications.* Dordrecht: Martinus Nijhoff.

Aquilera, D. C. (1990). *Crisis intervention: Theory and methodology* (6th ed.). St. Louis: Mosby.

Armenian, H., Morikawa, M., Melkonian, A., Hovanesian, A., Akiskal, K., & Akiskal, H. (2002). Risk factors for depression in the survivors of the 1988 earthquake in

Armenia. *Journal of Urban Health: Bulletin of the New York Academy of Medicine, 79*(3), 373–382.

Asarnow, J., Glynn, S., Pyrnoos, R. S., Nahum, J., Gunthrie, D., Cantwell, D. P., et al. (1999). When the earth stops shaking: Earthquake sequelae among children diagnosed for pre-earthquake psychopathology. *Journal of the American Academy of Child & Adolescent Psychiatry, 38,* 1016–1023.

Astin, M. C., Lawrence, K. J., & Foy, D. H. (1993). Risk and resiliency factors among battered women. *Violence and Victims, 8,* 17–28.

Atkeson, B., Calhoun, K., Resick, P., & Ellis, E. (1982). Victims of rape: Repeated assessment of depressive symptoms. *Journal of Consulting and Clinical Psychology, 90,* 1–13.

Attorney General's Task Force on Family Violence. (1984). *Final report.* Washington, DC: Government Printing Office.

Averill, J. R. (1982) *Anger and aggression.* New York: Springer-Verlag.

Averill, J. P. (1988). Disorders of emotion. *Journal of Social and Clinical Psychology, 6,* 247–268.

Averill, J. P., & Rosen, M. (1972). Vigilant and novigilant coping strategies and psychophysiological stress reactions during the anticipation of electric shock. *Journal of Personality and Social Psychology, 23,* 128–141.

Axford, S. N. (1999). Review of the Posttraumatic Stress Diagnostic Scale. In B. S. Plake, and J. C. Impara, (Eds.), *The supplement to the thirteenth mental measurement yearbook* (pp. 225–226), Lincoln, NE: The Buros Institute of Mental Measurements of The University of Nebraska.

Bandura, A. (1977). Self-efficacy: Toward a unifying theory of behavioral change. *Psychological Review, 84,* 191–215.

Bard, M., & Ellison, K. (1974). Crisis intervention and investigation of forceful rape. *Police Chief, 41,* 68–74.

Bard, M., & Sangrey, D. (1979). *The crime victim's book.* New York: Basic Books.

Bard, M., & Sangrey, D. (1980). *Things fall apart: Victims in crisis.* In L. Kivens (ed.), *Evaluation and change.* Minneapolis: Minnesota Medical Research Foundation.

Bard, M., & Sangrey, D. (1986). *The crime victim's book* (2nd ed.). New York: Brunner Mazel.

Barlow, D. H., & Craske, M. G. (1988, April). *Behavioral assessment and treatment of panic and avoidance.* Workshop, Eastern Psychological Association. Syracuse, New York.

Barlow, D. H.(1991). Disorders of emotion. *Psychological Inquiry, 2,* 58–71.

Barrera, M., Jr. (1986). Distinctions between social support concepts, measures, and models. *American Journal of Community Psychology, 14,* 413–445.

Barrera, M., Jr., Sandler, I. N., & Ramsay, T. B. (1981). Preliminary development of a scale of social support: Studies on college students. *American Journal of Community Psychology, 9,* 435–447.

Bastian, L. (1990). *Hispanic victims.* Washington, DC: Bureau of Justice Statistics, U.S. Department of Justice.

Baumeister, R. F. (1991). *Meaning of life.* New York: Guilford Press.

Beauchamp, N., Irvine, A. B., Seeley, J., & Johnson, B. (2005). Worksite-based Internet multimedia program for family caregivers of persons with dementia. *The Gerontologist, 45*(6), 793–801.

Beck Youth Inventories of Emotional and Social Impairment. (2005). Retrieved October 10, 2007, from http://www.beckinstitute.org

Beck. A. T. (1979). *Cognitive therapy and emotional disorders*. New York: International University Press.

Benner, P., Roskies, E., & Lazarus, R. S. (1980). Stress and coping under extreme conditions. In J. E. Dimsdale (Ed.), *Survivors, victims, and perpetrators: Essays on the Nazi Holocaust* (pp. 219–259). Washington, DC: Hemisphere.

Berkowitz, L. (1962). *Aggression: A special psychological analysis*. New York: McGraw-Hill.

Berkowitz, L. (1993). *Aggression: Its causes, consequences, and control*. New York: McGraw Hill.

Billings, A., & Moos, R. (1981). The role of coping responses and social resources attenuating the impact of stressful life events. *Journal of Behavioral Medicine, 4*, 39–147.

Bioterrorism Preparedness and Response Act of 2002 (Public Law 107–188). Retrieved November 20, 2007, from http://www.fda.gov/oc/bioterrorism/PL107–188.html

Bloom, B. L. (1963). Definitional aspects of the crisis concept. *Journal of Consulting Psychology, 27*, 498–502.

Blumberg, S. R., & Hokanson, J. F. (1983). The effect of another person's response style of interpersonal behavior in depression. *Journal of Abnormal Psychology, 92*, 196–209.

Bolger, N., Eckenrode, J. (1991). Social relationships, personality and anxiety during a major stressful event. *Journal of Personality and Social Psychology, 61*, 44–449.

Bolton, D., O'Ryan, D., Udwin, O., Boyle, S., & Yule, W. (2000). The long-term psychological effects of a disaster experienced in adolescence: II: General psychopathology. *Journal of Child Psychology and Psychiatry and Allied Disciplines, 41*, 513–523.

Bourdeaux, E., Kilpatrick, D., Resnick, H., Best, C., & Saunders, B. (1998). Criminal victimization, post traumatic stress disorder, and comorbid psychopathology among a community sample of women. *Journal of Traumatic Stress, 11*, 655–678.

Bowlby, J. (1980). *Attachment and loss*. New York: Basic Books.

Brewin, C. R., Andrews, B., Rose, S., & Kirk, M. (1999). Acute stress disorder and post traumatic stress disorder in victims of violent crime. *American Journal of Psychiatry, 156*(3), 360–366.

Briere, J. (1995). *Trauma symptom inventory (TSI) professional manual*. Psychological Assessment Resources. Retrieved October 24, 2007, from http://www.johnbriere.com/tsi.htm

Briere, J. (2007). Retrieved October 30, 2007, from http://www.johnbriere.com/

Briere, J., & Elliott, D. M. (1997). Psychological assessment of interpersonal victimization effects in adults and children. *Psychotherapy, 34*, 353–364.

Brock, S. E., Lazarus, P. J., & Jimerson, S. R. (Eds.). (2002). *Best practices in school crisis prevention and intervention*. Bethesda, MD: NASP Publications.

Brock, S. E., Sandoval, J., & Lewis, S. (2001). *Preparing for crises in the schools: A manual for building school crisis response teams*. New York: John Wiley & Sons.

Browne, A. (1987). *When battered women kill*. New York: Free Press.

Bruhn, C. (1991). Consumer perception of quality. *Perishables Handling Postharvest Technology of Fresh Horticultural Crops. Newsletter 72*, 4–9.

Burgess, A. W., & Holstrom, L. L. (1974). Rape trauma syndrome. *American Journal of Psychiatry, 131*, 981–986.

Burnam, M., Stein, J., Goldber, J., Siegel, J., Forsythe, A., & Telles, C., (1988). Sexual assault and mental disorders in a community population. *Journal of Consulting and Clinical Psychology, 50,* 843–850.

Burns, D. D., & Eidelson, R. J. (1998). Why are depression and anxiety correlated? A test of the tripartite model. *Journal of Consulting and Clinical Psychology, 66*(3), 461–473.

Campfield, K. M., & Hills, A. M. (2001). Effect of timing of critical incident stress debriefing (CISD) on posttraumatic symptoms. *Journal of Traumatic Stress, 14,* 327–340.

Caplan, G. (1964). *Principles of preventive psychiatry.* New York: Basic Books.

Carlson, B. E. (1996). Children of battered women: Research, programs and services. In A. R. Roberts (Ed.), *Helping battered women: New perspectives and remedies* (pp. 172–187). New York: Oxford University Press.

Carroll, E. M., Rueger, D. B., Foy, D. B., & Donahoe, C. P., Jr. (1985). Vietnam combat veterans with post traumatic stress disorder: Analysis of marital and cohabitating adjustment. *Journal of Abnormal Psychology, 94,* 329–337.

Cascardi, M., O'Leary, K. D., Schlee, A., & Lawrence, E. (1993). *Prevalence and correlates of PTSD in abused women.* Paper presented at the 27th Annual Conference of the Association for the Advancement of Behavior Therapy (AABT), Atlanta, GA.

Cassel, J. (1976). The contribution of the social environment to host resistance. *American Journal of Epidemiology, 104,* 107–123.

Centers for Disease Control and Prevention. (2001). *Recognition of illness associated with the intentional release of a biologic agent.* MMWR, 50(41), 893–897. Retrieved Sept. 27, 2007, from http://www.cdc.gov/mmwr/preview/mmwrhtml/mm5041a2.htm

Centers for Disease Control and Prevention. (2001). Retrieved October 5, 2007, from http://www.cdc.gov

Child Abuse Prevention and Treatment Act (CAPTA). (1988). Retrieved December 11, 2007, from http://www.acf.hhs.gov/programs/cb/laws_policies/cblaws/capta/index.htm

Child Welfare Information Gateway. (2007). Retrieved November 12, 2007, from http://www.childwelfare.gov/systemwide/laws_policies/statutes/define.cfm

Christensen, J. (1981). Assessment of stress: Environmental, interpersonal, and outcome issues. In P. McReynolds (Ed.), *Advances in Psychologcal Assessment.* San Francisco: Jossey-Bass.

Clark, L. A. (1989). The anxiety and depressive disorders: Descriptive psychopathology and differential diagnosis. In P. C. Kendall & D. Watson (Eds.), *Anxiety and depression: Distinctive and overlapping features* (p. 83–129). San Diego, CA: Academic Press.

Clark, A. A., & Hovanitz, C. A. (1989). Dimensions of coping that contribute to psychopathology. *Journal of Clinical Psychology, 45,* 28–36.

Clay, D., Anderson, W., & Dixon, W. (1993). Relationship between anger expression and stress in predicting depression. *Journal of Counseling and Development, 72,* 91–94.

Cobb, S. (1976). Social support as a moderator to life stress. *Psychosomatic Medicine, 38,* 300–314.

Code of Federal Regulations. 28 C.F.R. Section 0.85. Retrieved from http://www.gpoaccess.gov/cfr/index.html

Cohen, J. (1992). A power primer. *Psychological Bulletin, 112,* 155–159.

Cohen, M. (1998). The cost of mental health care for victims of crime. *Journal of Interpersonal Violence, 13*(1), 93–111.

Cohen, S., & Hoberman, H. M. (1983). Positive events and social supports as buffers of life change stress. *Journal of Applied Social Psychology, 13,* 93–111.

Cohen, S., & McKay, G. (1984). Social support, stress, and the buffering hypothesis: A theoretical analysis. In A. Baum, J. Singer, & S. Taylor (Eds.), *Handbook of psychology and health* (pp. 253–267). Hillsdale, NJ: Erlbaum.

Cohen, S., & Willis, T. (1985). Stress, social support and the buffering hypothesis. *Psychological Bulletin, 98,* 310–357.

Colegrove, M., Bloomfield, H., & McWilliams, P. (1976). *How to survive the loss of a love.* New York: Bantam Books.

Coleman, G., Gaboury, M., Murray, M., & Seymour, S. (eds.) (1999). *National Victim Assistance Academy.* Retrieved October 21, 2007, from http://www.ojp.usdoj.gov/ovc/assist/nvaa99

Collins, B., & Reed, G. (1994). Ten principles proposed as policy guidelines for mental health intervention research and mental health services among persons living with HIV/AIDS. *Psychosocial Rehabilitation Journal, 17*(4), 83–95.

Collins, G. (1978). Strategies for dealing with conflict: Crisis intervention. *Journal of Nursing Education, 5,* 39–46.

Collins, R. L., Taylor, S. E., & Skokan, L. A. (1990) A better world or a shattered vision? Changes in life perspectives following victimization. *Social Cognition, 8,* 263–285.

Cook, R., Smith, B., & Harrel, A. (1987). *Helping crime victims: Levels of trauma and effectiveness of services.* Washington, DC: U.S. Department of Justice, National Institute of Justice.

Corey, G. (1996). *Theory and practice of counseling and psychotherapy.* Pacific Grove, CA: Brooks-Cole.

Cox, T., & Ferguson, E. (1991). Individual differences, stress and coping. In C. L. Cooper & R. Payne (Eds.), *Personality and stress: Individual differences in the stress process* (pp. 7–30). Chichester, UK: Wiley.

Coyne, J. C., Wortman, C. B., & Lehman, D. R. (1988). The other side of support: Emotional over-involvement and miscarried helping. In B. H. Gottlieb (Ed.), *Social support: Formats, processes and effects* (pp. 305–330). Newbury Park, CA: Sage.

Currier, J. M., Holland, J. M., & Neimeyer, R. A. (2006). Sense-making, grief, and the experience of violent loss: Toward a mediational model. *Death Studies, 30,* 403–428.

Currier, J. M., Holland, J. M., Coleman, R. A., & Neimeyer, R. A. (2006). Bereavement following violent death: An assault on life and meaning. In R. Stevenson & G. Cox (Eds.), *Perspectives on violence and violent death.* Amityville, NY: Baywood.

Cutrona, C. E., & Russell, D. (1990). Type of social support and specific stress: Toward a theory of optimal matching. In I. G. Sarason, B. R. Sarason, & G. R. Pierce (Eds.), *Social support: An interactional view* (pp. 319–366). New York: Wiley.

Czaja, S. J., & Rubert, M. P. (2002). Telecommunications technology as an aid to family caregivers of persons with dementia. *Psychosomatic Medicine, 64,* 469–476.

Davidson, J. R. T., Book, S. W., Colket, J. T., Tupler, L. A., Roth, S., David, D., et al. (1997). Assessment of a new self-rating scale for post-traumatic stress disorder. *Psychological Medicine, 27,* 153–160.

Davis, R. C., & Friedman, L. N. (1985). The emotional aftermath of crime and violence. In C. R. Figley (Ed.), *Trauma and its wake* (pp. 90–112). New York: Brunner Mazel.

Decker, R. H. (1997). *When a crisis hits: Will your school be ready?* Thousand Oaks, CA: Corwin Press.

Deffenbacher, J. L., & Stark, R. S. (1992) Relaxation and cognitive-relaxation treatments of general anger. *Journal of Counseling Psychology, 39,* 158–167.

Deffenbacher, J. L., Oeting, E. R., Huff, M. F., Cornell, G. F., & Dallager, C. J. (1996). Evaluation of two cognitive behavioral approaches to general anger reduction. *CognitiveTherapy and Research, 20,* 551–573.

Deimling, G., & Harel, Z. (1983). Social integration and mental health of the aged. *Research on Aging, 6,* 515–527.

DiGiovanni, C. (1999). Domestic terrorism with chemical or biological agents: Psychiatric aspects. *American Journal of Psychiatry, 156,* 1500–1505.

De Haes, J. C., & van Knippenberg, F. C. (1985). The quality of life of cancer patients: A review of the literature. *Social Science Medicine, 20,* 809–842.

Doka, K. J. (Ed.). (1995). *Children mourning, mourning children.* Washington, DC: Hospice Foundation of America.

Dunkin, J., & Anderson-Hanley, C. (1998). Dementia caregiving burden: A review of the literature and guidelines for assessment and intervention. *Neurology, 51*(1), 53–60.

Dura, J. R., Stukenberg, K. W., Kiecolt-Glaser, J. K. (1990) Anxiety and depressive disorders in adult children caring for demented parents. *Psychology of Aging, 6,* 467–473.

Dyregov. A. (1998). Psychological debriefing: An effective method? *Traumatology, 4*(2), 6–25.

Eaves, C. (2001). The development and implementation of a crisis response team in a school setting. *International Journal of Emergency Mental Health, 3*(1), 35–46.

Eckenrode, J., & Wethington, E. (1990). The process and outcome of mobilizing social support. In S. Duck & R. C. Silver (Eds.), *Personal relationships and social support* (pp. 83–103). London: Sage.

Educational Service District 105, Yakima, Washington. (1997). *Quick response: A step-by-step guide to crisis management for principals, counselors, and teachers.* Alexandria, VA: Association for Supervision and Curriculum Development.

Ehrenreicht, J. H., & McQuaide, S. (2001). *Coping with disaster: A guide to psychosocial interventions.* Retrieved December 28, 2007, from http://www.mhwwb.org

Eisdorfer, C., Czaja, S. J., Lowenstein, D. A., Rubert, M. P., Arguelles, S., Mitrani, V. B., et al. (2003). The effect of a family therapy and technology-based intervention of caregiver depression. *The Gerontologist, 43,* 521–531.

Magnusson, D., & Ekehammer, B. (1975). Anxiety profiles, based on both situational and response factors. *Multivariate Behavior Research, 10*(1), 27–43.

Elias, R. (1984). Alienating the victims: Compensation and victim attitudes. *Journal of Social Issues, 40,* 103–116.

Ellis, E., Atkeson, B., & Calhoun, K. (1981). Short reports: An assessment of long term reaction to rape. *Journal of Abnormal Psychology, 90,* 263–266.

Endler, N. S. (1988). Hassles, health and happiness. In M. P. Janisse (Ed.), *Individual differences, stress and health psychology* (pp. 24–56). New York: Springer-Verlag.

Endler, N., & Parker, J. (1990). The multidimensional assessment of coping: A critical evaluation. *Journal of Personality and Social Psychology, 58,* 844–854.

Endler, N. S., & Parker, J. D. (1994). Assessment of multidimensional coping: Task, emotion and avoidance strategies. *Psychological Assessment, 6,* 50–51.

Endler, N. S., Cox, B. J., Parker, J. D., & Bagby, R. M. (1992). Self reports of depression and state-trait anxiety: Evidence for differential diagnosis. *Journal of Personality abd Social Psychology, 63* (5), 832–838.

Endler, N. S., Parker, J. D., & Summerfeldt, L. J. (1993). Coping with health problems: Conceptual and methodological issues. *Canadian Journal of Behavioral Science, 25,* 384–399.

Epston, D., & White, M. (1992). *Experience, contradiction, narrative and imagination: Selected papers of David Epston and Michael White.* Adelaide, South Australia: Dulwich Centre.

Everly, G. S., Jr. (1993). Psychotraumatology: A two-factor formulation of posttraumatic stress. *Integrative Physiological and Behavioral Science, 28*(3), 270–278.

Everly, G. S., Jr. (2006). *Mental health aspects of disasters.* Baltimore, MD: Johns Hopkins University Press.

Everly, G., & Lating, J. (2003). *Personality-guided therapy for posttraumatic stress disorder (Personality-Guided Psychology).* Washington, DC: American Psychological Association.Press.

Everly, G. S., Jr., & Mitchell, J. T. (1999). *Critical incident stress management (CISM): A new era and standard of care in crisis intervention* (2nd ed.). Ellicott City, MD: Chevron.

Everly, G. S., Jr., Flannery, R. B., Jr., Eyler V., & Mitchell, J. T. (2001). Sufficiency analysis of an integrated multi-component approach to crisis intervention: Critical incident stress management. *Advances in Mind-Body Medicine, 17,* 174–183.

Everly, G. S., Jr., Flannery, R. B., Jr., & Mitchell, J. T. (2000). Critical incident stress management: A review of literature. *Aggression and Violent Behavior: A Review Journal, 5,* 23–40.

Everly, G.S., Jr., Lating, J., & Mitchell, J. T. (2000). Innovation in group crisis intervention. In A. R. Roberts (Ed.), *Crisis intervention handbook: Assessment, treatment and research* (2nd ed., pp. 77–97), New York: Oxford University Press.

Fairchild, T. N. (1986). *Crisis intervention strategies for school-based helpers.* Springfield, IL: Charles C. Thomas.

Falsetti, S. A. (1997). The decision-making process of choosing a treatment for patients with civilian trauma-related PTSD. *Cognitive and Behavioral Practice, 4,* 99–121.

Falsetti, S. A., & Bernat, J. A. (2000). *Practice guidelines: Rape and sexual assault.* Retrieved October 29, 2007, from http://www.musc.edu/vawprevention/advocacy/rape.shtml

Falsetti, S. A., & Resnick, H. S. (1998). *Group cognitive behavioral therapy for women with PTSD and comorbid panic attacks.* Presented at the 32nd Annual Convention of the Association for the Advancement of Behavior Therapy, Washington, DC.

Falsetti, S. A., Resnick, H. S., Resick, P. A., & Kilpatrick, D. (1993). The modified PTSD symptom scale: A brief self-report measure of posttraumatic stress disorder. *Behavioral Therapist, 16,* 161–162.

Falsetti, S., Resnick, H., Dansky, B., Lydriad, R., Kilpatrick, D. (1995). The relationship of stess to panic disorder: Cause or effect. In C. M. Mazur (ed.), *Does stress cause psychiatric illness?* Washington, DC: American Psychiatric Press.

Federal Bureau of Investigation. (2003). *Crime in the U.S.: 2002.* Washington, DC: U.S. Government Printing Office.

Federal Bureau of Investigation. (2007). Supplementary Homicide Reports, 1976–2005. *Homicide Studies 4,* 317–340.

Feinberg, T. (1999). The Midwest floods of 1993: Observations of a natural disaster. In A. S. Canter & S. A. Carroll (Eds.), *Crisis prevention & response: A collection of NASP resources* (pp. 223–239). Bethesda, MD: National Association of School Psychologists.

Ferrell, B. R. (1993). Overview of breast cancer: Quality of life. *Oncology Patient Care* 3(3), 7–8.

Ferrell, B. R., & Dow, K. H. (1996). Portraits of cancer survivorship: A glimpse through the lens of survivors' eyes. *Cancer Practice, 4,* 76–80.

Foa, E. B., & Rothbaum, B. O. (1998). *Treating the trauma of rape: Cognitive behavioral therapy for PTSD.* New York: Guilford Press.

Foa, E. B., Hearst-Ikeda, D. E., & Perry, K. (1995). Evaluation of a brief cognitive behavioral program for the prevention of chronic PTSD in recent assault victims. *Journal of Consulting and Clinical Psychology, 63,* 948–955.

Foa, E. B., Riggs, D. S., Dancu, C. V., & Rothbaum, B. O. (1993). Reliability and validity of a brief instrument for assessing post-traumatic stress disorder. *Journal of Traumatic Stress, 6,* 459–473.

Foa, E. B., Rothbaum, B. O., Riggs, D. S., & Murdock, T. (1991). Treatment of post-traumatic stress disorder in rape victims: A comparison between cognitive behavioral procedures and counseling. *Journal of Consulting and Clinical Psychology, 59,* 715–723.

Foa, E. B., Dancu, C. V., Hembree, E. A., Jaycox, L. H., Meadows, E. A., & Street, G. P. (1999). A comparison of exposure therapy, stress inoculation training, and their combination for reducing posttraumatic stress disorder in female assault victims. *Journal of Consulting and Clinical Psychology, 59,* 715–723.

Folkman, S. (1997). Positive psychological states and coping with severe stress. *Social Science Medicine, 45*(8), 1207–1221.

Folkman, S. (1994). Personal control and stress and coping processes: A theoretical analysis. *Journal of Personality and Social Psychology, 46,* 839–852.

Folkman, S., & Lazarus, R. (1988). *Manual for the ways of coping questionnaire.* Palo Alto, CA: Consulting Psychologists Press.

Folkman, S., Lazarus, R. S., Dunkel-Schetter, C., Delongis, A., Gruen, R. J. (1986). Dynamics of a stressful encounter: Cognitive appraisal, coping and encounter outcomes. *Journal of Personality and Social Psychology, 50,* 571–579.

Frank, E., Turner, S. M., & Duffy, B. (1979). Depressive symptomatology in rape victims. *Journal of Affective Disorders, 1,* 269–277.

Freedy, J., Resnick, H., Kilpatrick, D., Dansky, B., & Tidwell, R. (1994). The psychological adjustment of recent crime victims in the criminal justice system. *Journal of Interpersonal Violence, 9,* 450–468.

Freeman, L. N., Shaffer, D., & Smith, H. (1996). Neglected victims of homicide: The needs of young siblings of murder victims. *Journal of American Orthopsychiatry, 66*(3), 337–345.

Friedman, K., Bischoff, H., Davis, R., & Person, A. (1990) *Victims and helpers: Reactions to crime.* Grant study funded by National Institute of Justice, Washington, DC.

Frieze, I., Hymer, S., & Greenberg, M. (1987). Describing the crime victim: Psychological reactions to victimization. *Professional Psychology: Research and Practice, 18,* 299–315.

Garofolo, J. (1979). Victimization and the fear of crime. *Journal of Research in Crime and Delinquency, 16,* 80–97.

Garofalo, J. (1997). Victimization and the fear of crime. *Journal of Research in Crime and Delinquency, 16,* 80–97.

George, L. K., & Gwyther, L. P. (1986). Caregiver well-being: A multidimensional examination of family caregivers of demented adults. *Gerontologist, 26*(3), 253–259.

Getzel, G., & Masters, M. (1984). Serving families who survive homicide victims. *Social Casework, 65,* 138–144.

Gillies, J., & Neimeyer, R. A. (2006). Loss, grief, and the search for significance: Toward a model of meaning reconstruction in bereavement. *Journal of Constructivist Psychology, 19,* 31–65.

Goenjian, A. K., Molina, L., Steinberg, A. M., & Fairbanks, L. A. (2001). Post traumatic stress and depressive reactions among adolescents after hurricane Mitch. *American Journal of Psychiatry, 158,* 788–794.

Golan, N. (1978). *Treatment in crisis situations.* New York: The Free Press.

Goldberger, L., & Brenitz, S. (Eds.) (1993). *Handbook of stress: Theoretical and clinical aspects* (2nd ed.). New York: Free Press.

Goodwin, J. (1988). *Post-traumatic stress disorders.* Washington DC: DAV.

Gormley, N. (2000). The role of dementia training programmes in reducing care-giver burden. *Psychiatric Bulletin 24,* 41–42.

Gotlib, I., & Cane, D. (1989). Self support reassessment of depression and anxiety. In P. C. Kendall & D. Watson (Eds.), *Anxiety and depression: Distinctive and overlapping features* (pp. 131–169). San Diego, CA: Academic Press.

Gotlib, I., Robinson, L. (1982). Responses to depressed individuals: Discrepancies between self-report and overserver-rated behavior. *Journal of Abnormal Psychology, 31,* 231–240.

Gourash, N. (1978). Help seeking: A review of the literature. *American Journal of Community Psychology, 6,* 413–424.

Gottfredson, G. D., Reiser, M., & Tsegaye-Spates, C. R. (1987). Psychological help for victims of crime. *Professional Psychology: Research and Practice, 18*(4), 316–325

Green, D. L., & Macaluso, B. (in press, a). A day in the life of a domestic violence social worker. In A. R. Roberts (Ed.), *Social workers' desk reference* (2nd ed.). New York: Oxford University Press.

Green, D. L., & Macaluso, B. (in press b). Social work best practices, roles and functions. In A. R. Roberts (Ed.), *Social workers' desk reference* (2nd ed.). New York: Oxford University Press.

Green, D. L., & Pomeroy, E. C. (2007). Crime victims: What is the role of social support? *Journal of Aggression, Maltreatment and Trauma, 15*(2), 97–113.

Green, D. L., Streeter, C., & Pomeroy, E. (2005) A multivariate model of the stress and coping process. *Stress, Trauma and Crisis, 8*(1), 61–73.

Haan, N. (1969). A tripartite model of ego functioning, values and clinical research applications. *Journal of Nervous and Mental Disease, 148,* 14–30.

Haan, N., (1977). *Coping and defending: Processes of self-environment organization.* New York: Academic Press.

Hall, A., & Wellman, B. (1985). Social support and social networks. In S. Cohen and S. L. Syme (Eds.), *Social support and health* (pp. 23–42). New York: Academic Press.

Hamberger, L. K., & Phelan, M. B. (2004). *Domestic violence screening and intervention in medical and mental healthcare settings.* New York: Springer Publishing.

Hanson, R. F., Kilpatrick, D. G., Falsetti, S. A., Resnick, H. S., & Weaver, T. (1996). Violent crime in psychological adjustment. In J. R. Freedy & S. E. Hobfall. (Eds.), *Traumatic stress: Theory and practice* (pp. 129–161). New York: Plenum.

Harvey, A. G., Bryant, R. A., & Tarrier, N. (2003). Cognitive behavior therapy for post traumatic stress disorder. *Clinical Psychology Review, 23,* 501–522.

Hendin, H. (1983). Psychotherapy for Vietnam veterans with posttraumatic stress disorders. *American Journal of Psychotherapy, 37*(1), 86–99.

Heppner, P. P. (1988). *The problem solving inventory manual.* Palo Alto, CA: Consulting Psychologist.

Herman, D., Felton, C., & Susser, E. (2002). Mental Health Needs in New York State Following the September 11th Attacks. *Journal of Urban Health: Bulletin of the New York Academy of Medicine, 79*(3), 322–331.

Hiley-Young, B., & Gerrity, E. T. (1994). Critical incident stress debriefing (CISD): Value and limitations in disaster response. *NCP Clinical Quarterly, 4*, 17–19

Hobfull, S. (1984). *The ecology of stress.* Washington, DC: Hemisphere.

Hobfull, S. E., & Lerman, M. (1988) Predicting receipt of social support: A longitudinal study of parents' reactions to their child's illness. *Health Psychology, 8*, 61–77.

Hobfull, S., & Vaux, R. (1993). Gender differences in preference to offer social support to death and dying. *Sociological Abstracts, 26*, 243–254..

Hobfull, S., Freedy, J., Geller, P., & Lane, C. (1990). Conservation of social resources: Social support resource theory. *Journal of Personal and Social Relationships, 7*, 465–476.

Hollon, S. F., & Kendall, P. C. (1980). Cognitive self-statements in dression: Development of an automatic thoughts questionnaire. *Cognitive Therapy and Research, 4*, 383–395.

Holohan, C. J., & Moos, R. H. (1990). Life stressors, resistance factors, and psychological health: An extension of the stress-resistance paradigm. *Journal of Personality and Social Psychology, 58*, 909–917.

Holohan, C. J., & Moos, R. H. (1992). Life stressors, personal and social resources and depression: A four year structural model. *Journal of Abnormal Psychology, 11*(1), 31–38.

Holohan, C. J., & Moos, R. H. (1994).Life stressoprs and mental health: Advances in conceptualizing stress resistance. In W. R. Avison & I. H. Gotlieg (Eds.), *Stress and mental health: Contemporary issues and prospects for the future* (pp. 213–238). New York: Plenum.

Homans, G. (1974). *Social behavior* (2nd ed.). New York: Harcourt, Brace & Jovanovich.

Homeland Security Act of 2002 (HR 5005-2). Retrieved January 3, 2008, from http://thomas.loc.gov/cgi-bin/bdquery/z?d107:H.R.5005

Horowitz, A. (1977). The pathways into psychiatric treatment: Some differences between men and women. *Journal of Health and Human Beahvior, 18*, 169–178.

House, J. S., Umberson, D., Landis, K. R. (1988). Structures and processes of social support. *American Review of Sociology, 14*, 293–296.

Houston, B. K., & Vavak, C. R. (1991). Cynical hostility: Developmental factors, psychological correlates and health behaviors. *Health Psychology, 10*, 9–17.

Idler, E. L. (1995). Religion, health and nonphysical sense of self. *Social Forces, 74*, 683–704.

Irwin, C., Falsetti, S., Lydriad, R., Ballenger, J., & Brener, W. (1996). Comorbidity of post traumatic stress disorder and irritable bowel movement. *Journal of Clinical Psychiatry, 57*, 576–578.

Jacobson, G., Strickler, M., & Mosley, W. (1968). Generic and individual approaches to crisis intervention. *American Journal of Public Health, 58*, 338–343.

Janis, I., & Mann, L. (1977). *Decision making.* New York: Free Press.

Janoff-Bulman, R. (1979). Characterological versus behavioral self-blame: Inquiries into depression and rape. *Journal of Personality and Social Psychology, 37*, 1798–1809.

Janoff-Bulman, R. (1989). Assumptive worlds and the stress of traumatic events: Applications of the schema construct. *Social Cognition, 7,* 113–136.

Janoff-Bulman, R. (1992). *Shattered assumptions.* New York: Free Press.

Janoff-Bulman, R., & Frieze, I. H. (1983). A theoretical perspective for understanding reactions to victimization. *Journal of Social Issues, 39,* 1–17.

Jernigan, D., Raghunathan, P., Bell, P., Brechner, R., Bresnitz, E., & Butler, J. (2002). Investigation of bioterrorism-related anthrax, United States, 2001: Epidemiologic findings. *Emerging Infectious Diseases, 8*(10), 1019–1028.

Johnson. T. C. (1989). Female child perpetrators: Children who molest other children. *Child Abuse and Neglect, 13,* 571–585.

Johnson, K. (1997). Professional help and crime victims. *Social Service Review, 71*(1), 89–110.

Jones, R. T., Fray, R., Cunningham, J. D., & Kaiser, L. (2001). The psychological effects of Hurricane Andrew on ethnic minority and Caucasian children and adolescents: A case study. *Cultural Diversity and Ethnic Minority Psychology, 7,* 103–108.

Jordan, K. (2005). What we learned from 9/11: A terrorism grief recovery process model. Retrieved November 24, 2007, from http://brief-treatment.oxfordjournals.org/cgi/content/full/5/4/240

Kahn, R., & Antonucci, T. (1993). Convoys over the life course: Attachment, roles, and social support. In P. Battes & O. Brin (Eds.), *Life span development and behavior* (pp. 253–285). New York: Academic Press.

Kaniasty, K. (1988). *Pretest of candidate measures: Results of two studies.* Violence: Psychological Reactions and Consequences. Louisville, KY: University of Louisville, Urban Studies Center.

Kaniasty, K., & Norris, F. (1994). Psychological distress following criminal victimization in the general population: Cross sectional, longitudinal, and prospective analysis. *Journal of Consulting and Clinical Psychology, 62*(1), 111–123.

Kaniasty, K., & Norris, F. (1997). Social support dynamics in adjustment to disasters. In S. Duck (Ed.), *Handbook of personal relationships: Theory, research and interventions* (2nd ed., pp. 595–619). New York, NY: John Wiley & Sons, Inc.

Karasek, R. A., Triantis, K. P., & Chaudhry, S. S. (1982). Coworker and supervisor support as moderators of associations between task characteristics and mental strain. *Journal of Occupational Behavior, 3,* 181–200.

Katz, B., & Burt, M. (1988). Self-blame: Help or hindrance in recovery from rape? In A. Burgess (Ed.), *Rape and sexual assault* (pp. 151–168). New York: Garland.

Keilitz, S. (2002). Improving judicial system responses to domestic violence: The promises and risks of integrated case management and technology solutions. In A. R. Roberts (Ed.), *Handbook of domestic violence intervention strategies* (pp. 147–171). New York: Oxford University Press.

Kennedy, M. (1999). Crisis management: Every school needs a plan. *American School & University, 71*(11), 25–27.

Kerlinger, F. (1986). *Foundation in behavioral research* (3rd ed.). Orlando, FL: Harcourt, Brace & Jovanovich.

Kessler, R. C., & McCleod, J. D. (1985). Social support and mental health in community samples. In S. Cohen & S. L. Syne (Eds.), *Social support and health* (pp. 219–240.). Orlando, FL: Academic Press.

Kilpatrick, D. (1983) Rape victims: Detection, assessment and treatment. *Clinical Psychologist 15* (4), 421–423

Kilpatrick. D. G. (1987). *Measures from research on rape victims.* Huntsville, AL: National Conference on Assessing the Impact of Child Sexual Abuse.

Kilpatrick, D., & Falsetti, S. (1994). The psychological adjustment of recent crime victims in the criminal justice system. *Journal of Interpersonal Violence, 9*(4), 450-461.

Kilpatrick, D. G., & Resnick, H. S. (1991). *The importance of being epidemiological: Implication for study of rape-related PTSD etiology.* Paper presented at the 25th annual convention of the Association for the Advancement of Behavior Therapy, New York.

Kilpatrick, D. G., Best, C. L., & Veronen, L. J. (1984). *Mental health consequences of criminal victimization: A random community survey.* Paper presented at the Annual Convention, American Psychological Association, Toronto, Canada.

Kilpatrick, D., Best, C., Veronen, L., Amick, A., Villeponteaux, L., & Ruff, G. (1985). Mental health correlates of victimization: A random community survey. *Journal of Consulting and Clinical Psychology, 53,* 866–873.

Kilpatrick, D. G., Edwards, C. N., & Seymour, A. E. (1992). *Rape in America: A report to the nation.* Arlington, VA: National Crime Victims Center.

Kilpatrick, D., Resick, P., & Veronen, L. (1981). Effects of a rape experience: A longitudinal study. *Journal of Social Issues, 37,* 105–122.

Kilpatrick, D. G., Resnick, H. S., Saunders, B. E., & Best, C. L. (1998) Rape, other violence against women, and posttraumatic stress disorder: Critical issues in assessing the adversity-stress-psychopathology relationship. In B. P. Dohrenwend (Ed.), *Adversity, stress, & psychopathology* (p. 161–176), New York: Oxford University Press.

Kilpatrick, D. G., Saunders, B. E., Veronen, L. J., Best, C. L., & Von, J. M. (1987). Criminal victimization: Lifetime prevalence, reporting to police, and psychological impact. *Crime and Delinquency, 33*(4), 3, 479–489.

Kilpatrick, D. G., Veronen, L. J., & Resick, P. (1982). Psychological sequelae to rape: Assessment and treatment strategies. In D. M. Doleys, R. I. Meredity, & A. R. Ciminero (Eds.), *Behavioral medicine: Assessment and treatment strategies.* New York: Plenum.

Klaus, P. A.(1994). *The cost of crime to victims.* Crime Data Brief, Bureau of Justice Statistics.

Kline, M., Schonfeld, D., & Lichtenstein, R. (1995). Benefits and challenges of school-based crisis response teams. *Journal of Social Health, 65,* 245–249.

Koenig, H. G., Westlund, R. E., George, L. K., Hughes, D. C., Blazer, D. G., & Hybels, C. (1993). Abbreviating the Duke Social Support Index for use in chronically ill elderly individuals. *Psychosomatics. 34,* 61–69.

Koss, M. P., Gidycz, C. A., & Wisniewski, N. (1987). Incidence and prevalence of sexual aggression and victimization in a national sample of higher education students. *Journal of Consulting and Clinical Psychology, 55,* 162–170.

Kraus, N. (1986). Chronic financial strain, social support, and depressive symptoms among older adults. *Psychology and Aging, 2,* 185–192.

La Greca, A. M., Silverman, W. K., Vernberg, E. M., & Prinstein, M. J. (1996). Symptoms of posttraumatic stress in children following Hurricane Andrew: A prospective study. *Journal of Consulting & Clinical Psychology, 64,* 712–723.

Lazarus, P. J., & Gillespie, B. (1996). Critical actions in the aftermath of natural disasters. *School Administrator, 53*(2), 35–36.

Lazarus, P. J., Jimerson, S. R., & Brock, S. E. (2002). Natural disasters. In S. E. Brock, P. J. Lazarus, & S. R. Jimerson (Eds.), *Best practices in school crisis prevention and intervention* (pp. 433–447). Bethseda, MD: NASP.

Lazarus, R. (1991). *Emotion and adaptation.* New York: Oxford University Press.

Lazarus, R., & Folkman, S. (1984). *Stress, appraisal and coping.* New York: Springer Publishing.

Lazarus, R. S., & Folkman, S. (1986). Cognitive theories of stress and the issue of circularity. In M. Appley & R. Trumbull (Eds.), *Dynamics of stress* (pp. 63–81). New York: Plenum.

Lazarus, R. S., & Folkman, S. (1987). Transactional theory and research on emotions and coping. In L. Laux & G. Vossel (Eds.), Personality in biographical stress and coping research. *European Journal of Personality, 1,* 141–169.

Leonard, K. E., & Blane, H. T. (1992). Alcohol and marital aggression in a national sample of young men. *Journal of Interpersonal Violence, 7,* 19–30.

Lerner, M. D., & Shelton. R. D. (1991). *Acute traumatic stress management: Addressing emergent psychological needs during traumatic events.* Commack, NY: The American Academy of Experts in Traumatic Stress.

Lichtenstein, R., Schonfeld, D., Kline, M., & Speese-Linehan, D. (1995). *How to prepare for and respond to a crisis.* Alexandria, VA: Association for Supervision and Curriculum Development.

Lindemann, E. (1944). Symptomatology and management of acute grief. *American Journal of Psychiatry, 101,* 141–148.

Lipovsky, J. (2002). *Treatment of child victims of child abuse and neglect.* Retrieved October 14, 2007, from www.childlaw.sc.edu

Lurigio, A. (1987). Are all victims alike? The adverse, generalized and differential impact of crime. *Crime and Delinquency, 33,* 452–467.

Lurigio, A., & Resick, P. (1990). Healing the psychological wounds of criminal victimization: Predicting postcrime distress and recovery. In A. Lurigio, W. Skogan, & R. Davis (Eds.), *Victims of crime: Problems, policies and programs* (pp. 50–68). Newbury Park, CA: Sage.

Maiuro, R. D. Cahn, T. S., Vitaliano, P. P., Wagner, B. C., & Zegree, J. B. (1988). Anger, hostility and depression in domestically violent versus generally assaultive men and nonviolent control subjects. *Journal of Consulting and Clinical Psychology, 56,* 17–23.

Mallinckrodt, B. (1989) Social support and the effectiveness of group therapy. *Journal of Counseling Psychology, 36*(2), 170–175.

Manzi, L. A. (1995). *Evaluation of the onsite academy's residential program.* Unpublished research investigation submitted to Boston College.

Marin, P. (1995). *Freedom and its discontents.* Hanover, NH: Steerforth Press.

Max, W., Rice, D. P., Finkelstein, E., Bardwell, R. A., & Leadbetter, S. The economic toll of intimate partner violence against women in the United States. *Violence and Victims, 19*(3), 259–272.

McCaul, K., Veltum, M., Boyechko, V., & Crawford, J. (1990). Understanding attributions of victim blame for rape: Sex, violence, and foreseeability. *Journal of Applied Social Psychology, 20,* 1–26.

McIntosh, D. N., Silver, R. C., & Wortman, C. B. (1993). Religion's role in adjustment to a negative life event: Coping with the loss of a child. *Journal of Personality and Social Psychology, 64,* 812–821.

Meneghan, E. (1989). Changes and psychological well-being: Variations in effects of gender and role repertoire. *Social Forces, 67*(3), 693–715.

Meichenbaum, D. (1974). *Cognitive behavior modification.* Morristown, NJ: General Learning Press.

Meyer, R. A. (2001). *Assessment for crisis intervention: A triage assessment model.* Pacific Grove, CA: Wadsworth.

Miller, S. M. (1987). Monitoring and blunting: Validation of a questionnaire to assess styles of information seeking under threat. *Journal of Personality and Social Psychology, 52,* 345–353.

Miller, S. M., Brody, D., & Summerton, J. (1988). Styles of coping with threat: Implications for health. *Journal of Personality and Social Psychology, 53,* 142–148.

Mitchell, J. (1988). Stress: The history and future of critical incident stress debriefings. *Journal of Emergency Medical Services, 7*–52.

Mitchell, J. T., & Everly, G.S. (1996). *Critical incident stress debriefing: An operations manual.* Ellicott City, MD: Chevron.

Mitchell, J. T., & Everly, G. S. (1997). *Critical incident stress debriefing: An operation manual for the prevention of traumatic stress among emergency services and disaster worker* (2nd ed.). Ellicott City, MD: Chevron.

Mittelman, M. S., Ferris, S. H., Shulman, E., Steinberg, G., & Levin, B. (1996). A family intervention to delay nursing home placement of patients with Alzheimer's disease. *Journal of the American Medical Association, 276,* 1725–1731.

Mittelman, M. S., Roth, D. L., Coon, D. W., & Haley, W. E. (2004). Sustained benefit of supportive intervention for depressive symptoms in caregivers of patients with Alzheimer's disease. *American Journal of Psychiatry, 161,* 850–856.

Moos, R., & Schaefer, J. (1993). Coping resources and processes: Current concepts and measures. In L. Goldberger & S. Breznitz (Eds.), *Handbook of stress: Theoretical and Clinical Approaches* (2nd ed., pp. 234–257). New York: Free Press.

Morgan, A. (2007). *What is narrative therapy?* Retrieved September 13, 2007, from http://www.dulwichecentre.com/au/alicearticle.html

Moss, M., Frank, E., & Anderson, B. (1990). The effects of marital status and partner support on rape trauma. *American Journal of Orthopsychiatry, 60,* 379–391.

Myer C. (1970). *Social work practice: A response to the urban crisis.* New York: Free Press.

Nadelson, C. C., Notman, M. T., Zackson, H., & Gornick J. (1982). A follow-up study of rape victims. *American Journal of Psychiatry, 139*(10), 1266–1270

National Center for Justice Reference Service. (2004). *National protocol for sexual assault medical forensic evaluations.* Retrieved October 15, 2007, from http://www.ncjrs.gov/

National Child Abuse and Neglect Data System. (2005). *Child Maltreatment 2005.* Retrieved February 20, 2008, from http://www.childwelfare.gov/systemwide/statistics/can.cfm

National Committee for the Prevention of Elder Abuse. (2005). Retrieved January 26, 2008, from http://www.preventelderabuse.org

National Crime Victimization Survey. (2005). Retrieved October 9, 2007, from http://www.ojp.usdoj.gov/bjs/cvict.htm

National Institute of Justice. (1996). *Conference on research priorities, transcript.* Washington, DC: National Institute of Justice.

National Institute of Mental Health. (2002). *Mental health and mass violence evidence-based early psychological intervention for victims/survivors of mass violence. A workshop to reach consensus on best practices* (NIH Publication No. 02–5138). Washington, DC: U.S. Government Printing Office.

National Organization of Parents of Murdered Children. (2007). *National Organization of Parents of Murdered Children.* Retrieved November 14, 2007, from http://www. pomc.org. Reprinted with permission.

National Organization for Victim Assistance. (1992). Retrieved March 5, 2007, from http://www.trynova.org

National Organization for Victim Assistance. (1998). *The road to victim justice: Mapping strategies for service* (Vol. 18, p. 3). Washington, DC: National Organization for Victim Assistance.

National Organization for Victim Assistance. (2001). Retrieved October 27, 2007, from http://www.trynova.org

National Victim Center and Crime Victims Research and Treatment Center. (1992). *Rape in America: A Report to the Nation.* Arlington, VA: National Center for Victims of Crime and Crime Victims Research and Treatment Center.

Nezu, A., & Roman, G. (1988). Social problem solving as a moderator of stress related depressive symptoms: A prospective analysis. *Journal of Counseling Psychology, 38,* 134–138.

Nezu, A. M., Nezu, C. M., Saraydarian, L., Kalmar, K., & Ronan, G. F. (1986). Social problem solving as a moderating variable between negative life stress and depressive symptoms. *Cognitive Therapy and Research, 10,* 489–498.

Nezu, A., Nezu, C., & Perri, M. (1989). *Problem solving therapy for depression: Theory, research and clinical guidelines.* New York: Wiley.

Newgass, S., & Schonfeld, D. (2005). School crisis intervention, crisis prevention, and crisis response. In A. R. Roberts (Ed.), *Crisis intervention handbook: Assessment, treatment, and research* (pp. 499–517). New York: Oxford University Press.

Neimeyer, R. (2005). *Narrative therapy workshop series.* Retrieved November 10, 2007, from http://www.cbh.hku.hk/news/200511-neimeyer.htm

Neimeyer, R. A., & Anderson, A. (2002). Meaning reconstruction theory. In N. Thompson (Ed.), *Loss and grief* (pp. 45–64). London: Palgrave.

Norris, F., & Kaniasty, K. (1991). The psychological experience of crime: A test of the mediating role of beliefs in explaining the distress of victims. *Journal of Social and Clinical Psychology, 10,* 239–261

Norris, F., & Kaniasty, K. (1996). Received and perceived social support in times of stress: A test of the social support deterioration deterrence model. *Journal of Personality and Social Psychology, 71,* 498–511.

Norris, F., Kaniasty, K., & Scheer, D. A. (1990). Use of mental health services among victims of crime: Frequency, correlates, and subsequent recovery. *Journal of Counseling and Clinical Psychology, 10,* 239–261.

North, C., Nixon, S., & Shariat, S. (1999). Psychiatric disorders among survivors of the Oklahoma City bombing. *JAMA, 282,* 755–762.

North, C., McCutcheon, V., Spitznagel, E., & Smith, E. (2002). Three year follow-up of survivors of a mass shooting episode. *Journal of Urban Health: Bulletin of the New York Academy of Medicine, 79*(3), 383–391.

Norwack, K. (1989). Coping style, cognitive hardiness, and health status. *Journal of Behavioral Medicine, 12,* 145–158.

Novaco, R. W., Hamada, R. S., Gross, D. M., & Smith, G. (1997). Anger regulation deficits in combat-related posttraumatic stress disorder. *Journal of Traumatic Stress, 10*(1), 17–36.

Oatleley, K., & Bolton, W. (1985). A social-cognitive theory of depression in reaction to life events. *Psychoanalytic Review, 92,* 372–388.

Ogawa, B. (1990). *Color of justice: Culturally sensitive treatment of minority crime victims.* Sacramento: Office of the Governor, State of California.

Ory, M. G., Williams, T. F., Err, M., Lebowitz, B., Robins, P., Salloway, J., et al. (1985). Families, informal support and Alzheimer's disease: Current research and future agendas. *Research on Aging, 7*(4), 623–643.

Pan, H., Neidig, P. H., & O'Leary, K. D. (1994). Predicting mild and severe husband to wife aggression. *Journal of Consulting and Clinical Psychology, 62,* 975–981.

Parad, H. J. (Ed). (1965). *Crisis intervention: Selected readings.* New York: Family Service Association of America.

Parad, H. J., & Caplan, G. (1960). A framework for studying families in crisis. *Social Work, 5,* 3–15.

Parkes, C. M. (1987) *Bereavement: Studies of grief in adult life* (2nd ed.). Madison, CT: International Universities Press.

Parkes, S. H., & Pillisuk, M. (1991). Caregiver burden: Gender and the psychological costs of caregiving. *American Journal of Orthopsychiatry, 61*(4), 501–509.

Pearlin, L. I. (1985). Social structure and processes of social support. In S. Cohen & S. Syme (Eds.), *Social support and health* (pp. 43–60). Orlando, FL: Academic Press.

Pearlin, L. I., Schooler, C. (1978). The structure of coping. *Journal of Health and Social Behavior, 19,* 2–21.

Perloff, L. (1983). Perceptions of vulnerability to victimization. *Journal of Social Issues, 39,* 41–61.

Peterson, C., Semmel, A., Abramson, L. Metalsky, G., & Seligman, M. (1982). The attributional style questionnaire. *Cognitive Therapy & Research, 6*(3), 287–300.

Pitcher, G., & Poland, S. (1992). *Crisis intervention in the schools.* New York: The Guilford Press.

Poland, S., & Pitcher, G. (1990). Best practices in crisis intervention. In A. Thomas & J. Grimes (Eds.), *Best practices in school psychology* (pp. 259–275). Washington, DC: National Association of School Psychologists.

Polinsky, M. L. (1994). Functional status of long term breast cancer survivors: Demonstrating chronicity. *Health and Social Work, 19*(3), 165–174.

President's Task Force on Victims of Crime. (1982). *President's Task Force on Victims of Violent Crime, final report.* Washington, DC: U.S. Government Printing Office.

Prigerson, H., Bierhals, J., Kasl, S., Reynolds, C., Shear, K., Day, N., et al. (1997). Traumatic grief as a risk factor for mental and physical morbidity. *American Journal of Psychiatry, 154*(5), 616–623.

Prinstein, M. J., La Greca, A. M., Vernberg, E. M., & Silverman, W. K. (1996). Children's coping assistance: How parents, teachers, and friends help children cope after a natural disaster. *Journal of Clinical Child Psychology, 25,* 463–475.

Raid, J. K., & Norris, F. H. (1996). The social influence of relocation on the environmental, social, and psychological stress experience of disaster victims. *Environment and Behavior, 28,* 163–182.

Rando, T. (1993). *Complicated mourning.* Champaign, IL: Research Press.

Rape, Abuse and Incest National Network. (2007). Retrieved October 16, 2007, from http://www.rainn.org/statistics/index.html?gclid=CIG4jYmclI8CFQ8bgQodHyi-HA

Redmond, L. (1989). *Surviving when someone you love is murdered*. Clearwater, FL: Psychological Consultation and Education Services.

Resick, P. (1988). Psychological effect of victimization: Implications for the criminal justice system. *Crime and Deliquency, 33,* 468–478.

Resick, P. A., & Schnicke, M. K.. (1992). Cognitive processing therapy for sexual assault victims. *Journal of Consulting and Clinical Psychology, 60*(5), 748–756.

Resick, P. A., & Schnicke, M. K.. (1993). *Cognitive processing therapy for sexual assault victims: A treatment manual*. Newbury Park CA: Sage Publications.

Resnick, H. (1997). Medical and mental health outcomes. *Behavioral Medicine, 23,* 65–79.

Resnick, H. S., Kilpatrick, D. G., Dansky, B. S., Saunders, B. E., & Best, C. L. (1993). Prevalence of civilian trauma and PTSD in a representative national sample of women. *Journal of Clinical and Consulting Psychology, 61,* 6–14.

Reynolds, S., & Gilbert, P. (1991). Psychological impact of unemployment interactive effects of vulnerability and protective factors on depression. *Journal of Counseling Psychology, 38,* 76–84.

Rheingold, A., Grier, J., & Whitworth, N. (2005). *Guide for survivors of homicide*. National Crime Victims Center. Charleston, SC. Retrieved November 19, 2007, from http://colleges.musc.edu/ncvc/

Richards, D. (2001). A field study of critical incident stress debriefing versus critical incident stress management. *Journal of Mental Health, 10,* 351–362.

Riggs, D., Dancu, C., Gershuny, B., Greenber, D., & Foa, E.(1992). Anger and PTSD in female crime victims. *Journal of Traumatic Stress, 5,* 613–625.

Robertiello, G. (2006). Common mental health correlates of domestic violence. *Brief Treatment and Crisis Intervention, 6*(2), 111–121.

Roberts, A. R. (1990). *Helping crime victims*. Thousand Oaks, CA: Sage Publications.

Roberts, A. R. (1991). *Contemporary perspectives on crisis intervention and prevention*. Englewood Cliffs, NJ: Prentice Hall.

Roberts, A. R. (1996). *Helping battered women: New perspectives and remedies*. New York: Oxford University Press.

Roberts, A. R. (1998). *Battered women and their families: Intervention strategies and treatment approaches* (2nd ed.). New York: Springer Publishing.

Roberts, A. R. (2000). An introduction and overview of crisis intervention. In A. R. Roberts. (Ed.). *Crisis intervention handbook: Assessment, treatment and research* (2nd ed., pp. 3–30). New York: Oxford University Press.

Roberts, A. R. (2002a). Assessment, crisis intervention, and trauma treatment: The integrative act intervention model. *Brief Treatment and Crisis Intervention, 2,* 1–22.

Roberts, A. R. (2002b). Duration and severity of woman battering: a conceptual model/ continuum. In A. Roberts. (Ed.). *Handbook of domestic violence intervention strategies* (pp. 64–79). New York: Oxford University Press.

Roberts, A. R. (2005). Bridging the past and present to the future of crisis intervention and crisis management. In A. R. Roberts (Ed.), *Crisis intervention handbook: Assessment, treatment and research* (3rd ed., pp. 3–35). New York: Oxford University Press.

Roberts, A. R., & Dziegielewski, S. F. (1995). Foundation skills and applications of crisis intervention and cognitive therapy. In A. R. Roberts (Ed.), *Crisis intervention and time-limited cognitive treatment* (pp. 3–27). Thousand Oaks, CA: Sage.

Roberts, A. R., & Everly, G. S. (2006). A meta-analysis of 36 crisis intervention studies. *Brief Treatment and Crisis Intervention, 6*(1), 10–21.

Roberts, A. R., & Kim, J. (2005). Exploring the effects of head injuries among battered women: A qualitative study of chronic and severe woman battering. *Journal of Social Service Research, 32*(1), 33–47.

Roberts, A. R., & Roberts, B. S. (2005). *Ending intimate abuse: Practical guidance and survival strategies.* New York: Oxford University Press.

Rock, M. L. (2000). Effective crisis management planning: Creating a collaborative framework. *Education & Treatment of Children, 23*(3), 248–265.

Rosenberg, M. (1989). *Society and the adolescent self-image* (rev. ed.). Middletown, CT: Wesleyan University Press.

Roth, S., & Newman, E. (1991). The process of coping with sexual trauma. *Journal of Traumatic Stress, 4,* 279–297.

Rothbaum, B., Foa, E., Riggs, D., Murdock, T., & Walsh, W. (1992). A prospective examination of post traumatic stress disorder in rape victims. *Journal of Traumatic Stress, 9*(4), 865–871.

Rycus, J. R., & Hughes, R. C. (in press). Recognizing indicators of child maltreatment. In A. R. Roberts (Ed.), *Social workers' desk reference* (2nd ed.). New York: Oxford University Press.

Sabbagh, L. (1995). Stress signs often missed in victims of violent crimes. *The Medical Post.* Retrieved September 7, 2007, from www.mentalhealth.com/mag1/p51-ptsd.html

Sales, E., Baum, M., & Shore, B. (1984). Victim readjustment following assault. *Journal of Social Issues, 40*(1), 117–136.

Sandoval, J. (Ed.). (2002). *Handbook of crisis counseling, intervention, and prevention in the schools* (2nd ed.). Mahwah, NJ: Lawrence Erlbaum.

Sarason, I. G., Sarason, B. R., & Shearin, E. N. (1986). Social support as an individual difference variable: Its stability, origins, and relational aspects. *Journal of Perosnality and Social Psychology, 50,* 845–855.

Saunders, B. E., Kilpatrick, D. G., Resnick, H. S., & Tidwell, R. P. (1989). Brief screening for lifetime history of criminal victimization at mental health intake: A preliminary study. *Journal of Interpersonal Violence, 4*(3), 267–277.

Schonfeld, D., Kline, M., & Members of the Crisis Intervention Committee. (1994). School-based crisis intervention: An organizational model. *Crisis Intervention and Time-Limited Treatment, 1*(2), 155–166.

Schonfeld, D. J., Lichenstein, R., Pruett, M. K., & Speese-Liehan, D. (2002). *How to prepare for and respond to a crisis.* Alexandria, VA: Association for Supervision and Curriculum Development.

Schuster, M., Stein, B., & Jaycox, L. (2001). A national survey of stress reactions after the September 11, 2001, terrorist attacks. *New England Journal of Medicine, 345,* 1507–1512

Shachter, B., & Seinfeld, J. (1994). Personal violence and the culture of violence. *Social Work, 39*(4), 347–350.

Shalev, A. Y., Freedman, S., Tuvi Peri, M. A., Brandes, D., Sahar, T., Orr, S., et al. (1996). Prosepctive study of post traumatic stress disorder and depression following trauma. *American Journal of Psychiatry, 155*(5), 630–637.

Shaw, J. A., Applegate, B., & Shorr, C. (1996). Twenty-one month follow up of children exposed to Hurricane Andrew. *Journal of the American Academy of Child & Adolescent Psychiatry, 35,* 359–366.

Shilne, K. (2003). *Bioterrorism: From panic to preparedness*. Retrieved September 15, 2007, from http://www.rand.org/publications/randreview/issues/rr.08.02/bioterrorism.htm

Shulman, N. (1990). Crisis intervention in secondary schools: Lessons from the Concord High School experience. In A. R. Roberts (Ed.), *Crisis intervention handbook* (pp. 63–77). Belmont, CA: Wadsworth.

Smith, M. E., & Kelly, L. M. (2001). The journey of recovery after a rape experience. *Issues in Mental Health Nursing, 2*(4), 337–352.

Spielberger, C. (1979). *Understanding stress. and anxiety*. New York: Harper.

Spielberger, C. (1996). *The anger expression scale*. Tampa, FL: Center for Research and Behavioral Medicine and Community Psychology.

Spielberger, C., Johnson, E., Russell, S., Crane, R., Jacobs, G., & Worden, T. (1985). The experience and expression of anger: Construction and validation of an anger expression scale. In M. A. Chessey & R. H. Rosenman (Eds.), *Anger and hostility in cardiovascular and behavioral disorders* (pp. 5–30). New York: Hemisphere/McGraw-Hill.

Standing Together Against Rape. (2007). *Rape myths and reality*. Retrieved October 1, 2007, from http://www.staralaska.com/scripts/home.asp

Stanton, A. L., Danoff-Burg, S., Cameron, C. L., & Ellis, A. P. (1994). Coping through emotional approach: Problems of conceptualization and confounding. *Journal of Personality and Social Psychology, 66*, 350–362.

Stark, E., & Flitcraft, A. (1988). *Violence among intimates: An epidemiological review*. In V. B. Van Hasselt, R. L. Morrison, A. S. Bellack, & M. Hersen (Eds.), *Handbook of family violence* (pp. 293–317). New York: Plenum.

Steinmetz, C. (1984). Coping with a serious crime: Self help and outside help. *Victimology, 9*, 324–343.

Stone, A. A., Helder, L. & Schneider, M. M. (1988). Coping with stressful events: Coping dimensions and issues. In L.H. Cohen (Ed.) *Life events and psychological functioning: Theoretical and methodological issues* (pp. 182–210). Newbury Park, CA: Sage.

Straus, M. A. (1986). Medical care costs of intrafamily assault and homicide. *Bulletin of New York Academy of Medicine, 6*(5), 556–561.

Straus, M. A., & Gelles, R. J. (1991). How violent are American families: Estimates from the National Family Violence Resurvey and other studies. In M. Straus & R. Gelles (Eds.), *Physical violence in American families: Risk factors and adaptations in 8,145 families* (pp. 95–112). New Brunswick, NJ: Transaction.

Strentz, T., & Auerbach., S. M. (1988). Adjustment to the stress of simulated captivity: Effects of emotion-focused vs. problem-focused preparation on hostages differing in locus of control. *Journal of Personality and Social Psychology, 55*, 652–666.

Terr, L. (1983). Chowchilla revisited: The effects of psychic trauma four years after a school-bus kidnapping. *American Journal of Psychiatry, 138*, 14–19.

Terr, L. (1990). *Too scared to cry*. New York: Harper and Row.

Terr, L. (1994). *Unchained memories: True stories of traumatic memories, lost and found*. New York: Basic Books.

Thibaut, J., & Kelley, H. (1959). *The social psychology of groups*. New York: Wiley.

Thoits, P. A. (1985). Social support and psychological well being: Theoretical possibilities. In I. G. Sarason & B. R. Sarason (Eds.), *Social support: Theory, research and application* (pp. 51–72). Boston: Martinus Nijhoff.

Thompson, M. P., & Norris, F. (1992). Crime, social status, and alienation. *American Journal of Community Psychology, 20,* 211–241.

Thompson, M. P., Norris, F. H., & Ruback, R. B. (1996). System influences on posthomicide beliefs and distress. *American Journal of Community Psychology, 24*(6), 785–805.

Tjaden, P., & Thoennes, N. (2000). *Extent, nature, and consequences of intimate partner violence: Findings from the National Violence against Women Survey.* Washington, DC: National Institute of Justice, U.S. Department of Justice.

Turner, F. (1996). *Social work treatment: Interlocking theoretical approaches.* New York: Free Press.

United States Department of Justice. (2005). *Crime in the United States.* Retrieved July 30, 2007, from http://www.fbi.gov/ucr/05cius/

United States Department of Veteran Affairs. Retrieved September 9, 2007, from http://www.ncptsd.va.gov/ncmain/ncdocs/assmnts/nc_chart_trauma_exp.html

Uniting and Strengthening America by Providing Appropriate Tools Required to Intercept and Obstruct Terrorism (USA PATRIOT ACT). (2001). USA Sections 802–811.

Valentiner, D. P., Holohan, C. J., & Moos, R. J. (1994). Social support, appraisals of teen controllability and coping: An integrative model. *Journal of Personality and Social Psychology, 66,* 1094–1102.

Valentiner, D. P., Foa, D. S., Riggs, D. S., & Gershuny, B. S. (1996). Coping strategies and post traumatic stress disorder in fremale victims of sexual and nonsexual assault. *Journal of American Psychology, 3,* 455–458.

van der Kolk, B. A., & van der Hart, O. (1989). The breakdown of adaptation in psychological trauma. *American Journal of Psychiatry, 146*(12), 1530–1540.

van der Veer, P. (1998). Cultural politics and the state. *Cultural Dynamics, 10*(3), 281–287.

van der Veer, P. (1994). *Religious nationalism: Hindus and Muslims in India.* Berkeley: University of California Press.

Vargas, L. A., Loya, F., & Hodde-Vargas, J. (1989). Exploring the multidimensional aspects of grief reactions. *American Journal of Psychiatry, 145,* 1484–1488.

Vaux, R. (1986). *Social support: Theory, research and intervention.* New York: Praeger.

Von Bertalanffy, L. (1968). *General system theory: Foundations, development, applications.* New York: George Braziller.

Von Hentig, H. (1948). *The criminal and his victim.* New Haven, CT: Yale University Press.

Walker, L. A. (1984). *Battered women syndrome.* New York: Springer Publishing.

Wallace, H. (1998). *Victimology.* Needham, MA: Allyn and Bacon.

Wanko, M. A. (2001). *Safe schools: Crisis prevention and response.* Lanham, MD: Scarecrow Press.

Wasserstein, S.B., & La Greca, A. M. (1998). Hurricane Andrew: Parent conflict as a moderator of children's adjustment. *Hispanic Journal of Behavioral Sciences, 20,* 212–224.

Watson, R. J., & Watson, R. S. (2002). *The school as a safe haven.* Westport, CT: Bergin & Garvey.

Whitaker, C. (1990). *Black victims.* Washington, DC: Bureau of Justice Statistics, U.S. Department of Justice.

White, N. E., Richter, J. M., & Fry, C. (1992). Coping, social support and adaptation to chronic illness. *Western Journal of Nursing Research, 4*(2), 212–224.

Whittier, S., Coon, D., & Aaker, J. (2001). *Caregiver support interventions.* Retrieved December 5, 2007, from http://cssr.berkeley.edu/pdfs/famcare_04.pdf

Wilson, J. P., Smith, W. K., & Johnson, S. K. (1985). A comparative analysis of PTSD among various survivor groups. In C. R. Figley (Ed.), *Trauma and its wake: The study and treatment of PTSD* (pp. 142–172)New York: Brunner/Mazel.

Winkel, F., & Vrij, A. (1993). Facilitating problem- and emotional-focused coping in victims of burglary: Evaluating a police crisis intervention program. *Journal of Community Psychology, 21,* 97–113.

Winkel, F., & Vrij, A. (1995). Chapter 19. In G. Davies, S. Lloyd-Bostock, M. McCurran, & C. Wilson (Eds.), *Psychology, law, and criminal justice: International developments in research and practice* (pp. 363–373). Berlin: Walter de Gruyter.

Wirtz, P., & Harrell, A. (1987). Victim and crime characteristics, coping responses, and short and long term recovery from victimization. *Journal of Consulting and Clinical Psychology, 55,* 866–871.

Wolfgang, M. E. (1958). *Patterns of criminal homicide.* Philadelphia: Patterson Smith.

Worden, J. W. (1991). *Grief counseling and grief therapy.* New York: Springer Publishing.

Yassen, J., & Glass, L. (1984, May-June). Sexual assault survivors group: A feminist practice perspective. *Social Work,* 252–257.

Young, M. A. (1994). *Responding to communities in crisis.* Washington, DC: National Organization for Victim Assistance.

Young, M. A. (1997). *The community crisis response team training manual.* Washington, DC: National Organization for Victim Assistance.

Zeidner, M., & Endler, N. (1998). *Handbook of coping: Theory, research, applications.* New York: Wiley & Sons.

Zeidner, M., & Saklofske, D. (1996). Adaptive and maladaptive coping. In M. Zeidner & N. S. Endler (Eds.), *Handbook of coping: Theory, research and applications* (pp. 505–531). New York: John Wiley and Sons.

Zenere, F. J. (2001). Tremors of trauma: Responding to the El Salvador earthquakes. *NASP Communique, 29*(7), 10–11.

Zilberg, N. J., Weiss, D. S., & Horowitz, M. J. (1982). Impact of Event Scale: A cross-validation study and some empirical evidence supporting a conceptual model of stress response syndrome. *Journal of Consulting and Clinical Psychology, 50,* 407–414.

Index

Note: The italicized *f* and *t* following page numbers refer to figures and tables, respectively.

Handbook of Forensic Mental Health With Victims and Offenders

Assessment, Treatment, and Research

David W. Springer, PhD, LCSW
Albert R. Roberts, PhD, DABFE, Editors

Together for the first time: all your forensic social work best practice needs in one volume. From expert testimony advice to treating HIV-positive incarcerated women, this handbook contains the most current research and tested field practices for child welfare through adulthood in the civil and criminal system.

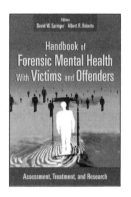

Encompassing a wide range of treatments, roles, specialized practices, research, and diagnoses, the *Handbook of Forensic Mental Health* will guide practicing professionals through the forensic social work issues they encounter on a daily basis, such as:

- Prevention of prisoner sudden deaths
- Expert witness testimony in child welfare and women battering
- Treating dually diagnosed adolescents
- The overrepresentation of African Americans for juvenile delinquency
- Jail mental health services for adults
- Drug courts and PTSD in inmates with substance abuse histories
- Recidivism prevention
- Basic tasks in post-trauma intervention with victims and offenders
- Culture and gender considerations in restorative justice

Edited by renowned psychologist Dr. Albert R. Roberts and social worker Dr. David W. Springer, with contributions by leaders in the field, this handbook should top the list of must-haves for all forensic social workers.

2007 · 650pp · hardcover · 978-0-8261-1514-0

11 West 42nd Street, New York, NY 10036-8002 • Fax: 212-941-7842
Order Toll-Free: 877-687-7476 • Order Online: www.springerpub.com

SPRINGER PUBLISHING COMPANY

Battered Women and Their Families, Third Edition

Intervention Strategies and Treatment Programs

Albert R. Roberts, PhD, DABFE, Editor

"[M]any challenges, problems, intervention strategies, assessment and treatment methods, and empowerment approaches are documented in this book by one of the most brilliant clinical researchers in North America today—Dr. Albert Roberts—together with the highly experienced chapter authors. This is the most practical, evidence-based, inspirational, and well-written book on family violence that I have read in the past 10 years. Every social worker, counselor, nurse, and domestic violence advocate should read this book."

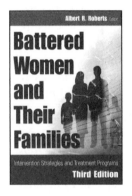

—From the Foreword by **Barbara W. White,**
Dean and Centennial Professor in Leadership,
School of Social Work, University of Texas at Austin.
Former President, Council on Social Work Education (CSWE),
and Former President, National Association of Social Workers (NASW).

The definitive work on battered women is now in a timely third edition. Considered the complete, in-depth guide to effective interventions for this pervasive social disease, *Battered Women and Their Families* has been updated to include new case studies, cultural perspectives, and assessment protocols. In an area of counseling that cannot receive enough attention, Dr. Roberts' work stands out as an essential treatment tool for all clinical social workers, nurses, physicians, and graduate students who work with battered women on a daily basis.

New chapters on same-sex violence, working with children in shelters, immigrant women affected by domestic violence, and elder mistreatment round out this unbiased, multicultural look at treatment programs for battered women.

2007 · 656pp · hardcover · 978-0-8261-4592-5

11 West 42nd Street, New York, NY 10036-8002 • Fax: 212-941-7842
Order Toll-Free: 877-687-7476 • Order Online: www.springerpub.com